Managing Your Firm's 401(k) Plan

Founded in 1807, John Wiley & Sons is the oldest independent publishing company in the United States. With offices in North America, Europe, Australia and Asia, Wiley is globally committed to developing and marketing print and electronic products and services for our customers' professional and personal knowledge and understanding.

The Wiley Finance series contains books written specifically for finance and investment professionals as well as sophisticated individual investors and their financial advisors. Book topics range from portfolio management to e-commerce, risk management, financial engineering, valuation and financial instrument analysis, as well as much more.

For a list of available titles, please visit our Web site at www.WileyFinance.com.

Managing Your Firm's 401(k) Plan

*A Complete Road Map
to Managing Today's
Retirement Plans*

Edited by MATT SMITH

WILEY

John Wiley & Sons, Inc.

Published by John Wiley & Sons, Inc., Hoboken, New Jersey.
Published simultaneously in Canada.

For general information on our other products and services or for technical support, please contact our Customer Care Department within the United States at (800) 762–2974, outside the United States at (317) 572–3993 or fax (317) 572–4002.

Wiley also publishes its books in a variety of electronic formats. Some content that appears in print may not be available in electronic books. For more information about Wiley products, visit our web site at www.wiley.com.

Library of Congress Cataloging-in-Publication Data:

Managing your firm's 401(k) plan : a complete roadmap to managing today's retirement plans / edited by Matt Smith.
    p. cm. – (Wiley finance series ; 564)
    Aon Consulting.
    Includes bibliographical references and index.
    ISBN 978-0-470-55300-8 (cloth); 978-0-470-7587-2 (ebk); 978-0-470-87588-9 (ebk); 978-0-470-87589 (ebk)
    1. 401(k) plans–Management.   2. Compensation management–United States.
I. Smith, Matthew X., 1961-   II. Aon Consulting.
    HD7105.45.U6M325 2010
    658.3'253–dc22

                                                                    2010012322

Printed in the United States of America

10 9 8 7 6 5 4 3 2 1

Contents

Preface

401(k) plans hold *trillions* of dollars of retirement wealth in the United States. What started as a way to save a little extra money for retirement has now turned into a critical source of retirement security for millions of people. This is serious business.

Managing a 401(k) plan is not an easy task, yet thousands of corporate officers, finance, and human resource professionals across the country are handed this responsibility. The decisions they make *will* have a meaningful effect on the retirement wealth of their co-workers. *Managing Your Firm's 401(k) Plan* is a resource for anyone who has responsibility for the design or management of the employer's 401(k) plan.

There are many sources for information about design and management of 401(k) plans. Many of these sources are highly technical in nature, while others are oversimplified. What we've tried to accomplish with this book is to present a practical and objective overview of the important issues that you need to know about your 401(k) plan. The content in this book will enable you to be an informed consumer of plan services and an empowered manager of your 401(k) plan.

This book is not just a technical manual, although there is a fair amount of technical detail contained. We do not expect you to come to this book with a great deal of technical knowledge, although if you do, we feel there is a lot here that will interest you as well. A great deal of effort was put into keeping the content in this book interesting and at the same time tethered to the technical aspects of the laws and regulations that govern 401(k) plans.

Also, it will help you think through or reexamine fundamental questions about your plan: What should your role be in helping your employees reach a secure retirement, why should you sponsor a 401(k) plan, how does your plan design affect better participant decisions, what kinds of risks are you assuming by sponsoring a plan, or by not sponsoring a plan?

HOW THE BOOK IS ORGANIZED

The opening chapter of this book provides a context for why the 401(k) plan is becoming more important in the United States. 401(k) plans have been around since the early 1980s. What is different today that is making them so important to our retirement security? As baby boomers reach retirement, they will spend more years in retirement than previous generations and their expenses will likely be higher. As this is happening, employers are shifting more of the responsibility for retirement to their employees by changing from defined benefit (DB) to defined contribution (DC) plans. The shift from DB to DC is putting the 401(k) plan at the center of the retirement spotlight, and as a result, the individual is left to manage many of the risks associated with retirement, including funding, investment, longevity, and spending risk.

In this new DC-dominant era of employer-sponsored retirement plans, the employer's role is being redefined. This is the topic of Chapter 2. Why do employers sponsor 401(k) plans and what roles do they play are questions we address. As the employer's role evolves, so does the standard for 401(k) plan stewardship. Seven areas of plan stewardship are discussed from the perspective of how they are changing.

The main purpose of every 401(k) plan is to help individuals become ready for retirement, but how is retirement readiness measured? A place to start is to understand the concept of income replacement ratio. The amount of income someone needs in retirement as a percentage of his preretirement income is an income replacement ratio. This concept is covered in detail in Chapter 3. Also in Chapter 3, we cover ways to improve retirement readiness by making your 401(k) plan as effective as possible.

In Chapter 4, we talk about the basics of establishing a 401(k) plan: how they work, establishing plan objectives, benchmarking plan design features, and documentation requirements for the plan and trust.

Plan governance and related fiduciary issues are the topics covered in Chapter 5. Here we define who a plan fiduciary is, her basic duties, and the selection and monitoring of outside fiduciaries. Also discussed are establishing roles and responsibilities for managing your 401(k) plan, including the setup and operations of a benefits committee and using plan assets to pay expenses.

Being a plan fiduciary involves risk, so we include a chapter on protecting yourself as a plan fiduciary. Over the past decade, high profile incidents such as the collapse of Enron and scandals in the mutual fund industry have changed the fiduciary landscape for 401(k) plans. These are covered in Chapter 6 along with the consequences of a breach of fiduciary duty, the voluntary fiduciary correction program, ERISA bonding requirements, and fiduciary indemnification strategies.

The core of any 401(k) plan is its investments. Chapter 7 covers investment topics, including creating an investment policy statement and the plan's investment menu, the use of prediversified portfolios such as target date funds, selecting and monitoring investment managers, understanding investment related expenses and complying with Code Section 404(c). Also discussed in Chapter 7 is the use of company stock in 401(k) plans, default investment options, the mapping of assets from one fund to another, advice and education options, brokerage accounts and mutual fund windows, and socially responsible investment options.

When it comes to plan operations, most plan sponsors think of their recordkeeper. While the plan's recordkeeper does a tremendous amount of the day-to-day plan operations, the plan sponsor still has the responsibility for overseeing the work as well as the ultimate responsibility for the record-keeper's actions. Chapter 8 covers monitoring your service providers, operational and regulatory compliance, and special considerations related to changing plan recordkeepers.

The ultimate goal of any 401(k) plan is to distribute benefits to retirees. Chapter 9 covers distribution-related issues including vesting rules, distributable events, and forms of distributions. Also covered are optional plan design features specifically addressing both terminated employees and employees who may need to take a distribution while still employed. Finally, we discuss taxation considerations and special distribution situations such as qualified domestic relations orders.

Chapter 10 discusses how business transactions affect 401(k) plans. For the purposes of this book we define a *business transaction* as a structural change to the plan sponsor's business, such as a merger, acquisition, spin-off, or major downsizing. It is not often that the 401(k) plan is at the top of CEOs' minds when companies are planning a business transaction. However, as you'll see in Chapter 10, a business transaction can trigger a tremendous amount of work related to the plan. In addition to the effect of business transactions, we also cover the topic of plan terminations, providing a detailed checklist of related activities.

Effectively communicating your 401(k) plan to your employees is critical to your plan's success. Chapter 11 provides you information on how to develop and measure your communications strategy, branding your communications program, and managing your communications vendors.

It is fitting that our last chapter is about helping participants manage their retirement income because this is the final role a 401(k) plan plays in providing retirement security for the individual. Today, most DC plans only distribute cash payments to retirees, either as lump sums or as installments. Retirees must then deal with the risks associated with managing their retirement income on their own. What help if any should plan sponsors provide retirees in the income phase of retirement? Chapter 12 provides the plan sponsor with information and context for answering this question. Topics covered include whether income products should be offered inside a plan or out, the risks related to managing retirement income, an analysis of eight retirement income product types and how they managed these risks, and additional product features that might be included as part of a retirement income solution.

We hope you find the information in this book useful. If it helps you to understand the design and purpose of your plan more clearly, helps you establish better governance practices, or even prevents you from making a simple compliance error, then it will have been worth our time writing and your time reading this book.

Acknowledgments

My role in the development of this book has been one of both editor and co-author. Producing a book is always a team effort and I was fortunate to have had the support of many of my Aon Consulting colleagues during this project.

I would like to thank Kathryn Haley and Cecil Hemingway for their support and encouragement of this project, Amol Mhatre for co-developing the themes in the *employer's role* section of Chapter 2, Scott Fisher for co-developing content in Chapters 2 and 3, and Laura Moran for her development support and coordination. Several of my colleagues sacrificed their free time to provide much appreciated content review: Susan Alford, Tony Andrews, Juliette de Carteret, Michael Schachet, Martha Spano, Arnie Stone, and Steve Stone.

Listed here are the names of authors and contributors by chapter:

- Chapters 1, 2, 3, 6, 7, and 12: Matt Smith
- Chapter 4: Terri Vaughan, Craig Harris, and Rhonda Jinks
- Chapter 5: Jan Raines and Joe Steen
- Chapter 8: Leslie Smith and David Swallow
- Chapter 9: Linda Boarman and Mike Miller
- Chapter 10: Bridget Steinhart and Gena Buchwald
- Chapter 11: Melissa Burke and Lynn Devany

The content in Chapter 3 regarding *replacement ratios* came from Aon Consulting's *2008 Replacement Ratio Study*. This study was completed under the direction of Dr. Bruce Palmer, professor and chair emeritus of the Department of Risk Management and Insurance, Robinson College of Business, Georgia State University. Also working closely with Dr. Palmer on this study were professionals from Aon Consulting, including Ron DeStefano, E.A., Michael Schachet, F.S.A., Jeff Paciero, F.S.A., and Chris Bone, F.S.A.

Portions of the content in Chapters 4, 5, 6, and 7 were derived from the following research briefs prepared by Aon Consulting:

Fiduciary Fundamentals Under ERISA—Editor: Drew McCorkle, JD. Contributors: Jill Carson, JD, CEBS, Scott Fisher, Laura Philip, Jan Raines,

Stephanie Rosseau, JD, CEBS, Arnold Stone, Thomas O. Toale, Terri Vaughan, CPA, CEBS, and Cynthia Zaleta.

Fiduciary & Investment Issues: Beyond the Basics—Editor: Drew McCorkle, JD. Contributors: Dennis Blair, JD, CEBS, Jill Carson, JD, CEBS, James Danaher, Jay Desjardins, Scott Fisher, Barry Newman, JD, Laura Philip, Jan Raines, Stephanie Rosseau, JD, CEBS, Terri Vaughan, CPA, CEBS, and Cynthia Zaleta.

I would also like to thank Laura Walsh, Bill Falloon, and Meg Freeborn at John Wiley & Sons—Laura and Bill for providing us the opportunity to develop this book, and Meg for her patience, advice, and support throughout the editing process.

Matt Smith

CHAPTER 1

The Importance of the 401(k) Plan

Retirement in the United States is getting more attention every year. The reasons include the baby boom generation reaching retirement age, people spending more years in retirement, rising retirement expenses, and the shift from employer-sponsored defined benefit (DB) plans to defined contribution (DC) plans.

In addition, the traditional sources of retirement security, *government*, *employer*, and *individual* are all straining under the weight of competing economic priorities, causing us to reexamine how these sources interact to provide a secure retirement. Emerging at the center of the new retirement architecture in the United States is the 401(k) plan.

BABY BOOMERS HAVE REACHED RETIREMENT AGE

The baby boom generation, defined by the U.S. Census Bureau as everyone born in the years 1946 through 1964, is having a profound effect on the retirement landscape in the United States. The baby boom generation has left its imprint on each life stage it has passed through. Now it is retirement's turn. In 2008, there were approximately 44 million Americans in the 10-year age cohort from age 45 to 54.[1] For comparison, the 10-year age cohort from age 25 to 34 numbered approximately 40 million. That comparison might not seem dramatic, but keep in mind that the younger age cohort will continue to shrink in size over the next 20 years because of normal mortality. For additional comparison, the current 10-year age cohort from age 65 to 74 number approximately 19.5 million.

The baby boom effect on retirement is multifaceted. Boomers are transitioning from net savers to net spenders as they pull dollars out of their retirement accounts rather than putting new contributions in; they are looking for help for the first time with ways to ensure they don't outlive their accumulated wealth; there will be an increase in demand for health care products and services; and a higher proportion of the population in retirement will cause the Social Security retirement dependency ratio to increase dramatically.

PEOPLE ARE SPENDING MORE YEARS IN RETIREMENT

People are spending more years in retirement because they are retiring earlier than planned and living longer than in the past. While the normal retirement age most people think of is 65, research shows that many are retiring earlier. According to the Employee Benefit Research Institute's (EBRI) 2010 Retirement Confidence Survey (RCS), 28 percent of the individuals surveyed who were still working (workers) indicated that they planned on retiring before age 65. However, of the individuals surveyed who were already retired, 61 percent said they actually retired before age 65. An excerpt from the survey report sheds some light as to why people are retiring earlier than planned.

> *The RCS has consistently found that a large percentage of retirees leave the work force earlier than planned (41 percent in 2010). Many retirees who retired earlier than planned cite negative reasons for leaving the work force before they expected, including health problems or disability (54 percent); changes at their company, such as downsizing or closure (26 percent); and having to care for a spouse or another family member (19 percent). Others say changes in the skills required for their job (16 percent) or other work related reasons (11 percent) played a role. Some retirees mention a mix of positive and negative reasons for retiring early, but just 5 percent offer only positive reasons.*

In addition to retiring earlier than planned, increased life expectancy is causing the number of years people spend in retirement to be longer than in the past. Around the year 1900, average life expectancy at birth in the United States was just over 49 years. It has been increasing ever since. Measured every 10 years (based on the 10-year censuses that we have), it finally passed age 70 in 1970, hitting 70.8 years. By the time of the 2000 census, it had reached 76.9 years.

For retirement planning purposes, we are also interested in the average number of years a person is likely to live once they've reached retirement age. In 1900, a survivor to age 65 could expect to live an additional 11.9 years (on average). In 1970, the average remaining life expectancy at 65 had increased to 15 years. In 2000, this figure was 17.9.[2]

It is a fact that people are spending more years in retirement. The effect this has on retirement planning is clear. Either spending rates must come down to allow retirement assets to last longer or additional wealth must be accumulated to fund the same standard of living for these additional years.

EXPENSES IN RETIREMENT ARE INCREASING

If a person wishes to maintain their pre-retirement standard of living in retirement, it will usually require less annual income in retirement than in pre-retirement. The reason is that there are some expenses that go down in retirement such as transportation, taxes, clothing, and savings for retirement. Aon Consulting, in conjunction with Georgia State University, has conducted a Replacement Ratio Study every few years since 1980. This study examines the federal government's Consumer Expenditure Survey (CES) data to determine how people at various income levels spend their income. By examining these data, the study determines what percentage of a person's pre-retirement income they need to replicate their pre-retirement standard of living once they stop working and retire. The 2008 edition of this study concludes that a person making an annual salary of $30,000 per year would need 90 percent of his pre-retirement income to maintain the same standard of living. This percentage is termed an *income replacement ratio*. Someone making $90,000 per year would require an income replacement ratio of 78 percent.

These income replacement ratios are based on a snapshot in time. As such, they do not project changes in spending patterns or variances in expense increases among different expense categories. One area of expense that is likely to increase in the future for retirees is health care. We know anecdotally that health care costs have been increasing at rates of two and three times the rate of inflation in recent years, and retirees spend a higher percentage of their income on health care than pre-retirees. So, what might these income replacement ratios be if we factored in higher health care costs in the future? When the income replacement ratios are recalculated assuming health care costs will increase in retirement by an additional $400 per month (which represents the combined costs of Medicare Parts B and D premiums, and an amount for supplemental coverage) the $30,000 per year individual's ratio increases from 90 percent to 102 percent. The $90,000 per year individual's ratio increases from 78 percent to 82 percent.

THE SHIFT FROM DB TO DC

Over the past several decades, there has been a steady trend of shifting the risks and responsibilities associated with retirement from institutions to individuals. One of the most obvious manifestations of this trend is the shift from DB plans to DC plans as the primary employer-sponsored retirement program. Nineteen ninety-six was the last year in which there were more assets in private DB plans than in private DC plans, when each held approximately $1.6 trillion. Private DC plans include profit sharing, money purchase, and 401(k) plans. Governmental or not-for-profit DC plans are not included in this statistic and usually take the form of 457 or 403(b) plans. By the year 2011, it is estimated that private DC plans will hold $4.2 trillion, while private DB plans will hold $2.5 trillion.[3]

Another comparison, this time conducted by researchers at the National Bureau of Economic Review (NBER) estimates that the assets currently in DB plans versus 401(k) plans are roughly equal (at the time this chapter was written in 2010). By the year 2040, however, it is estimated that there will be four times the assets in 401(k) plans as in DB plans.[4] For workers entering the workforce today, it is highly likely that their primary source of employer-sponsored retirement will be in the form of a defined contribution account rather than a defined benefit. We discuss later in this chapter some of the risks that are transferred to the individual as employers move from DB to DC retirement programs.

SHARING RESPONSIBILITY

There is a popular analogy comparing retirement security in the United States to that of a three-legged stool. The legs in this analogy are represented by government (Social Security), employer (employer-provided retirement benefits), and individual (personal savings). Because of the converging factors discussed at the beginning of this chapter, the three-legged stool is beginning to list to one side. Social Security is facing solvency concerns in the coming decades if changes are not made. As was stated earlier, employers are moving toward DC plans. This move shifts most of the risks associated with retirement to the individual. And finally, personal wealth accumulation is being strained because of lower personal savings rates, lower housing values (a large source of personal wealth for many Americans), and lower investment portfolio values due to the global economic downturn.

The Government as a Source of Retirement Security

Social Security is the federal government's contribution to Americans' retirement security. (We say it's the federal government's contribution even though the source of Social Security's funding is payroll taxes.) Individuals reaching retirement age just as the Great Depression was unfolding found themselves literally in the streets with no resources to maintain a decent standard of living. As a result, the U.S. government initiated a Social Security program in 1935, the largest part of which is a retirement pension for workers reaching retirement age. Americans are depedent on Social Security, but the system may face solvency problems in the coming decades because of longer life expectancies and the sheer numbers of workers who will draw benefits as the baby boomer generation begins to reach retirement age.

At the time Social Security was enacted, the average life expectancy was about 65 years of age. More specifically, the average life expectancy of a female was 67 and 63 for a male. Coincidentally, the normal retirement age to qualify for Social Security was 65. In 1935, people spent fewer years in retirement simply because they didn't live as long after retiring as they do today. The length of time someone spends in retirement (by definition a time when no income is generated by working) greatly affects the amount of financial resources needed to fund such a retirement.

At the end of the 1930s, the average expected remaining years of life for a person at age 65 was 12.8. By the year 2000, this figure had increased to 17.9 years, for an increase of 5.1 years. This means that during this period alone, the average length of time a person aged 65 spends in retirement has increased by 40 percent.[5]

Another factor that will strain the Social Security system is the dependency ratio in the United States. The *dependency ratio* is a measure of the number of nonworking dependents relative to the number of persons of working age. When measured this way (including children and older dependents) the dependency ratio in the United States peaked in 1965 when there were 94.7 dependents for every 100 persons of working age in the United States.[6] If we consider the dependency ratio of just older dependents, however, (which is a better indication of the burden to be borne by Social Security in the future), the ratio is estimated to increase dramatically, as can be seen in Table 1.1.

Since its inception, there have been changes to the Social Security system, partly in response to the demographic changes just discussed. First of all, the age at which a worker can start to receive full retirement benefits from the system has increased. Anyone born in 1937 or before can start receiving full retirement benefits at age 65. Workers born after that date will have to wait longer. The phase-in to older normal retirement dates gradually increases until those who were born in 1960 or after will have to wait until they are 67 to start receiving full retirement benefits from the Social Security system.[7]

Another change has been in the tax rate to which workers' wages are subjected.[8] The Old-Age, Survivors, and Disability Insurance (OASDI) tax rate was 1 percent of wages from 1937 to 1949.[9] In 1955, the rate was 2 percent; in 1960, the rate was 3 percent; in 1969, 4.2 percent; in 1978,

TABLE 1.1   Dependency Ratio

Year	All Dependents*	Persons 65 and Older*
1950	72.5	13.8
1965	94.7	18.2
1980	75.0	19.5
2010 (est.)	65.6	20.9
2040 (est.)	81.7	37.2
2080 (est.)	86.1	42.1

*Number of dependents per 100 persons of working age.
Source: Congressional Research Service.

5.05 percent; in 1988, 6.06 percent; and from 1990 to the present, it has been 6.2 percent.

Are these changes enough to prevent solvency problems down the road? Soon the amount of payments flowing out of the system to retirees and beneficiaries will increase dramatically relative to taxes coming into the system from workers. Eventually, the system will pay out more in benefits than it takes in from taxes. Once this happens, the system will begin to draw down on the trust surplus that has been built up from past tax revenue surpluses. If no other changes are made to Social Security (increased taxes or reduced benefits) the trust surplus will run out in the next 20 to 30 years.

Every year, every American who has paid into the U.S. Social Security system is sent a statement of benefits from the Social Security Administration. Printed on the front page of a Social Security statement from mid-2009 are the following two paragraphs:

> *Social Security is a compact between generations. For decades, America has kept the promise of security for its workers and their families. Now, however, the Social Security system is facing serious financial problems, and action is needed soon to make sure the system will be sound when today's younger workers are ready for retirement.*
>
> *In 2017 we will begin paying more in benefits than we collect in taxes. (A recent revision of this estimate suggests this actually may occur in 2010 due to the 2008–2009 global recession.) Without changes, by 2041 the Social Security Trust Fund will be exhausted* *

*These estimates are based on the intermediate assumptions from the Social Security Trustees' Annual Report to the Congress.

and there will be enough money to pay only about 78 cents for each dollar of scheduled benefits. We need to resolve these issues soon to make sure Social Security continues to provide a foundation of protection for future generations.

The Employer as a Source of Retirement Security

In the mid-twentieth century, as the United States's economy was growing rapidly after World War II, U.S. employers competed vigorously for workers. Employee turnover was expensive and employers looked for ways to tie workers to the company. There arose an unwritten pact between employer and employee that went something like "the employer will take care of the employees, the employees will take care of the customers, and business will be good." A common feature of this pact between employer and employee became the employer-provided pension plan. The employer pension usually took the form of a defined benefit plan whereby an employee working for an entire career with the same employer would receive a significant percentage (in many cases 100 percent) of their pre-retirement income in the form of a lifetime pension. In some of these plans the benefit included annual cost of living increases for the retirees.

Before 1975, there were fewer rules governing the funding and operation of defined benefit plans. Employers could operate their plans on a pay-as-you-go basis. Profits from production of current workers could be used to fund the benefit payments promised to retired workers. As long as the worker-retiree dependency ratio was favorable, the system worked. But this system was fraught with potential problems. When business declined or the ratio between workers and retirees began to shift, employers became stuck with liabilities in excess of their ability to pay. The laws governing defined benefit plans in the United States have tightened significantly over the years. Employers are now required to meet certain funding limits. Pension liabilities of public companies that used to be less than transparent now must be fully disclosed. Investment losses experienced by pension trusts must now be made up in a shorter time frame than in the past, causing a level of funding volatility that has become unbearable for many corporations. In addition to regulatory changes, the social compact between employer and employee has eroded. Today, employers have less visibility as to what their organization will look like in the future. Without this visibility, it is often unclear what type of workforce they will need even in as little as a few years into the future. For some employers, making a long-term pension commitment to their workers seems to make less sense than it did in the past, especially given the financial challenges associated with operating a defined benefit plan.

These are some of the main reasons why employers have shifted away from defined benefit plans toward defined contribution plans. In contrast, DC plans are always fully funded. There is no pension liability for the CEO or CFO to worry about. The employer has flexibility in determining what level of benefit the company will fund. As for the employee, she no longer has to work her entire career with a single employer to realize a meaningful retirement benefit. With the exception of some relatively short-term vesting requirements, employees are free to take their entire benefit with them when they move on to the next employer. In some ways, both the employer and employee benefit from the move toward DC plans, but there are challenges as well. When moving from a DB to a DC plan, employers are shifting certain risks from themselves to the employee. In a DC system, the employee takes on a greater level of the funding, investment, longevity, and spending risks related to his retirement security.

Funding Risk　　In most DC plans, when employers determine their level of contribution, they do so regardless of whether that contribution is sufficient to enable their employees to reach their wealth accumulation needs at retirement. The employees, of course, can adjust their contributions each year within the limits of the law. However, unlike in a DB plan, there are no actuarial calculations in DC plans to determine the level of funding needed to reach a certain "defined benefit." The funding risk inherent in a DC plan is therefore twofold. First, it is difficult for the employee, or the employer, to know if their contribution levels are sufficient to reach the participant's wealth accumulation goals. Second, even if the amount were known, the individual may not have the financial flexibility to adjust her contribution year to year to stay on track.

Investment Risk　　In a DB plan, the consequence of plan investments experiencing lower returns than expected is the employer contributing more money to the plan. In a DC plan, the consequence is the employee must contribute more money to their account or settle for a lower final account balance at retirement. The investment outcomes, whether good or bad, are absorbed by the employee's account. The investment risk borne by the participant is compounded in most cases by allowing participants to direct the investment of their accounts.

Longevity Risk　　DB plans offer longevity protection to the plan participant by offering an annuity form of benefit at retirement. Depending on the form of annuity, there may or may not be a survivor benefit when the participant dies. If the participant lives longer than expected, the defined benefit plan funds the additional cost of longevity by continuing to pay the participant his monthly benefit. If the participant dies earlier than expected, the defined benefit plan realizes a mortality credit (which offsets the cost of those living longer than expected). This describes the pooling of longevity risk that takes place in DB plans. With a DC plan, participants don't earn a monthly benefit; they accumulate an account balance. They can spend their account in retirement as fast or as slowly as they wish, but if they live longer than expected, however, they may run out of money.[10] This describes longevity risk, the risk of outliving your money. We discuss in Chapter 12 the ways a DC plan sponsor can help participants deal with longevity risk.

Spending Risk   In a DB plan, participants who reach retirement have earned the promise of a monthly pension from the plan sponsor. Unless the participants elect to forgo an annuity form of benefit and accept a lump sum payment, the participants will receive their benefit in monthly installments. They are not able to take an advance on future payments or borrow against their pension (at least not from the plan itself). This process imparts a spending discipline on the retiree. With a DC plan, though, participants who reach retirement age have access to their entire account at once. They may decide to take that account and buy an annuity, which imposes the same spending discipline as the DB pension, but very few DC participants buy annuities with their accounts upon retirement. This access to their entire account balance at once introduces spending risk to the DC participant. In cases of financial emergencies, having access to more than just one month's worth of retirement wealth can be a good thing. In many cases, however, spending risk manifests itself in the inability to spend in a disciplined manner or, spending at a rate that is too fast relative to the retiree's ultimate length of life. In this second example, spending risk and longevity risk are closely related.

The Individual as a Source of Retirement Security

In our traditional view of retirement security, the individual is the third source. Just as we've seen with Social Security and employer-provided retirement, the individual has challenges as well. For all but those on the doorstep of retirement, retirement seems a distant concern. Most people have more financial needs than they can satisfy and these needs compete with saving for retirement. Unfortunately, as the funding burden for retirement has been shifted to the individual, the national savings rate has dropped considerably. Putting off saving for retirement until later in life is difficult to overcome. Inertia is one of the many behavioral challenges that we as humans are hardwired with that gets in the way of sound retirement planning.

Lower Savings Rates   From 1952 to 2008, the average annual savings rate in the United States was just above 7 percent.[11] This savings rate is represented by the percentage of after-tax income that is not spent at the end of every year. Where this money ultimately ends up is another matter altogether and the exact method for calculating the national savings rate is always a popular subject for debate. What is important for our discussion here is not merely the absolute value of the national savings rate but how it has changed in the past few decades. For example, the average savings rate for the eight-year period from 1971 to 1978 was 9.72 percent. Thirty years later, the average savings rate for the eight-year period from 2001 to 2008 was 2.65 percent. There are two insights that might be drawn from these very different periods. First, the average for this most recent period is significantly below the long-term average of 7 percent. If personal savings becomes a more important source of retirement security in the future, a national savings rate below 3 percent is unlikely to be enough. Second, and possibly the unexpected bright side to this story, the savings rate for the 1970s might be a foreshadow of savings rates to come. If it turns out that the economic climate in the 2010s is similar to that of the 1970s, we may soon see dramatically higher savings rates than we've experienced recently.

Behavioral Challenges   There is an abundance of evidence that individuals often act irrationally when making financial decisions. The field of study that looks at the psychology behind how we make financial decisions is known as behavioral finance. Daniel Kahneman, a pioneer in the field of behavioral finance, won the Nobel Prize for Economics in 2002 for "having integrated insights from psychological research into economic science, especially concerning human judgment and decision-making under uncertainty."[12] More recently still, the field has been extended even further by researchers seeking to understand which parts of the brain are involved with specific types of financial decision making: hence the name *neuroeconomics* for this new science.

What we've learned so far from these new fields of studies is that humans have decision-making tendencies that cause suboptimal outcomes in their financial lives. In other words, we often behave badly when it comes to money. Most of these tendencies are hardwired in our brains. But now that we know they exist, we need to work around them to give ourselves the best chance at reaching our financial goals. Inertia causes people to delay participation in savings programs. Too many investment choices causes choice overload, which results in lower participation and often-inappropriate investment portfolios. Overconfidence and the tendency to chase last year's best returning funds too often results in lower investment returns than the capital markets are willing to deliver.

CONCLUSION

Today and in the future, individuals will be asked to take on more responsibility for the provision of their own retirement security. It is uncertain how reliable government and employer sources will be. 401(k) plans offer individuals several advantages: automatic features such as payroll deduction and automatic enrollment that can mitigate bad behavioral tendencies; employer contributions that help with the funding burden; and tax-advantaged treatment of contributions and earnings that allows for faster and greater wealth accumulation. 401(k) plans also usually provide lower investment and administration fees than the individual would experience in a retail setting.

CHAPTER 2

The Role of the Employer

A s we saw in Chapter 1, the importance of the 401(k) plan in providing retirement security has been increasing. While the nature and importance of the 401(k) plan evolves, so does the role of the employer in providing this retirement benefit. We discuss in this chapter how the employer's role is changing.

WHY DO EMPLOYERS SPONSOR 401(K) PLANS?

There is no law requiring employers to offer a retirement program yet encouraging (or possibly requiring at some time in the future) employers to provide their employees with access to a retirement savings program was an element of President Obama's financial regulatory reform initiative that he announced in July 2009. In some cases, employers are required to sponsor a 401(k) plan as a result of a collectively bargained agreement, but these plans represent a relatively small percentage of the 401(k) plans in existence today.

Could it be that employers just feel it is the right thing to do? Is this enough of a reason to spend the time, effort, and expense to sponsor a plan? There is a general feeling among employers that they have some responsibility to help their employees reach a secure retirement. In 2009, consulting firm Deloitte and the International Foundation conducted a 401(k) benchmarking survey in which they asked employers how they viewed their responsibility to prepare their employees for retirement. Twenty-three percent responded that they felt their only responsibility was to offer a competitive retirement plan. On the other end of the spectrum, 14 percent responded that they felt "very responsible" to prepare their employees for retirement. The remainder, 63 percent, felt their responsibility included "taking an interest whether their employees are tracking toward a comfortable retirement (that is, offering options that allow participants to plan for a reasonable replacement ratio)."[1]

Many employers believe that sponsoring a 401(k) plan is a sound business decision. They feel that it gives them a competitive advantage or at the very least prevents their competition from gaining a competitive advantage over them. 401(k) plans are seen as a tool to recruit, retain, and reward the workers needed to compete and be successful.

A final reason that is beginning to be discussed more among employers is the notion that a 401(k) plan can be a workforce management tool. First, there is evidence that financial stress causes lost production in the workplace. An employer with an effective retirement program, in which the benefits are well communicated to the participants, has a better chance at reducing stress in the workplace because of financial factors.[2] A 401(k) plan can also be a useful transition tool for employers who need to transition older workers out of the workplace but want to do so knowing that their older workers are financially able to have a secure retirement. A retirement program that is effective at helping workers accumulate enough for retirement helps ease the transition to a younger workforce.

WHAT ROLES DO EMPLOYERS PLAY?

There is a continuum of roles an employer can play in helping their employees prepare for retirement. On one end of the continuum we will place the label "Paternal." The fully paternalistic employer feels an obligation for providing his employees with a level of income in retirement that is comparable with the level of income during their working years. Whether or not any employer is actually at this end of the continuum, many employers have leaned this way, particularly those in industries that aggressively compete for specialized talent. We often see employers at this end of the continuum sponsoring defined benefit plans that provide a 100 percent or more of final pay retirement benefit.

At the other end of the continuum, we place the label "Libertarian." Employers in this group believe in allowing their employees full freedom to do as they wish with their compensation. Instead of providing an employer-sponsored retirement benefit, they give their employees the equivalent in the form of cash compensation. If the employees wish to set aside some of their cash compensation into a retirement program, such as an IRA, then so be it. The employer is not involved in deciding how to allocate their compensation in this way. Again, what we are describing here is one extreme end of the continuum. We are not saying there are employers occupying this end of the continuum per se, but if there were, they would be characterized by the mindset that "cash is king." They choose to pay their people higher cash salaries and let them decide how much to save for retirement for themselves (see Figure 2.1).

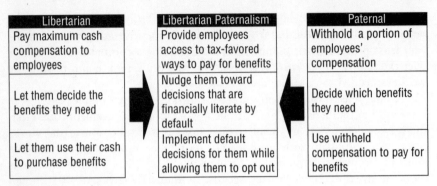

Libertarian	Libertarian Paternalism	Paternal
Pay maximum cash compensation to employees	Provide employees access to tax-favored ways to pay for benefits	Withhold a portion of employees' compensation
Let them decide the benefits they need	Nudge them toward decisions that are financially literate by default	Decide which benefits they need
Let them use their cash to purchase benefits	Implement default decisions for them while allowing them to opt out	Use withheld compensation to pay for benefits

FIGURE 2.1   Libertarian Paternalism Continuum

In real life, most employers are somewhere between these two end points on the continuum. We see employers moving toward a middle ground that can be labeled *libertarian paternalism*. We explain this apparently contradictory term a little later in this chapter.

We just described employers at each end of the continuum. What do employers look like who are in the middle? These employers feel they should neither do it all for their employees nor leave them entirely to their own devices. What should they do with their retirement programs? As it turns out, there are many things an employer can do that guides the employee in the right direction, yet leaves the ultimate responsibility up to them. Within the confines of a 401(k) plan, we have identified five actions a plan sponsor might consider. These include providing access to a tax-deferred savings program (such as a 401(k) plan); offering sensible choices through thoughtful plan design; leveraging institutional buying power; providing funding assistance in the form of an employer contribution; and practicing sound plan stewardship. We discuss each of these in detail on the following pages.

Provide Access

The most fundamental action an employer can take to help their employees reach a secure retirement is to sponsor a 401(k) plan. Even if the employer does not contribute to the plan and all plan expenses are paid by plan participants, sponsoring a plan is of real value to employees. It is true that individuals have the ability to contribute to an IRA, but a 401(k) plan has a couple of advantages over an IRA. Contribution limits are higher for 401(k) participants. For instance, IRA contribution limits in 2010 are $5,000 for individuals age 49 and under, and $6,000 for those 50 and older.

In comparison, 401(k) limits in 2010 are $16,500 for individuals age 49 and under, and $22,000 for those 50 and older. In addition, fees for investments and account maintenance (administration) are generally higher for IRAs than with 401(k) plans.

Develop and Offer Financially Literate Choices

Evidence from the field of behavioral finance, neuroeconomics, and observation of 401(k) plans over the past decades tells us that individuals often make poor choices about saving for retirement. We also know that there is no such thing as a neutral frame to a choice. That is, the way a choice is presented (framed) influences the choice itself. Whether it is the order of names on a ballot, the organization of food items at a school cafeteria, or the way investment choices are placed on a 401(k) enrollment form, the framing matters.

Employers, therefore, are the choice architects for their employees. The choice architect concept is covered in detail in the book *Nudge* by authors Richard Thaler and Cass Sunstein, and refers to someone who is responsible for "organizing the context in which people make decisions."[3] An example of choice architecture at work in 401(k) plans is the use of automatic features. For example, rather than merely allowing employees to participate in the company 401(k) plan, an automatic enrollment feature initiates the employee's participation unless she makes an affirmative decision to opt out of the plan. Another example is the operation of a default fund, where the investment of a participant's contributions are automatically invested if the participant does not make an affirmative decision as to where her account is to be invested. Many employers are using a target date fund, balanced fund, or professionally managed account as the plan's default investment. Historically, these types of investments have shown to be more diversified than the funds' participants tend to choose on their own. And finally, more and more plans are implementing automatic escalation of the participant's contribution rate unless the participant makes a deliberate decision to not have their contribution increased. As an example of this feature, a participant who was automatically enrolled into the plan at a 3 percent contribution level would have his contribution rate increased by a percentage point or two every year until the rate reached some predetermined maximum, such as 10 or 15 percent.

By implementing these automatic features, the employer has framed each choice. If the default is to enroll in the plan, invest in a diversified portfolio, and to increase the contribution rate each year, then more employees will make these choices (or let inertia work to their benefit by doing nothing). Whether consciously or subconsciously, the employee is affected by the frame of the choice. The default carries an implied endorsement of the employer. The fact that these features are supported by the Pension Protection Act of 2006 (PPA) strongly suggests at the very least an implied endorsement by Congress.

The notion that there is no such thing as a neutral frame for a choice, and that employers are choice architects, whether they want to be or not, brings us back to the concept we mentioned earlier—libertarian paternalism. This concept is also discussed in more detail in *Nudge*. Here the authors explain: "We are keenly aware that this term is not one that readers will find immediately endearing. Both words are somewhat off-putting, weighted down by stereotypes from popular culture and politics that make them unappealing to many. Even worse, the concepts seem to be contradictory....We argue that if the terms are properly understood, both concepts reflect common sense—and they are far more attractive together than alone."

Libertarians believe that people should be free to do what they like. Paternalism seeks to steer (or nudge) people in directions that is thought will improve their lives. It is therefore legitimate for choice architects to try to influence people's behavior in order to make their lives longer, healthier, and better while at the same time allowing them considerable freedom to do what they like. After all, they can always opt out of the default choice if they wish.

Leverage Buying Power

Generally speaking, 401(k) plans with large assets or plans that have a high average participant account balance pay the lowest investment and administration fees. It therefore follows that plan sponsors should be aware that as their plans grow, their ability to negotiate lower fees on behalf of their plan(s) increases. In some cases, employers who have both defined benefit and defined contribution plans can combine their purchasing power across both plans to negotiate lower fees than either plan would be able to negotiate separately. When using the combined purchasing leverage of both plans, employers must be careful not to make a decision that is in the best interest of one plan but at the cost of the other.

Provide Funding Assistance

If a worker were to save a consistent percentage of her paycheck from the very beginning of her career to the day she retires, *and* her salary stayed consistent in real dollars for her entire career, *and* her account earned a steady investment return of 7 percent each year, the percentage she would need to save to reach a reasonable income replacement ratio would be fairly low, somewhere in the range of 6 percent of pay. The problem is that in reality this never happens. Something else happens. Pay and contribution rates fluctuate, investment returns experience volatility, bad investment decisions are made, hardship withdrawals are taken, or account balances are spent when the participant changes jobs. These things happen to most people. So, the 6 percent contribution that is enough when we run the calculation on our spreadsheet is, all of a sudden, not enough when we are out in the real world. Most people need to save more than 6 percent of pay, and if their employer can help with the funding, they have a better chance of reaching a secure retirement.

At the time this chapter was written, the most common employer matching contribution was 50 percent of the first 6 percent of compensation. In other words, for every dollar the employee contributes to the plan (up to 6 percent of his compensation) the employer will match that contribution by putting in an additional 50 cents. If the employee contributes 6 percent of his pay, the employer will contribute 3 percent (for a total of 9 percent). Based on 2008 data, Vanguard found that the average total contribution, including employee and employer amounts, going into a participant's account was 10.4 percent. However, this figure only considers employees who chose to participate. When all eligible employees were added to the calculation (including those who were eligible but contributing nothing to the plan) the average total contribution was 7.6 percent.[4]

Provide Sound Stewardship

In the early years of 401(k) plans, many plans were started as supplementary savings programs. That is to say that these plans were supposed to be in addition to the main or real retirement program, which was typically a DB plan. While the laws governing 401(k) plans have consistently held that plan fiduciaries must adhere to a strict standard of always acting in the best interest of the plan participants and beneficiaries, the common stewardship practices for 401(k) plans did not start out in a fully evolved form. With a DB plan, the effect of decisions regarding plan oversight and operations was generally felt by the plan sponsor. For example, if plan assets underperformed because of lax investment oversight, the plan sponsor was on the hook to make up the difference because it still owed the participants benefits defined under the plan. The plan participant typically did not feel the effect. Stewardship processes for DB plans therefore evolved within this context. However, things are different in DC plans. The effects of many of the decisions regarding plan investments and operations are felt directly by the participants, not the plan sponsor. To be clear, if the investment funds in the DC plan were of poor quality relative to other fund options that could have been used, the participants were the ones who incurred the cost.

Over the years, the best practice stewardship model for 401(k) plans has evolved with the understanding that the plan fiduciaries have an obligation to make sound decisions that are in the best interest of the plan participants. This is so even though they as plan sponsors are not a direct beneficiary of these decisions. Chapter 5 is dedicated to the specifics of being a good plan fiduciary. We discuss here seven trends we see in the evolution of 401(k) plan stewardship. For each trend, we describe where plan stewards may have been in the past and where they are heading.

Plan Management   The trend: *From* relinquishing plan management to recordkeepers *toward* acting as empowered managers.

There are many high quality recordkeepers in the 401(k) industry who do a great job of managing their clients' 401(k) plans. However, this does not mean that the management of a 401(k) plan should be relinquished to the recordkeeper. The plan sponsor may feel the plan is on auto-pilot and all is running smoothly. The plan sponsor should still take an active and empowered role in the management and oversight of the plan. The plan sponsor cannot delegate plan stewardship responsibility to the recordkeeper no matter how effective the recordkeeping process seems to be. We discuss in detail later in this book service provider oversight that we call "vendor management." Sound vendor management is part of plan sponsor oversight responsibilities and involves setting clear expectations about service standards, measuring key service metrics on a regular basis, and providing clear feedback to providers as to what is going well and what needs improvement. Clearly, managing the recordkeeper is part of good plan stewardship and the recordkeeper cannot oversee itself.

Governance   The trend: *From* nonexistent or casual governance processes *toward* having prudent and consistent governance processes.

There is an old saying that "prudence is process." Sound plan governance means that those responsible for oversight and management are identified, their responsibilities are clearly documented, they have the expertise to carry out their duties or have access to experts to assist them, they meet regularly to review and discuss appropriate information, and they make and document their decisions. In short, there is a prudent and consistent process in place and the process is followed.

Investment Oversight   The trend: *From* nonexistent or inexpert investment oversight *toward* expert investment oversight.

To be done well, the selection and ongoing evaluation of investments requires specific expertise. Even trained experts struggle with this task at times. The 401(k) plan fiduciaries are ultimately responsible for selecting and evaluating the funds in their plan. This is typically done through an investment or benefits committee. (Throughout this book there are references to committees. The words *plan, retirement, investment, benefits* and *fiduciary* are used to describe committees. In many cases these committee names are interchangeable. The name of the committee is not as important as the committee's charter, the responsibilities they are formally given.) Chapter 7 is dedicated to investment oversight issues. We want to make the point here that if the plan sponsor or committee does not have expertise in investment oversight, they have an obligation to seek out such expertise from someone outside the committee. Many plan sponsors believe their plan recordkeeper provides investment oversight. But, in many cases the recordkeeper is only reporting results or providing publicly available information. The level of investment oversight needed is typically much more detailed than this. More importantly many recordkeepers, due to their affiliation with investment management businesses, lack the necessary independence and objectivity, which is our next stewardship topic.

Independence and Objectivity   The trend: *From* decision makers with potential conflicts of interest *toward* independent and objective decision making.

Plan sponsors need to be aware of how companies and individuals are compensated as it relates to decisions made about their 401(k) plan. Does the recordkeeper make more profit if the plan uses investment funds the recordkeeper (or an affiliate) manages? Does the investment advisor make a higher fee, or the broker a higher commission, depending on the services or products chosen by the plan sponsor? Product and service providers, as well as their employees and agents, should be paid a fair amount for their efforts. As a matter of fact, it is in everyone's best interest that the organizations and individuals who serve 401(k) plans make a fair and sustainable profit. Otherwise, the participants suffer in the long run because the services these organizations provide, when done correctly, directly benefit all participants. However, plan sponsors need to have a keen understanding of how these entities are paid, especially when these entities are providing information that plan sponsors will ultimately use in their decision making.

Fee Transparency   The trend: *From* lack of fee transparency *toward* absolute fee transparency.

There are two areas of fee transparency that are important. First, the plan sponsor should have a crystal clear view of all fees charged by service providers and investment managers regardless of who ends up paying these fees. Second, plan participants should have access to easy-to-understand fee information regarding any fees they are paying. One of the problems with fee transparency is that some fees are simply not disclosed to the plan sponsor, the plan participants, or both. Often, fees that are disclosed are reported in such an arcane or complicated fashion that the average participant does not have a reasonable chance of understanding exactly what she is paying. Transparency and ease of understanding will eventually be solved through fee disclosure laws and associated regulations. At the time this chapter was written, several bills had been introduced into Congress regarding fee disclosure to plan sponsors and plan participants.

Value for Fees Paid   The trend: *From* unclear value for fees paid *toward* clear value for fees paid.

Fee transparency is a prerequisite to ensuring you are receiving good value for the fees you are paying. This does not mean you must hire the cheapest service provider or use the cheapest investment funds available, but rather you should have a clear understanding what value is being delivered for the fees being paid. We have found that plan sponsors may be paying for services that are not being used or valued by participants. In these cases, the plan sponsor has an opportunity to negotiate other services for these fees or a reduction in, or elimination of, these fees. A case in point is employee communications. Many times, the recordkeeper has a communications budget built into the administration fee being charged to the plan. We have seen plan sponsors unaware that they have a budget that can be used for this purpose. If this portion of the overall fees is eventually charged to plan participants, it is the sponsor's fiduciary duty to make the best use of this fee or negotiate a fee reduction.

Flexibility   The trend: *From* slow to change *toward* flexibility to change when needed.

Employers and plan fiduciaries should have the ability to make changes to their plan features and operations when needed. As an example of "slow to change," let's take the case of a plan that was relatively small in asset size just a few years ago and uses mutual funds for all of its investment choices. Today, the plan's assets may have grown considerably from where they were a few years ago. As the plan grows in size, it can become eligible for other investment structures such as commingled investment trusts or separate accounts that may offer fee advantages over the current mutual funds in the plan. If the plan sponsor relies on other parties to make them aware of these opportunities, years could pass before this detail is noticed or brought to the sponsor's attention.

CONCLUSION

Employers in the United States are not required to sponsor 401(k) plans, and as such, they get to choose what role they play in providing this benefit. Their choices are defined by a continuum framed at one end by a libertarian point of view and at the other end by a paternalistic point of view. Most employers seem to choose somewhere between these end points. A libertarian paternalism is beginning to emerge in which employees are given the freedom to do what they wish while they are at the same time being gently nudged toward making decisions that are financially literate by default.

Behind the scenes, the evolution of plan stewardship continues. Plan sponsors are beginning to take a more active role in the management of their plans, applying prudent and consistent governance processes, including expert investment oversight, seeking more independent and objective advice to help them make better decisions, demanding greater fee transparency, getting greater value for the fees they pay, and preserving their flexibility to make changes to their plan as the need arises.

CHAPTER 3

Measuring Retirement Readiness

How can we tell if someone is financially ready for retirement? The answer is different for everyone, but with a basic measurement tool we can get to a meaningful starting point. We introduced in Chapter 1 the Replacement Ratio Study conducted by Aon Consulting in conjunction with Georgia State University. This study attempts to define retirement readiness by calculating a person's needed income replacement ratio. Much of the content in the first half of this chapter comes from Aon's 2008 Replacement Ratio Study.

The first part of this chapter discusses replacement ratios in detail. The second part covers five areas of 401(k) plan management that can improve retirement readiness.

REPLACEMENT RATIOS

A replacement ratio is a person's gross income *after* retirement, divided by his or her gross income *before* retirement. For example, assume someone earns $50,000 per year before retirement. Furthermore, assume that his gross income after retirement is $40,000 from Social Security and other sources. This person's replacement ratio is 80 percent because:

$$\$40,000 \ / \ \$50,000 = 0.8, \text{ or } 80 \text{ percent}$$

The Aon/Georgia State Replacement Ratio study analyzes the replacement ratio individuals need to maintain their pre-retirement standard of living after retirement. Generally, a person doesn't need as much gross income after retiring, primarily because of four factors:

1. Income taxes go down after retirement. This is because extra deductions are available for those over age 65, and taxable income usually decreases at retirement.

TABLE 3.1   Replacement Ratio for Individual Retiring at 65

	Pre-Retirement (A)	Post-Retirement (B)	Replacement Ratio (B) Divided by (A)
Gross Income	$60,000	$46,972	78%
Taxes*	(10,967)	(49)	
Savings†	(2,225)	0	
Age- and Work-Related Expenses‡	(34,253)	(34,368)	
Amount Left for Other Living Expenses	12,555	12,555	

*Tax rates and Social Security amounts are based on the laws in effect on January 1, 2008.
†Savings are assumed to stop at retirement.
‡Age- and work-related expenses are listed in detail in the full version of the 2008 Replacement Ratio Study.

2. Social Security taxes (FICA deductions from wages) end completely at retirement.
3. Social Security benefits are partially or fully tax-free. This reduces taxable income and, therefore, the amount of income needed to pay taxes.
4. Saving for retirement is no longer needed.

In addition to these factors, changes in age- and work-related expenditures that occur at retirement also influence the amount of income someone needs in retirement. Changes in these expenditures, however, vary from person to person.

Table 3.1 shows that a 78 percent Replacement Ratio would allow a person earning $60,000 to retire at age 65 in 2008 without reducing her standard of living. Because taxes and savings decrease at retirement, this person is just as well off after retirement with a gross income of only just $46,972.

The primary data source for this information is the U.S. Department of Labor's Bureau of Labor Statistics' Consumer Expenditure Survey (CES). This is essentially the same database that is used to construct the Consumer Price Index. The CES is done annually, and Aon used data from the most recent years available at the time—2003, 2004, and 2005. These data include information on 12,823 working consumer units and 6,498 retired consumer units.

Table 3.2 shows the baseline case results for the 2008 Replacement Ratio Study. The baseline case assumes a family situation in which there is one wage earner who retires at age 65 with a spouse aged 62. Thus, the family unit is eligible for family Social Security benefits, which are 1.375 times the wage earner's benefit. The baseline case also takes into account age- and work-related expenditure changes after retirement, in addition to pre-retirement savings patterns and changes in taxes after retirement.

Figure 3.1 illustrates three significant points about the replacement ratio calculations:

TABLE 3.2   2008 Replacement Ratio Findings

Pre-Retirement Income ($000)	Social Security–Provided Replacement Ratio	Private and Employer-Provided Replacement Ratio	Total Replacement Ratio Needed
20	69	25	94
30	59	31	90
40	54	31	85
50	51	30	81
60	46	32	78
70	42	35	77
80	39	38	77
90	36	42	78

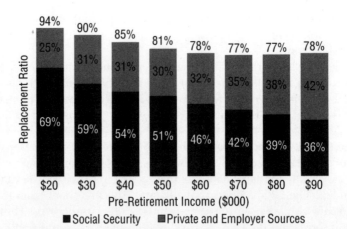

FIGURE 3.1   Required Replacement Ratios Broken Down by Source

- Social Security replaces a larger portion of pre-retirement income at lower wage levels. This is by design. Social Security has the effect of redistributing income from higher paid to lower paid individuals.
- Total replacement ratios that are required to maintain a person's pre-retirement standard of living are highest for the very lowest paid individuals. This is primarily for two reasons. First, before they retire, lower paid individuals save the least and pay the least in taxes as a percentage of their income. Thus, they spend a higher percentage of their income and need higher Replacement Ratios to maintain that level of expenditures. Second, age- and work-related expenditures do not decrease by as much, as a percentage of income, for the lower paid individuals. This also means they need more income after retirement (as a percentage of their pre-retirement income) than the higher paid individuals.
- After reaching an income level of $60,000, the total required replacement ratios remain fairly constant at 77 to 78 percent. This is primarily because post-retirement taxes increase as income levels increase. Post-retirement taxes increase from 0.1 percent of post-retirement income for a $60,000 person to 6.7 percent for a $90,000 person. To pay the additional taxes, higher paid individuals need more retirement income.

One reason the highest income individuals pay more tax after retirement is that as much as 85 percent of a married couple's Social Security benefit is taxable when retirement income (including 50 percent of Social Security) goes above $44,000. It is important to note that at the time this chapter was written (2010) the $44,000 threshold is not indexed like other tax break points. As time goes on and the nominal dollar value of Social Security benefits increase, more and more of a person's Social Security benefit will be taxed.

The Effect of Income on the Replacement Ratio

The year 2008 marked the first time that there was some usable Consumer Expenditure Survey (CES) data available at income levels above $90,000. These data are less complete than at income levels at $90,000 and below. Using the available data, the replacement ratio calculations were extended to income levels of $150,000, $200,000, and $250,000.

Table 3.3 shows that the ratios continue to trend upward as income levels increase. Although higher pre-retirement taxes paid by higher income individuals have a decreasing effect on replacement ratios, higher post-retirement taxes have an even more powerful effect and drive the ratios upward. The net effect is that higher replacement ratios are needed as income increases.

TABLE 3.3 Replacement Ratios at Higher Income Levels

Pre-Retirement Income ($000)	Social Security (%)	Private and Employer Sources (%)	Total Replacement Ratio (%)
80	39	38	77
90	36	42	78
150	23	61	84
200	17	69	86
250	14	74	88

It would be difficult for high income individuals to generate sufficient retirement income solely from Social Security and an employer's qualified plans. These individuals generally need to receive a substantial portion of their retirement income from other sources such as personal savings or a nonqualified arrangement sponsored by their employer.

Lump Sums

Retirement adequacy has traditionally been measured by replacement ratios. However, in situations in which savings accounts (some combination of IRAs, personal savings, and balances in 401(k) or similar plans) are a person's largest source of retirement income, it is also useful to define how large a lump sum needs to be to provide an adequate retirement income stream. The answer depends on a number of factors, such as:

■ How long will a person live after retirement? Those who live longer after retiring need larger lump sums. It is also true that people retiring at younger ages generally need more than people retiring at older ages, because they have longer remaining lifetimes. In addition, females generally need more than males because, on average, they live longer than men. A male retiring at age 65 lives an average of 18.3 additional years, while the average female lives an additional 20.5 years. Lifestyle, health, and other factors also influence one's lifespan.
■ How much will inflation increase a retiree's cost of living after retirement? The higher the rate of inflation, the larger the lump sum needed.
■ What rate of investment return will the lump sum earn in retirement? The higher the rate, the smaller the lump sum needed at retirement.

Examples of how different rates of investment return affect the lump sum needed are shown in Table 3.4. Table 3.4 shows the lump sum amount needed at retirement to provide an income of $100 per month for life to an average male or female retiring at age 65. While invested, the lump sum

TABLE 3.4   Lump Sum Needed at Retirement to Provide a
$100 Monthly Income

	Assumed Annual Rate of Investment Return After Retirement		
	4%	6%	8%
Male	$19,509	$16,160	$13,669
Female	$21,635	$17,571	$14,633

TABLE 3.5   Lump Sum Needed (as a Multiple of Final Pay) at Retirement from Private and Employer Sources

Pre-Retirement Income ($000)	Replacement Ratio Needed (% of final pay)	Equivalent Lump Sum Needed (as a multiple of final pay)	
		Male	Female
20	25	4.0	4.5
30	31	5.0	5.5
40	31	5.0	5.5
50	30	4.8	5.4
60	32	5.2	5.7
70	35	5.6	6.3
80	38	6.1	6.8
90	42	6.8	7.5

is assumed to return 4 percent, 6 percent, or 8 percent per year. In all cases, the $100 payment is assumed to increase 3 percent per year to allow the retiree to keep up with inflation.

As you can see in Table 3.4, the lump sum needed at retirement is about 45 percent more if the investments return is 4 percent, rather than 8 percent. Also, on average, women need about 9 percent more than men across the board because they live longer.

Since the amount of the lump sum needed at retirement depends on so many factors, it is hard to know exactly how much to target. One approach is to target the amount that's needed to buy an annuity that will provide the desired level of retirement income. Using this approach, and annuity prices that were quoted to Aon at the time the 2008 study was written, lump sum amounts needed at retirement were calculated. These amounts, expressed as a multiple of a person's salary at retirement, are shown in Table 3.5.

The lump sum multiples shown in Table 3.5 are in addition to income that is expected to be provided by Social Security. Individuals with a defined benefit plan will have part of their post-retirement income provided through that program. Thus, they won't need as large a lump as those indicated in Table 3.5.

We've seen here how to calculate a replacement ratio. Next we'll look at how to help individuals and groups of individuals improve their retirement readiness.

IMPROVING RETIREMENT READINESS

Employers are becoming more interested in determining the retirement readiness of their workforce and how levels of retirement readiness affect their ability to manage their employee group. There are several challenges associated with making these determinations. Most employers do not have access to all of the data that affect retirement readiness calculations, including wealth outside the employer's sponsored plans, retirement benefits accrued with other employers, and complete career compensation history.

While it might not be possible to get a precise read on a group of employees' retirement readiness, there are steps that can be taken to improve the effectiveness of your 401(k) plan. In the following section we discuss five areas of a plan design and management that can positively affect retirement readiness: participation rates, contribution rates, investment fees and performance, participant performance, and post-retirement income efficiency. At the end, we briefly discuss the common forms of leakage from 401(k) plans.

Participation Rates

By their nature, 401(k) plans are voluntary. Based on the analysis provided by one major 401(k) recordkeeper, we know that when left to make the decision on their own, only about 60 percent of individuals elect to participate in an employer-sponsored 401(k) plan.[1] Despite massive amounts of communication directed at employees and a mainstream understanding of 401(k) plans, inertia prevents participation rates from being higher.

As early as 1984, employers began experimenting with automatically enrolling their employees into 401(k) plans.[2] It was called "negative enrollment" (or "negative election") at the time because the employee had to make an election to *not* be enrolled into the plan. The negative enrollment moniker did not stick and we now know the practice as automatic enrollment. Congress made it easier for plan sponsors to automatically enroll their employees with the passage of PPA in 2006. By superseding state laws that might have prevented this practice and by providing fiduciary relief to plan sponsors using automatic enrollment, PPA became the turning point for the adoption of automatic enrollment. Keep in mind that regardless of whether automatic enrollment is used, participants always have the right to opt out of participation if they so choose.

A common concern of plan sponsors regarding automatic enrollment is that it can create unreasonable administrative cost and complexity. This can be especially true if the workforce is subject to high turnover, or is very young, paid at a lower rate, or both. All of these conditions tend to result in a large number of small account balances. These concerns have merit, and employers must make their own cost-benefit decisions regarding automatic enrollment. However, the long-term participation rates for plans using automatic enrollment are significantly higher (84 percent according to the same recordkeeper referenced earlier) than for purely voluntary plans.

Contribution Rates

Paying off college debt, starting a family, establishing a household, saving for college, and everyday living expenses are just a few of the demands that compete for the dollars that could otherwise be contributed to a 401(k) account. The average contribution rate among those participating in 401(k) plans is about 7 percent of pay.[3] This figure is an average for those who participate in these plans and it does not take into consideration those who do not, and thus contribute zero percent of pay. After adding in employer contributions, the average percent of pay contribution is about 10.4 percent.

It is literally impossible to determine the exact percentage of pay any one individual needs to set aside for retirement without knowing the circumstances that apply to each situation. In some cases 10.4 percent will be enough, but in many cases it will not. Regardless of what the appropriate percentage may be, employers have ways to help raise employee contribution rates.

Interestingly, average contribution rates for participants in automatic enrollment plans are lower (6.3 percent) than those in purely voluntary plans (7.6 percent). On the surface this may look like the automatic enrollment feature has a dampening effect on contribution rates. However, the real impact is that more employees are participating in the automatic enrollment plan and those additional participants (those who would have otherwise contributed zero percent) are now having their contribution rates added to the calculation. They are contributing at a percent lower than the average but at least they are now contributing. The most common initial default contribution rate for plans utilizing automatic enrollment is 3 percent of pay.

One way to raise the contribution rates for those who are automatically enrolled is to use another automatic feature, the automatic escalation, or increase, of contributions. Auto escalation is the practice of increasing the participants' contribution rate each year. This practice is also endorsed by PPA. The most common rate of auto escalation is a 1 percent annual increase. The annual increase continues until the participant's contribution rate reaches a predetermined level such as 10 or 15 percent of pay. The combination of auto enrollment and escalation results in more people contributing and at higher levels than they would have if they were left to make the decision on their own.

As more employees become familiar with automatic enrollment and escalation, a potential side effect emerges. Let's assume a person changes employers every seven years and makes no contribution elections, yet they contribute at a 3 percent rate in their first year (because they were automatically enrolled in the plan at that percentage rate). Then, their contribution rate increases at 1 percent increments in years two through seven, topping out at 10 percent just as they are ready to move on to their next employer. When they start their next job, they start over at a 3 percent contribution level. This creates a saw-toothed pattern of contribution rates with relatively low contribution rates for many years during their career (their first few years with each employer).

There are a couple of ways to address this problem. One solution is to use a higher initial default contribution rate, say 7 percent or more. Several recordkeepers who have tracked the opt-out rates of participants in auto enrollment plans have reported that there is not significantly higher opt-out rates in plans using higher initial default contribution rates (above 3 percent). Another solution is to escalate contributions at a faster rate than 1 percent per year. It is obvious but worth stating that using a 2 percent escalation rate gets contribution rates moving upward twice as fast as a 1 percent rate, boosting the growth rate in contribution percentage by a full 100 percent.

Investment Fees and Performance

While contributions to a retirement account provide the basis for wealth accumulation, investment returns can represent as much as 90 percent of the total value of all benefits ultimately paid out.[4] It's common to hear the advice that a plan should use investments that have low fees and superior performance. In practice, choosing high quality investments that give your participants the best chance at superior returns over a long-term horizon, and at fees that are reasonable, is at best, difficult to do. Fortunately, there are well-established processes that can be followed that will yield a reasonable chance of having investment options with superior performance and reasonable fees.

The place to start is to get professional help. If the plan has a benefits or retirement committee with members who are trained in investment analysis, then they may already have the expertise they need. If the committee does not have the internal expertise, they have an obligation to seek expert advice. Given the nature and challenges of this process, outside assistance is almost always beneficial. (We cover this topic in greater detail in Chapter 7.) An investment consultant can help ensure that the funds in the plan meet the fee and performance standards set out in the plan's investment policy statement. Regular monitoring (at least quarterly) of the plan's investments is the foundation of a sound fiduciary process.

Beyond regular monitoring, there are structural considerations that can affect the fees (and in turn the performance) of investments. For example, it is true that many mutual funds have multiple share classes with different fees for each share class. The lower fee share classes are usually only offered to larger investors. As plan assets grow, the plan may qualify for lower fee share classes for the funds in the plan. Plan sponsors should check with their fund managers regularly to ensure they are using the lowest fee share class available.

Share class is not the only avenue that can save money on investment fees. Many investment funds are available in a fund type that is cheaper than a mutual fund. For example, commingled investment trusts (CITs) often charge lower fees and may be available as an alternative to a mutual fund that is already being used in the plan. While CITs often require higher minimum investments than mutual funds they are worth investigating as the plan assets grow.

Another potential way to capture lower investment fees is to manage the number of fund choices in the plan. In terms of efficiency, it almost always makes sense to have as few funds as possible in order to capture economies of scale that allow the plan to qualify for lower fee options. This must be balanced with providing sufficient investment choice to allow participants to appropriately diversify their portfolios, but this can usually be accomplished while at the same time avoiding unnecessary duplication in fund type or investment style. A lower fund count tends to lead to higher total assets per fund. Higher asset levels per fund can help a plan qualify for lower fee share classes, or even CITs as discussed in the previous paragraphs, saving considerable participant expense in the process.

This approach yields additional benefits. When plans offer too many investment choices, they can cause participant confusion and anxiety, which can lead to suboptimal investing behavior. As a practical example, think of a plan that offers participants a choice of three funds in the same asset class and style. If those three funds are substantially similar in style and quality, the plan sponsor may consider consolidating the three funds into one with the resulting fund having an account balance equal to the previous three. Now, at a higher balance, the plan may qualify for a lower share class for the resulting fund. It is important to keep in mind, that the plan fiduciaries must consistently balance any potential fee savings against the effect any reduction in fund choice might have on each participant's ability to appropriately diversify her portfolio. The resulting decisions should always be in the best interest of plan participants and beneficiaries.

Participant Performance

Participant performance is a separate and distinct topic from investment performance. While fund investment performance focuses strictly on the funds themselves, participant performance has to do with the actual returns the participants experience in their accounts. A plan can have an investment lineup that features many of the best available funds in each category, but if participants use the funds inappropriately, they could end up with lower investment returns than they should. How much lower? Research has shown that participants who create their own investment portfolios versus those who delegate this task (through the use of target date funds, balanced funds, or model portfolios) experience lower investment returns by as much as 250 to 300 basis points per year.[5] The main driver for the difference has to do with the investing behavior of the participants.

When it comes to investing their retirement accounts, participants fall into one of three broad categories: those who want someone else to make all the investment decisions for them (do it for me), those who want some help but also want the final say in their investment choices (help me do it), and those who want maximum flexibility and the freedom to do whatever they want (I'll do it myself). The majority of participants fall into the "do it for me" category.

The realization that participants organize themselves into these groups has led many plan sponsors to create a tiered structure to their investment lineup. The first tier is usually made up of a series of target date or target risk funds (also known as lifecycle and lifestyle funds) that are easier for participants to assess and select. In most cases, the participant is best served by choosing a single fund in this category, in which the diversification and rebalancing are done for the participant within the fund. It is now common for these types of funds to be used as the default investment for those who are automatically enrolled in the plan. The second tier typically contains a broad range of funds, often referred to as the Core Menu, organized into distinct asset classes sufficient in range to allow a participant to create a well-diversified portfolio. The due diligence the plan sponsor provides for these funds ensures the participants are working with high quality building blocks as they build their own portfolios. The third tier (if the plan sponsor chooses a third tier) is often an open platform of investments such as a mutual fund window in which the participant can access a very broad range of investments. The participant should be aware when investing in this tier that he is virtually on his own when it comes to levels of risk and diversification in the resulting portfolio. The plan sponsor is best advised to make this fact clear to these participants, and some have taken this to the level of securing written acknowledgment of the essentially self-service nature of the due diligence effort participants need to expend in this tier.

The point of explaining the three-tiered structure is to emphasize that most participants are likely to be better off in the first tier. They are better off from the standpoint of both reduced anxiety, and are likely to be better off from an investment performance perspective. Industry experience suggests that any effort to encourage the use of tier one–type investments, whether it be through designating them as the plan default investment or through communication efforts emphasizing these funds, will likely result in better participant investment performance.

Post-Retirement Income Efficiency

In the book *The Retirement Plan Solution: The Reinvention of Defined Contribution,* the authors introduce the 10/30/60 Rule, which states that for every dollar spent in retirement from a DC account, 10 percent comes from contributions made to the account before retirement, 30 percent comes from investment earnings earned before retirement, and 60 percent comes from investment earnings earned after retirement. However, this rule only holds true if the individual is able to gradually draw down the retirement account at a rate that allows the assets to last for most or all of her remaining lifetime. If the account is spent too fast, the individual loses a substantial opportunity for investment returns.

There are many reasons why individuals inefficiently manage their income in retirement. Some of the main reasons include: not knowing what a reasonable spending rate is, lack of discipline to adhere to a sensible spending plan, and unexpected or unplanned-for expenses. Policy makers and employers are now beginning to look at ways they can encourage retirees to manage their income more efficiently. Chapter 12 explores this topic and potential solutions in greater detail. The point is that the efficient management of retirement income, whether it be through planning, discipline, or investment vehicles such as annuities, can greatly extend the length of time an individual's wealth will last in retirement.

A Word about Plan Leakage

Leakage refers to dollars leaving the plan that are used for a purpose other than retirement. Hardship distributions and participant loans that are not paid back upon termination are a couple of the most common forms of leakage from 401(k) plans. While it would be an easy fix to just eliminate these plan features, from a practical standpoint, many employees would not participate if they didn't have these safety valve features available to them.

Still, some of this leakage is unnecessary and may be prevented. One tactic a plan sponsor may consider is to provide financial advice at the point of origination. For instance, requiring plan participants to meet with a financial advisor to explore other ways to solve their financial hardship before a hardship distribution is approved may eliminate unnecessary hardship distributions. The personal privacy of the participant, time commitment, and the cost of the financial advice are all factors a plan sponsor must weigh before implementing such a program.

CONCLUSION

Retirement readiness can be determined only on an individual basis, but a replacement ratio methodology provides a solid foundation from which to begin. Lower income earners will need a smaller percentage of income replacement from private and employer sources, yet may have more competing needs for their discretionary income in their pre-retirement years, making saving for retirement difficult. Higher income earners will need to rely more heavily on private sources for income since they face funding limitations in employer-sponsored tax-qualified retirement accounts. They will also have a much smaller portion of the income replaced by Social Security than will lower income workers.

Regardless of where employees are on the retirement readiness scale, there are a number of ways to improve the effectiveness of a 401(k) plan in helping to boost their wealth accumulation. These include improving participation and contribution rates, ensuring the plan has reasonably priced high quality investment options, encouraging the use of prediversified investment portfolios, and providing plan participants with distribution options that support a sensible spending plan once in retirement.

CHAPTER 4

Establishing a 401(k) Plan

Most 401(k) plans are sponsored by for-profit taxable organizations, but others, including nongovernmental tax-exempt organizations and Native American tribal governments, may sponsor 401(k) plans as well. There are a few grandfathered 401(k) plans in existence for governmental entities. In general, however, governmental entities can no longer establish new 401(k) plans.

There are places in this book where we refer to a 401(k) plan as a *qualified plan*. This term reflects the fact that 401(k) plans meet the qualifications of the Internal Revenue Code (Code). Meeting the qualifications of the Code allows employers to deduct contributions made to the plan as business expenses and for employees to defer the taxes related to contributions made on their behalf.

We begin this chapter with a brief overview of how a typical 401(k) plan works followed by a discussion on establishing plan objectives and benchmarking plan design features against a peer group. Also discussed in this chapter are plan setup topics including plan documentation and trust requirements.

HOW A 401(K) PLAN WORKS

The general concept of a 401(k) plan is simple enough—an employee chooses to defer a portion of her current pay, and instead sets that money aside in a retirement account. The deferred pay and investment income on her retirement account is not immediately subject to federal (and, in most cases, state) income tax, therefore minimizing the impact of the reduction in take-home pay. Over the course of the employee's working career, her contributions will continue going into her account on a regular basis, allowing her to take advantage of dollar-cost averaging and hopefully earn an adequate investment return. Upon retirement, the employee will be able to withdraw from the accumulated balance to provide a revenue stream (to supplement Social Security and any other pension benefit). At that time, the money withdrawn will be subject to income taxes (unless the account is a Roth account).

The operation of a 401(k) plan is, of course, much more complicated than the simple description given here—there are numerous legislative requirements and fiduciary responsibilities associated with sponsoring a plan, and the specific activities associated with any plan will depend on its particular design. Still, the basic premise of how a plan works can be summarized as follows.

To begin with, a determination must be made as to which employees are eligible to participate in the plan. Have all employees been notified of the eligibility requirements? Are they covered under the plan on the basis of their job code or employment status? Have they met the age and service requirements of the plan (if any)? Upon meeting the plan's eligibility requirements, each employee is allowed to make a formal election to participate in the plan and defer income (the exception would be for a plan that uses an automatic enrollment process). The term *salary deferral* is also used to refer to deferred income. Salary deferral elections may be made on paper with a signature, or taken electronically, but it must be properly collected and documented in advance. Most often, the election is made as a percentage of pay to be withheld (resulting in an automatic increase in contributions coincident with any future increase in pay), but some plans allow specific dollar elections. Each employee should be allowed to modify or suspend this initial enrollment election in the future. Although the plan sponsor may restrict the timing and frequency of any changes, most do not.

After the salary deferral election instructions have been provided by the employee, the employer will begin deducting the appropriate amount from their pay and calculating tax withholding accordingly. Any money withheld each pay period will need to be segregated from corporate assets and deposited as quickly as possible into the plan trust and invested.

A 401(k) plan can be set up so that each participant elects how his own contributions will be invested, or the plan sponsor (or its designated fiduciary) can make that decision on behalf of all plan participants. Most plans use the first method, and are referred to as "participant-directed." Under this scenario, employees will need to make a formal election regarding the investment of their contributions; again, this election must be properly collected and documented. Typically, investment elections are collected at the time of enrollment, and can be modified periodically in the future (again, the plan sponsor may set limits on the frequency or timing of any changes).

When speaking of a 401(k) plan, the *401(k)* refers to the section of the Code that allows employees to defer income as described earlier. However, the vast majority of 401(k) plans include an additional provision allowing for the employer also to contribute to the plan on behalf of participants. The employer can deduct the cost of those contributions as a business expenses. The employer tax deduction and the privilege that the employee enjoys of deferring income tax on the contributions and trust earnings have driven the popularity of these plans among both employees and sponsors. Eligibility for employer contributions does not have to be the same as eligibility for employee deferrals. Many employers make their contributions in the form of a match. An employer *match* is a contribution made by the employer that is contingent upon the employee also making a contribution. For example, a dollar-for-dollar match is when an employer contributes one dollar to the plan for every dollar the employee contributes. Employer matching contributions encourage employees to contribute so they can receive the employer benefit, thus increasing the total dollars contributed as well as the probability of meeting long-term savings goals. An employer contribution may also take the form of a nonelective contribution, in which employees receive the benefit regardless of whether they are contributing any of their own money. (Nonelective employer contributions are sometimes referred to as profit sharing contributions.)

The plan sponsor can dictate the timing of the sponsor's contributions, although the IRS provides guidelines for the contributions to be tax-deductible. In most cases in which the employer contribution is a match, it is funded at the same time as the employee salary deferrals (that is, each pay period), although a less frequent basis is permissible (such as annually). Restrictions can be put in place regarding the allocation of employer contributions; for example, in situations in which the contribution is funded annually after year-end, it is common to require that the employee be actively employed on the last day of the plan year, and work at least 1,000 hours during the plan year. The employer contribution can also be set up as a discretionary contribution, whereby the employer decides for each plan year whether to make the contribution. Clearly, plan sponsors have a great deal of flexibility in determining the specific design of their contribution(s) to a 401(k) plan, but under any design, a determination of eligibility and a calculation of the benefit will have to be done.

In addition, the sponsor can specify that employees do not "own" the employer contributions and related investment earnings until they have completed a certain amount of service, as a means of encouraging employees to stay. This is accomplished through the use of a vesting schedule. Employees who sever their employment before meeting the required vesting conditions will forfeit some or all of their employer contributions. There are, however, legislative limits on the length of any vesting schedule in a 401(k) plan (this is covered in greater detail in Chapter 9). Keep in mind that the existence of a vesting schedule will increase the administrative complexity of the plan—someone will be responsible for calculating the vested balance of all participants.

A plan can allow employees to roll over distributions received from other qualified plans. Rollovers have become extremely common as job changers now are more likely to have 401(k) accounts from previous employers. Documentation about the money that is being rolled over is usually required, and must be reviewed to determine whether the rollover meets the requirements as outlined by the plan and the Code and Regulations— this process will ensure that only qualified money is allowed in the plan.

Regulations further define how the Internal Revenue Code is to be applied. Regulations can be issued by the Department of the Treasury, where the Internal Revenue Service (IRS) resides or by the Department of Labor (DOL). Therefore, in this book we use the terms DOL Reg, Treasury Reg, or Reg(s) to refer to the Regulations that govern specific aspects of 401(k) plans.

Once an employee has enrolled in the plan, ideally there would be little else for him to do until retirement, other than monitor the contribution and earnings activity in the account, and evaluate whether he is saving enough or if money is invested properly for him to meet his retirement goals (not to imply that this is an easy task!). However, a 401(k) plan may serve other purposes to the employee before retirement. The plan sponsor may permit participants to periodically borrow against their accounts and pay themselves back, usually through payroll deduction. Or, the plan may be designed to allow for various in-service withdrawals. *In-service* refers to distribution. plan participants still employed with the employer. In-service withdrawals are typically permitted from specific accounts only (such as rollover contributions or salary deferrals) or only under certain conditions (for example, after a certain amount of service or due to hardship).

Once an employee has terminated employment with the plan sponsor, she may then elect to take a final distribution of her account balance. Since the employee may not actually be retiring at that point, but may be moving to a new employer, 401(k) plan benefits are designed to be portable. The account can be rolled over from one employer's 401(k) plan to another, or to an IRA, until the individual retires or needs to access the funds. A lump sum payment is the most common form of final distribution from a 401(k) plan. In fact for many plans a lump sum is the only distribution option. Some plans offer other options, such as installments, partial payments, or annuity options, which provide the participant with additional flexibility. A more detailed summary of both in-service withdrawals and forms of distribution is included in Chapter 9.

This has been a brief description of how a typical 401(k) plan works. In summary, the main design decisions an employer must make when establishing a 401(k) plan are:

- Which employees should be covered under the plan?
- What are the eligibility requirements for both employee and employer contributions?
- Should the plan use automatic enrollment and automatic escalation of contributions (and at what percentages)?
- If employer contributions are to be made, how is the contribution amount determined and what formula will be used?
- Will the employer contribution be fully vested or subject to a vesting schedule?
- What investment options will be made available in the plan, and will the participants be permitted to direct the investment of their accounts?
- Which investment will be used as the plan default?
- Will loans or in-service withdrawals be made available to the active employees?
- What forms of distribution from the plan will be permitted?

To help make these design decisions, an employer should carefully consider the objectives of the plan. This topic is the focus of the next section.

ESTABLISHING PLAN OBJECTIVES

When establishing a new plan or redesigning an existing plan, defining clear plan objectives is imperative. This process is generally the responsibility of a management team appointed by the compensation committee and ultimately the responsibility of the board of directors (or in the case of a not-for-profit entity, the board of trustees). Since finance and human resources often have different views about employee benefits, the best plan designs are collaborative. Involving the management teams from both human resources and finance in the design process usually results in a better outcome, with all parties understanding the genesis of the design. Individuals who are familiar with plan operations should also be involved in the plan design process to ensure that the design details will mesh with accounting and payroll systems. A plan has a better chance of success if the employees responsible for ongoing plan operations understand and appreciate the benefit. Operational details should be automated where possible to avoid unnecessary expense and difficulties.

The following questions can be useful in helping a plan sponsor define the objectives for the plan.

Why is the 401(k) being established? While the obvious answer is "to provide a benefit for retirement," most employers cannot fully provide the entire contribution needed for an adequate retirement benefit (the finance side), yet they feel an obligation (the human resources side) to give employees the tools and the encouragement with which they can provide for themselves. Since a 401(k) plan has become a standard benefit in most companies, recruiting good employees would likely be more difficult if a plan did not exist.

What is the desired perception of the plan by current and prospective employees?

- Is the plan primarily a tool for recruiting new employees or a tool for retaining current employees, or both?
- How does the plan compare to the plans of the competition?
- Is the plan an important part of the benefits package, or are other benefits, such as health care or time off programs, better suited to recruiting or retaining employees?
- If employee retention is important, should length of service be rewarded in the plan design either by the use of a vesting schedule or by providing a larger contribution to employees who have worked longer?
- Should age affect the employer contribution rate for an employee?

Who has the primary responsibility for retirement savings: the employee or the employer?

- What portion of retirement savings should the employer provide? (25 percent, 50 percent, 75 percent, or 100 percent)
- Is there a belief that the employer should provide a base contribution to cover the lowest paid employees?
- Since a 401(k) generally places a significant responsibility on the employee to save for retirement, to what extent will employee savings be encouraged?
- How will the plan design encourage or accommodate a combined employee and employer contribution rate that is sufficient to generate adequate retirement savings?
- Should the employer take a paternalistic approach that encourages employee savings for retirement through the:
  - Enrollment process?
  - Matching contribution?
- For an existing plan, what percentage of employees participate today? If this percentage is less than desired, should the plan design be used to push the percentage higher? How would this affect the budget if participation increased?

What is the budget?

- Is there long-term strategy to spend no more than most employers on the retirement plan?
- What percentage of compensation is being spent on the plan today and where will the budget require this to be in the next one to five years?
- Should retirement benefits vary among different business units or certain jobs? If so, in what way should they differ? Do they differ today?

What investment strategy is considered appropriate for your employees?

- Will a significant number of employees want the investments chosen for them?
- Will the vast majority of employees want to pick investments from a very broad array of choices?
- How important is a stable value fund or guaranteed interest option?

Another helpful step in the process is to benchmark your plan (or your proposed plan design) against other employers of like size, geography, or industry. Benchmarking plan design features are covered in the next section.

BENCHMARKING PLAN DESIGN FEATURES

You must be able to measure something before you can manage it. This is certainly true in managing a retirement plan, particularly as it relates to providing a competitive benefit. Employers want to know how their plans stack up against the competition and how this affect their businesses.

Before starting, an employer should determine where they want to be in relation to the competition. Do they want to be at the median, slightly better than median, or slightly below median? How do their business objectives influence this decision? Whatever the target, it is beneficial to have a sense of where the target is before benchmarking the plan.

What Should Be Benchmarked?

Benchmarking starts with determining which plan features to measure. A good place to start is to look back at the design considerations listed earlier in this chapter. This list represents the design features most plan sponsors are interested in benchmarking. The list is repeated here:

- Which employees are covered under the plan?
- What are the eligibility requirements for both employee and employer contributions?
- Is automatic enrollment and automatic escalation of contributions used (and at what percentages)?
- If employer contributions are made, how is the contribution amount determined and what is the formula?
- Is the employer contribution fully vested or subject to a vesting schedule?
- What investment options are available in the plan, and are participants permitted to direct the investment of their accounts?
- Which investment is used as the plan default?
- Are loans or in-service withdrawals available to the active employees?
- What forms of distribution does the plan permit?

The next task is to define a peer group, the other organizations with which to compare the plan. Comparisons are most often done by industry and by geography, meaning that organizations generally compare themselves with specific competitors in their industry or with organizations in a specific locale, or a combination of the two. These types of comparisons, often called custom benchmarking studies, can be costly and time consuming, but tend to yield very useful information.

Another, less costly, approach is to compare the plan to information contained in publicly available industry surveys. A number of industry groups (for example, the Profit Sharing Council of America, *Plan Sponsor* magazine, and so forth) conduct periodic surveys that contain very useful information. In some cases, the information is provided by industry or organization size.

Determining which other organizations to measure the plan against is typically a function of cost, time, and the questions to be addressed. For example, is the key question: "What is the optimal number of investment funds to offer?" If yes, this could likely be addressed quickly by looking at public survey data. On the other hand, if the issue is to determine what employer-provided benefits other firms in your industry offer, this would likely require more time and the need to gather information on specific competitors.

After the benchmarking study is done, the next step is to develop a plan to address the issues that have been identified.

This benchmarking discussion has focused exclusively on benchmarking plan design features and how they compare to other organizations with which the employer competes for talent. However, it is also important to benchmark plan operational costs against comparable plans. Unwittingly paying excessive fees creates serious fiduciary risk by causing a drag on participant investment returns. Excessive fees also impair a participant's ability to accumulate wealth and fund a secure and adequate retirement. The fiduciary risk associated with excessive plan fees is addressed in Chapter 5.

PLAN SETUP

So far, our focus has been on the reasons for sponsoring a plan, what it is expected to accomplish, and how to determine a design to meet employer and employee goals. Once these decisions are made, an employer is then faced with the mechanics of getting a valid plan in place and the ongoing task of plan operations and periodic changes that may be either desired or required by law.

To be a valid plan, the plan must be written and must be communicated to employees.

Plan Documentation Requirement

Every 401(k) plan is required to have a written plan document. The written plan document may consist of more than one document but collectively these documents must lay out the plan operations within the rules defined by the Employee Retirement Income Security Act (ERISA), the Code and applicable rules and regulations.

One mistake that must be avoided is to deduct salary deferrals from an employee's paycheck before there is a valid written plan document. Once the plan is established then the employee's salary deferrals can be made and deposited into the plan. The order of this process is very important. Also, in most cases the employer must also establish a trust to hold the plan assets.

There are various choices allowed with regard to the plan design, all within the parameters of the law, but ERISA dictates that named fiduciaries take responsibility for plan operations and for safeguarding plan assets.

Trust Requirement for Plan Assets

The plan assets of a 401(k) plan must be held in trust by one or more trustees or may be held under certain annuity contracts. Like the plan, the trust document must also be in writing. The trustees must be either named in the trust agreement or the plan document or appointed by a named fiduciary. Once the trustee is named or appointed, the trustee has exclusive authority and discretion to manage and control the assets of the plan, subject to certain exceptions.[1] These trustees are responsible for holding, safeguarding, and investing the plan assets. In some cases, a 401(k) plan will be "self-trusted" by individuals who are employees of the employer, but generally a financial institution is hired to serve this function. A trustee may have sole discretionary control over how the assets are invested, in which case the trustee takes full fiduciary responsibility for this function. For most 401(k) plans, however, the trustee is a *directed trustee* that merely invests plan assets in investment funds as directed by plan participants. The fund options are selected and monitored by a plan investment committee. As a directed trustee, the responsibility is to carry out the direction of the investment committee and plan participants so long as they are not in violation of ERISA, the plan document or trust. Directed trustees are discussed in greater detail in Chapter 5.

Communication of Plan Provisions to Employees

Keep in mind that a valid plan must be communicated to employees. Although the legal plan documents must be made available to participants upon request, plan sponsors are required to provide participants with a summary of the plan provisions (Summary Plan Description, or "SPD"), that is easy to read and understand.

CONCLUSION

The intention of this chapter is to provide much of the information needed to establish a 401(k) plan. We covered the basics of how a 401(k) plan works, establishing objectives for your plan, and the benchmarking of plan design features. Also covered were the plan documentation and trust requirements.

CHAPTER 5

Plan Governance and Fiduciary Issues

In Chapter 2, we discussed how following prudent and consistent governance processes was a key element of sound plan stewardship. In this chapter we discuss in greater detail the governance and fiduciary issues related to 401(k) plans. As you will see, not all of the legal requirements a 401(k) plan must comply with are defined with crystal clear language. We find words such as *reasonable* and *prudent* in the rules and regulations leaving us to interpret and apply their meaning. This makes governance a tricky business for plan fiduciaries. Generally, a fiduciary is someone in a position of trust who has the responsibility to act on the behalf of others. We provide a more specific definition of *plan fiduciary* later in this chapter.

Most employer-sponsored pension plans, including 401(k) plans, are subject to the fiduciary responsibility rules of ERISA.[1] ERISA was signed into law on Labor Day in 1974. In addition to being created to curb abuses in the use of employee benefit plan assets and to avoid conflicts between state regulations, ERISA was implemented to establish a single national standard for the conduct of employee benefit plan fiduciaries. ERISA standards were developed using components of various state trust laws. ERISA includes a preemption clause that supersedes state pension laws and, in that regard, has clarified plan fiduciaries' work by creating a uniform set of guidelines by which qualified retirement plans should be governed.

The DOL, in conjunction with its Employee Benefits Security Administration (EBSA), enforces the fiduciary aspects of ERISA. In this context, the DOL is concerned with whether assets held in employee benefit plans are used exclusively for the benefit of plan participants and beneficiaries. A plan fiduciary must make decisions solely in the interest of participants and beneficiaries and not in the interest of the fiduciary or any third parties (including the plan sponsor). Before any decision is made, the fiduciary should be able to affirmatively answer the question, "Is it in the best interest of the plan's participants and beneficiaries to take this action?"

The most important word to remember from this chapter is *process*. Having a sound 401(k) governance process is key to success in fulfilling your fiduciary responsibilities. While not specifically stated in ERISA, some courts have opined that process is more important than results since process is under fiduciaries' direct control.

Many events of the past have raised public awareness of the responsibility and potential liability of plan sponsors and fiduciaries. Some of these events include:

- Collapse of high profile companies such as Enron, WorldCom, and others and the effect their collapse had on those companies' 401(k) plans
- Scandals in the mutual fund industry
- Unusual volatility of investment markets
- Calls for increased fee transparency
- Increased activity of the DOL

Also, although the Sarbanes-Oxley Act of 2002 (SOA)[2] focuses on corporate abuses by regulating public companies and accounting firms, it also directly regulates some aspects of defined contribution plans by requiring notices to participants which could allow them to avoid losses similar to those suffered by participants in Enron's defined contribution plans. SOA's main impact on 401(k) plans involves timing and administrative details related to when plans change recordkeepers or investment options. A detailed discussion of this is included in Chapter 8 in the section "Changing Recordkeepers."

We go into further detail in Chapter 6 about the effects that the scandals in the mutual fund industry and Enron litigation have had on the rules governing 401(k) plans. In this chapter, we cover who is a plan fiduciary, basic fiduciary duties, selecting and monitoring outside fiduciaries, responsibilities of directed trustees, prohibited transaction rules, and establishing roles and responsibilities for managing a 401(k) plan.

WHO IS A PLAN FIDUCIARY?

The term *fiduciary* is given a broad, functional definition by ERISA. Generally, anyone who has or exercises control over plan assets (manages assets or decides how they are used) is a fiduciary. In addition, some individuals are fiduciaries by virtue of the role they take with regard to the plan. Fiduciary liability under ERISA is personal to the individual serving in a fiduciary capacity and, generally, is not dischargeable in bankruptcy.[3]

A person or entity is a fiduciary of a 401(k) plan *to the extent* that that person or entity:

- Exercises any discretionary authority or control over the management of the plan or management or disposition of its assets

- Provides investment advice for a fee or other compensation, directly or indirectly, or has authority to do so
- Has discretionary authority or responsibility in the administration of the plan[4]

Examples of fiduciaries include administrators who have discretion over assets, trustees, and investment advisors. Corporate directors and officers may also be fiduciaries of the plan if they exercise authority over the plan or its assets. This extends to those who appoint fiduciaries, so that an organization's board of directors is a fiduciary if they appoint the fiduciary committee. While the board may have delegated their committee tasks, they are still responsible for monitoring other fiduciaries. There are certain statutory ERISA fiduciaries—ERISA requires that plans identify a trustee, a named fiduciary, and a plan administrator, each of whom will be considered a fiduciary in view of their relationship to the plan. In December 2009, the DOL announced their plan to publish a proposed regulation sometime in 2010 to amend the regulatory definition of fiduciary to include more persons, such as pension consultants. At the time of this writing, the proposed regulation has not been issued.

Trustee

The assets of a 401(k) plan must be held in trust, and the trust must have one or more trustees.[5] The trustees may be individuals or entities. For example, the trustee of a plan may be an employee or employees, may be a committee duly authorized by the plan sponsor or may be a bank or trust company. There is a trust exemption for any assets of a plan that consist of insurance contracts or policies issued by an insurance company qualified to do business in the applicable state, which most typically affects 401(k) plans (or 403(b) plans) funded by a group annuity contract.

The DOL has stated that a plan trustee is always a fiduciary.[6] The trustee has exclusive authority and discretion to manage and control the assets of the plan unless:

- The plan expressly provides that the trustees are subject to the direction of a named fiduciary who is not a trustee, in which case the trustees shall be subject to proper directions of the named fiduciary
- Authority to manage, acquire, or dispose of assets is delegated to one or more investment managers
- Plan participants direct the investments of their assets[7]

In cases in which two or more trustees hold plan assets, each must use reasonable care to prevent a co-trustee from committing a breach, and they must jointly manage and control the assets of the plan. However, the trustees may enter into an agreement, authorized by the trust agreement, to allocate specific responsibilities, obligations, or duties among trustees. If this happens, a trustee is not liable for the acts and omissions of another trustee that has accepted those specific duties.[8] For example, a trust agreement may allow for the delegation of specific responsibilities among the trustees. Pursuant to an agreement, Trustee A is responsible for the management of plan assets, and Trustee B is responsible for the distribution of plan assets to participants. If Trustee B makes improper distributions to participants, Trustee A will not be held liable for the improper distribution if he has no knowledge of it. Also, if assets are held in more than one trust, a trustee is not liable for the acts and omissions of the trustee of any other trust.[9] If Trustee A is aware of a breach by Trustee B, however, Trustee A must take reasonable steps to remedy the breach.

Outside businesses, such as banks or trust companies, will usually consider themselves to be a *directed trustee* with limited fiduciary responsibilities. Trust documents and trust service agreements provided by directed trustees will typically include provisions that acknowledge their limited fiduciary liability. The fiduciaries providing the direction to the trustee will retain the fiduciary liability relative to the direction they are providing (or lack thereof).

It should be noted, however, that it is possible for a directed trustee to realize fiduciary liability. We cover the responsibilities of directed trustees later in this chapter.

Named Fiduciary

A *named fiduciary* is a "fiduciary who is named in the plan document or who, pursuant to a procedure specified in the plan, is identified as a fiduciary"[10] and "has the authority to control and manage the operation and administration of the plan." All plans governed by ERISA must provide for at least one named fiduciary. Individuals or entities, such as the trustee, plan sponsor, or a plan committee, may be designated as the named fiduciary. Plan sponsors are most often indicated as the named fiduciary. In designing the plan's governance structure, the plan sponsor should consider the merits of assigning a plan committee as the named fiduciary so as to delineate a fiduciary chain of authority or control over plan assets, being careful to consider that authority is duly authorized by the company's board and that fiduciary liability is properly insured or indemnified (indemnification is discussed in greater detail later in Chapter 6).

In certain circumstances, it may be advisable to employ an independent fiduciary who operates independently from the named fiduciary or fiduciary committee. We also cover independent fiduciaries later in this chapter.

Plan Administrator

The term *plan administrator* is one of the more commonly misunderstood 401(k) terms. The plan administrator, as a defined plan term, is not the plan's vendor (for example, recordkeeper, or third-party administrator). The plan administrator is the person or entity designated in the plan document as such. If none is designated, the plan sponsor will be the plan administrator.[11]

Under ERISA, the plan administrator has extensive responsibilities for the day-to-day operations of the plan. These responsibilities make the plan administrator a fiduciary.[12] As with the named fiduciary designation, individuals or entities, such as the trustee, plan sponsor, or a plan committee, may be designated as the plan administrator. While plan sponsors are commonly designated as plan administrator, consideration should be given to the designation of a plan committee as the plan administrator, as noted in the preceding section.

Functional Definition

While trustees, named fiduciaries and plan administrators are statutory fiduciaries, the definition of a fiduciary is functional in nature. The extent to which an individual or entity has discretion or exercises control over plan administration or assets defines a fiduciary. Claiming that someone is not a fiduciary will not prevent that person from being a fiduciary. For example, in one case, although an individual had not agreed to be a fiduciary and indeed had claimed not to be a fiduciary, her actions with respect to plan assets caused her to be a fiduciary. By signing off on the sale of plan assets and making plan investments, she became a fiduciary.[13] In another situation, a person who was not otherwise associated with a plan, but embezzled plan assets, was found to be a fiduciary. By holding plan assets and exercising discretion over their use, the embezzler became a fiduciary.[14]

BASIC FIDUCIARY DUTIES

At its core, ERISA sets out the basic duties that all fiduciaries must follow. They must discharge their duties solely in the interest of plan participants and beneficiaries. Plan fiduciaries' duties fall within the following four categories:

1. Exclusive Benefit rule—This Duty of Loyalty rule requires that fiduciary actions must be for the exclusive purpose of providing benefits to

participants (or their beneficiaries) and defraying reasonable expenses of administering the plan

2. Prudent Expert rule—ERISA's Duty of Prudence requires that fiduciaries act with the care, skill, prudence, and diligence under the circumstances that a prudent person, acting in a like capacity and familiar with such matters, would use in the conduct of an enterprise of a like character and with like aims

3. Duty to Diversify Plan Investments rule—They have the responsibility of diversifying the investments of the plan so as to minimize the risk of large losses, unless under the circumstances, it is clearly prudent not to do so

4. Follow Plan Documents—They must act in accordance with the documents and instruments governing the plan, as long as the documents and instruments are consistent with ERISA[15]

Also, although not expressly mentioned in ERISA, a critical obligation of plan fiduciaries is to monitor all plan operations and service providers.

Exclusive Benefit Rule

The exclusive benefit rule requires that a fiduciary discharge her duties with respect to a plan solely in the interest of the participants and beneficiaries and not for the benefit of any other person or entity.[16]

The exclusive benefit rule does not prohibit a fiduciary from serving in more than one capacity. Thus, a corporate officer may, and often will, function in dual roles as a business manager and plan fiduciary. Whether a person is serving as a business manager or a fiduciary will determine whether his actions are settlor functions (business or plan sponsor–related) or nonsettlor (fiduciary) functions.

A *settlor* is the person or entity that establishes a trust. Plan assets are held in a trust, so those functions of the employer/plan sponsor in their capacity as employer/plan sponsor are referred to as "settlor functions."

As a business manager, a corporate officer can act solely in the interest of the stockholders. The corporate officer may also make decisions that balance the interests of stockholders with those of plan participants. For example, in the role of business manager, a corporate officer may make nonfiduciary settlor decisions with regard to the plan, such as establishing, designing, amending, or terminating the plan.[17] The impact of these decisions on plan participants and beneficiaries is a business issue, not a fiduciary issue. Settlor functions are to be distinguished from administrative functions, which are necessary for plan operations. Examples of administrative expenses include such activities as recordkeeping, allocating contributions, processing benefit requests, and so on.

As a fiduciary, the corporate officer must act solely in the interest of the participants and beneficiaries, regardless of whether these decisions would benefit the company, stockholders, or other entities. For example, if employer stock ceased to be a prudent investment, and liquidating the employer stock would be seen as a failure of the company's management, continuing to offer employer stock to avoid executive embarrassment would violate the exclusive benefit rule. As another example, placing plan assets with a banking entity for the purpose of securing a line of corporate credit would be a violation of the exclusive benefits rule. Incidental benefits to the plan sponsor will not result in a violation of the exclusive benefit rule as long as the fiduciary concludes that the transaction is in the best interest of plan participants and beneficiaries.[18]

Prudent Expert Rule

The second fiduciary duty is to act "with the care, skill, prudence, and diligence under the circumstances then prevailing that a prudent man, acting in a like capacity and familiar with such matters, would use in the conduct of an enterprise of a like character and with like aims."[19] Many refer to this ERISA standard as the "prudent expert rule," as this is a stricter standard than the traditional prudent man rule defined in the common law of trusts. Under ERISA, fiduciary actions are compared to a prudent man *familiar with such matters,* in other words, an expert.

A prudent fiduciary should:

- Have the necessary knowledge and skills to carry out their duties.
- Establish and follow written procedures (that is, have a documented process).
- Keep written records of actions taken.
- Review published information of what other professionals are doing.

Fiduciaries must either have the necessary knowledge and skills required to carry out their duties, seek expert advice, or delegate those tasks for which they do not have the required knowledge and skill. This is especially important in structuring a fiduciary committee, as committee members must demonstrate an appropriate level of expertise (more details are provided on establishing a committee later in this chapter). Therefore, it is crucial that individuals with appropriate credentials and experience are identified as fiduciaries, and that a properly documented governance process be established. Even though they may delegate responsibility to others or act on advice given to them, fiduciaries retain liability for their own actions, as well as the actions of those to whom they delegate. Therefore, they must follow a diligent process for the selecting and monitoring outside experts and service providers.

In a speech to CEOs in May 2004, then U.S. Secretary of Labor Elaine Chao made the point that designating another person or entity to manage a plan does not relieve the CEO—or other named fiduciary—of responsibility or liability. She points out that "the CEO or designated official has a responsibility to monitor the performance of the fiduciary of the plan," and to take "action if the designated fiduciary makes imprudent decisions."[20]

Diversify Plan Investments

Under the third fiduciary duty, a fiduciary must diversify the investments of the plan so as to minimize the risk of large losses.[21] For 401(k) plans, the diversification requirement is not violated by acquiring or holding a substantial amount of qualifying employer real property or qualifying employer securities. ERISA Section 404(c) provides fiduciaries of participant-directed individual account plans (that is, 401(k) plans) with limited relief from fiduciary liability for participants' investment losses by offering a range of at least three diversified core investment alternatives and meeting other criteria. Realistically, however, a fiduciary should carefully weigh the pros and cons of offering overly risky investments, less diversified funds (for example, sector funds) and individual securities, considering the extent to which participants may (or may not) be able to appropriately use these investment vehicles to create a diversified portfolio and limit their risk of large losses. See Chapter 7 for more details on 404(c) requirements and other investment considerations.

Following the Plan Document

The final basic fiduciary responsibility requires a fiduciary to act in accordance with the documents and instruments governing the plan.[22] While the particular documents and instruments are not clearly defined in ERISA, the two most obvious documents are the plan document and trust agreement. The trust document may be part of the plan document or may be a separate document. Other common documents that may fall into this category include collective bargaining agreements, loan policies, funding policies, group annuity contracts, fiduciary committee meeting minutes, and board of directors' resolutions. Many communications with plan participants and beneficiaries may be considered to be part of the plan and subject to the fiduciary rule that the plan document be followed. For example, some courts have found that the SPD controls the plan document if the two documents conflict.[23]

Although fiduciaries are required to follow the terms of the plan document (and other instruments governing the plan), they are prohibited from following the document if it would be in conflict with ERISA to do so.[24] It is possible that there may be no fiduciary violation, however, if the fiduciary fails to follow the plan because of an erroneous interpretation of the plan, particularly when the fiduciary relies on expert advice.[25]

It is extremely important to regularly review the plan documents (for example, adoption agreement, basic plan document, loan policy, and SPDs) to ensure their accuracy and consistency. Failure to follow the terms of plan documents can lead not only to ERISA litigation and the need for corrective action, but can also create Code qualification issues that can be costly to address and correct.

ALLOCATING OR DELEGATING FIDUCIARY RESPONSIBILITY

It is not uncommon for fiduciaries to delegate duties to other persons, or institutions, to carry out the fiduciaries' responsibilities.[26] Delegating their responsibility does not relieve fiduciaries of liability. Fiduciaries have a continuing duty to monitor the performance of those to whom they delegate authority. The plan document should be reviewed to ensure that delegation language is clear. For example, it could provide that a named fiduciary may employ one or more persons to render advice with regard to any responsibility such fiduciary has under the plan or appoint an investment manager or managers to manage any assets of a plan.[27]

Also, the plan may expressly provide procedures for delegating non-trustee fiduciary responsibilities among named fiduciaries and to persons other than named fiduciaries.[28] These delegated responsibilities typically include day-to-day plan administration, benefit distributions, and claims review.

Although not expressed as one of the four basic fiduciary responsibilities, a fundamental aspect of ERISA's fiduciary responsibility is the requirement to exercise diligence in selecting and monitoring service providers to the plan. Fiduciaries should monitor the activities of service providers at regular intervals (for example, quarterly, semi-annually, or annually) and document their monitoring efforts and conclusions. For example, if a named fiduciary hires a third-party recordkeeper to perform day-to-day operations, the named fiduciary should monitor the recordkeeper's activities and performance to determine whether it is in the best interest of the plans' participants and beneficiaries to continue the recordkeeper's services. If the fiduciary determines that replacing a service provider would be in the best interest of the participants and beneficiaries, the fiduciary must do so.

Selecting and Monitoring Outside Fiduciaries

Fiduciary committees are increasingly seeking the support of investment advisors and others who will take on fiduciary status. However, a fiduciary committee cannot completely eliminate its fiduciary exposure by retaining an independent fiduciary or co-fiduciary. The fiduciary committee and its members retain responsibility for prudently selecting and monitoring outside fiduciaries.

If structured properly, the arrangement with outside fiduciaries can effectively expand primary responsibility for particular decisions to the outside fiduciaries. It is important that fiduciary committees ensure that any outside fiduciaries:

- Are qualified to provide the services being delegated to them
- Have sufficient resources to stand behind their potential liability
- Do not attempt to protect themselves with exculpatory contract provisions that attempt to limit the amount of their liability or lower the standard of conduct (for example, gross instead of ordinary negligence) that would result in liability[29]

The current environment of participant litigation, the DOL's enforcement, and the complexity of the investment markets are causing fiduciary committees to evaluate whether to engage the services of an outside independent fiduciary or co-fiduciary. An independent fiduciary or a co-fiduciary can:

- Provide specialized fiduciary expertise to the committee
- Share responsibility with the fiduciary committee and other fiduciaries
- Demonstrate the prudence, loyalty, and diligence of the plan's fiduciaries

It is important when hiring an outside fiduciary to understand the extent of their responsibility and therefore liability under ERISA. ERISA allows a plan sponsor to delegate the responsibility of selecting, monitoring, and replacing plan investments to an ERISA Section 3(38) "investment manager." This manager is then considered an ERISA Section 405(d)(1) "independent fiduciary" of the plan. An ERISA Section 3(38) fiduciary can only be a bank, an insurance company, or a registered investment advisor (RIA) as defined by the Investment Advisers Act of 1940. An ERISA Section 3(38) fiduciary has legal discretion as a decision maker and is therefore legally liable for those decisions. A fiduciary with 3(38) status may consult with the plan sponsor regarding its investment decisions, but regardless has the authority to act with or without the sponsor's approval.

In contrast, an ERISA Section 3(21) limited-scope fiduciary has less legal authority and therefore less liability for decisions made regarding plan investments than an ERISA Section 3(38) fiduciary. The 3(21) limited-scope fiduciary's role is typically relegated to assisting, advising, and making recommendations to the plan sponsor regarding plan investment decisions.[30]

The reasons for retaining an independent fiduciary or a co-fiduciary are quite different, as we discuss in the next two sections.

Independent Fiduciary   As the name indicates, an independent fiduciary operates independently from the fiduciary committee. Indeed, an independent fiduciary is usually retained to make decisions on behalf of the plan participants without input from the committee. A person or entity filling this role is called upon most often when a committee would be in a conflict of interest situation or when the committee has insider information that cannot or will not be disclosed to plan participants.

For example, if employer stock is held in a plan, and the fiduciary committee anticipates a corporate transaction that will almost certainly have a dramatic impact on share price, an independent fiduciary may be retained to make decisions about employer stock as an investment option. Similarly, if a significant expense may be charged against plan assets, rather than be paid by the plan sponsor, and there is uncertainty whether the expense can properly be paid from plan assets, the fiduciary committee may hire an independent fiduciary to evaluate the decision of whether the expense is reasonable and payable from plan assets. Because of the expense of retaining an independent fiduciary, it is somewhat uncommon for an independent fiduciary to be involved on an ongoing basis.

Co-Fiduciary   Co-fiduciaries usually do not operate independently but are involved in the decision making with the plan's fiduciary committee. The prefix *co* to fiduciary indicates that there are multiple fiduciaries that are one another's co-fiduciaries.

As is the case with all fiduciaries, co-fiduciaries must be prudent and loyal to the extent that they exercise discretion or control over plan assets or plan management. Importantly, co-fiduciaries are liable for the fiduciary breaches of other plan fiduciaries if they:

- Enable the breach
- Participate in the breach
- Do not take reasonable steps to correct the breach if they become aware of it[31]

This applies equally to the fiduciary committee and outside fiduciaries. Consequently, it is important for all involved to be alert to the actions taken by other fiduciaries.

Responsibilities of Directed Trustees

Directed trustees are hired to hold plan assets and to carry out the specific directions of the plan fiduciaries regarding those assets. This is where the term *directed* comes from. Even though they only act upon the direction upon the plan fiduciaries, directed trustees still have responsibilities as fiduciaries themselves. A directed trustee's responsibilities include acting in the sole interest of plan participants and beneficiaries, acting only in accordance with the plan document, and acting only in accordance with ERISA. This next section covers in greater detail a directed trustee's responsibility to follow ERISA.

Follow ERISA   Even if a directed trustee is given a direction that is in accordance with the plan document, he must not follow a direction he knows or should know is contrary to ERISA. The following list of directed trustee responsibilities is a summary of the DOL's Field Assistance Bulletin (FAB), 2004–03 issued in December 2004, in part as a response to problems brought to light following the collapse of Enron.

Prohibited Transaction Determinations.   A directed trustee must follow processes that are designed to avoid prohibited transactions. A directed trustee could satisfy this obligation by obtaining and relying on appropriate written representations from the directing fiduciary.

Prudence Determinations.   A directed trustee does not have an independent obligation to determine the prudence of every transaction and does not have to duplicate or second-guess the work of plan fiduciaries that have discretionary authority over the management of plan assets.

Duty to Act on Nonpublic Information.   The directed trustee need only question the directing fiduciary's instructions for market transactions involving publicly-traded securities on a generally recognized market in rare circumstances, such as when a directed trustee possesses material nonpublic information about a security that is necessary to make a prudent decision. In this situation, the directed trustee has a duty to inquire about the fiduciary's knowledge and consideration of the information with respect to the direction. However, the possession of nonpublic information by one part of an organization will not be generally imputed to those providing directed trustee services where the organization maintains procedures designed to prevent the illegal disclosure under securities, banking, or other laws.

Note: Although the DOL appears to be acknowledging the value of ethical walls to solve problems, it does not appear ready to describe how they would work under ERISA. In a footnote to FAB 2004–03, the DOL states: "The [DOL] expresses no view as to whether, or under what circumstances, other procedures established by an organization to limit the disclosure of information will serve to avoid the imputation of information to a directed trustee."

Duty to Act on Public Information. The directed trustee will rarely have an obligation to question the prudence of a direction to purchase publicly traded securities at the market price solely on the basis of publicly available information. Even a steep drop in a stock's price, by itself, would not indicate that a named fiduciary's direction to purchase or hold stock is imprudent and not a proper direction. However, the DOL describes two circumstances where a directed trustee may have to question the direction based on public information:

1. When there are clear and compelling public indicators (for example, 8-K filing by the SEC, bankruptcy filing)
2. Situations where a fiduciary who is a corporate employee gives an instruction to buy or hold stock of his company subsequent to the company, its officers, or directors, being formally charged by state or federal regulators with financial irregularities

Note: The exception is if an independent fiduciary was appointed to manage the plan's investment in company stock, a directed trustee could follow the proper directions of the independent fiduciary without having to conduct its own independent assessment of the transaction.

Effect of Questioning Directions on Fiduciary Status. The DOL says the nature and scope of a directed trustee's fiduciary responsibility does not change merely because the directed trustee, in carrying out its duties, raises questions concerning whether a direction is "proper" or declines to follow a direction.

Co-Fiduciary Duties. A directed trustee may be liable as a co-fiduciary if they have knowledge of a fiduciary breach of another fiduciary and does not take reasonable steps to remedy the breach.

THE PROHIBITED TRANSACTIONS RULE

Plan fiduciaries are prohibited from being a party to certain plan transactions. In this context, ERISA was drafted to prohibit transactions that have the potential of abuse. Essentially, all transactions involving a plan and anyone who has dealings with the plan are prohibited, unless the transaction is necessary for the customary day-to-day operation of the plan. ERISA and the Code broadly define the transactions that are prohibited and then provide exceptions that allow plans to operate reasonably.

ERISA prohibits a fiduciary from engaging in a prohibited transaction directly or indirectly with a "party in interest." The Code imposes penalty excise taxes on any "disqualified person" who participates in a prohibited transaction.[32] Although similar and very broad, the definitions of party in interest and disqualified person are not identical. Most, but not all, prohibited transactions are subject to an excise tax that must be paid by any disqualified person who participates in the prohibited transaction. To avoid the penalty taxes, a fiduciary must have a basic understanding of the prohibited transaction rules.

Under ERISA, the following are prohibited transactions, unless an exemption applies:

- Sale or exchange, or leasing of any property between the plan and a party in interest
- Lending of money or extension of credit between the plan and a party in interest
- Furnishing of goods, services, or facilities between a plan and a party in interest
- Transfer to, or use by, or for the benefit of a party in interest of the income or assets of the plan
- Any act by a party in interest who is a fiduciary who deals with the income or assets of the plan in his own interest or for his own account
- Receipt of any consideration for his own personal account by a party in interest who is a fiduciary from any party dealing with the plan in connection with a transaction involving the income or assets of the plan
- Acting in any transaction involving a plan on behalf of a party (or representing a party) whose interests are adverse to the interests of the plan or the interests of its participants or beneficiaries
- Acquiring, on behalf of the plan, any employer security or employer real property that is not "qualified" or that exceeds certain limits[33]

A prohibited transaction under the Code includes the same list, with the exception of the last two items.[34]

Party in Interest or Disqualified Person

The definitions of a party in interest or disqualified person are intended to include everyone who could improperly influence a plan to engage in a prohibited transaction. The definitions of a party in interest under ERISA and a disqualified person under the Code are broad and complex.[35] To put it simply, a party in interest includes:

- A fiduciary
- A person providing services to the plan
- An employer whose employees are covered by the plan
- A 50 percent or greater owner of an employer
- A family member of any of the preceding
- A union or other employee organization whose members are covered by the plan
- An entity that is owned 50 percent or more by any of the preceding (except family members)
- An employee, officer, director, or 10 percent owner of the employer, the union, a service provider, or a related entity
- A partner or joint venturer of the employer, the union, or a service provider

The IRS's definition of a disqualified person is slightly narrower than the definition of party in interest under ERISA. Therefore, parties who meet the ERISA rules will also meet the Code's rules. However, the reverse is not true.

Employer Real Property and Securities

ERISA's prohibited transaction rules place limits on a plan's acquisition of employer real property and employer securities.[36] Only "qualifying employer real property" and "qualifying employer securities" may be held by a plan. In general, "qualifying employer real property" means parcels of employer real property if a substantial number of such parcels are dispersed geographically and are suitable for more than one use. "Qualifying employer security" means an employer security that is a stock, a marketable obligation, or an interest in a publicly traded partnership.

EXEMPTIONS FROM PROHIBITED TRANSACTION RULES

Recognizing that the prohibited transaction rules are so broad and inclusive that they would interfere with proper plan operations, a number of transactions are exempted from the prohibited transaction rules by statutory exemptions.[37] Also, plan fiduciaries and parties in interest (or disqualified persons) may request individual exemptions from the DOL, and the DOL may grant class exemptions.[38]

Statutory Exemptions

Among the most important statutory exemptions to the prohibited transaction rules are:

Office Space and Necessary Services.   A party in interest may contract or make reasonable arrangements for the provision of office space, legal, accounting, and other services necessary for the establishment or operation of a plan if no more than reasonable compensation is paid.[39] One basis for determining reasonableness is a comparison of what the plan would be required to pay for similar services or facilities provided by a provider who is not a party in interest.

Participant Loans.   Loans made by a plan to parties in interest who are plan participants if such loans:

- Are available to all such participants on a reasonably equivalent basis
- Are not made available to highly compensated employees[40] in an amount greater than the amount made available to other employees
- Are made pursuant to specific plan provisions governing such loans
- Bear a reasonable rate of interest
- Are adequately secured[41]

While plan loan provisions are common, it is not widely understood that a very common fiduciary breach found upon DOL audit is the failure of employees to repay participant loans in accordance with the terms of the plan and loan documents. If the employer does not timely default the unpaid loans in accordance with IRS regulations, the DOL may find the failure of the loan repayment to be a prohibited loan from the plan to the employee.

Loans to ESOPs.   A loan to an Employee Stock Ownership Plan (ESOP) is not prohibited as long as the loan is primarily for the benefit of plan participants, the loan is at a reasonable rate of interest, and certain other conditions are satisfied.[42] To the extent an ESOP loan is secured, the only permissible plan security is qualifying employer securities.[43]

Banks and Similar Financial Institutions.   To the extent a bank becomes a trustee of a plan's assets, it becomes a fiduciary to the plan. Plans and parties in interest may also use these same banks for customary banking services.[44]

Class Exemptions

The DOL has granted various class exemptions. A class exemption is an exemption to the prohibited transaction rules that applies to everyone in that group.[45] An example of a class exemption is one that permits mutual fund companies to offer their own open-ended mutual funds in their own retirement plans.[46]

Individual Exemptions

The DOL also has the authority to grant individual exemptions from the prohibited transactions rules for particular transactions, on a case-by-case basis.[47] An example of an individual prohibited transaction exemption is that of a terminating plan that owns real estate and must sell the real estate to liquidate the plan. The only realistic purchaser of the real estate is the plan sponsor. Selling the real estate to the plan sponsor would be a prohibited transaction. Just the same, in order to receive a reasonable price, it would be in the best interest of the participants and beneficiaries for the plan to sell to the plan sponsor. A transaction of this type may not be entered into without the DOL's approval, and the DOL will likely require there to be an independent fiduciary to represent the interests of the participants and beneficiaries in this type of transaction.

Excise Taxes and Other Penalties

The penalty imposed by the Code for prohibited transactions, in connection with a qualified plan, is a two-tiered excise tax, payable by the disqualified person who participated in the prohibited transaction. The initial excise tax is 15 percent of the amount involved for each year or partial year from the time the transaction occurs until it is corrected, a deficiency notice is mailed, or the tax is assessed.[48] The initial tax is intended to encourage the correction of prohibited transactions. If a prohibited transaction is not corrected in a timely manner, a second-tier tax is imposed equal to 100 percent of the amount involved in the prohibited transaction.

If the DOL audits the plan and determines that a fiduciary breach has occurred and requests that the fiduciaries engage in a settlement to voluntarily correct the violation in consideration, the DOL will not file a lawsuit. In this situation, the DOL will also assess a 20 percent penalty on the applicable recovery amount.[49] The fiduciaries should consider engaging a consultant familiar with DOL audits early on in the process to develop correction strategies that may avoid assessment of DOL penalties.

The penalty is mandatory unless the Secretary of the DOL waives or reduces the penalty upon finding that the fiduciary acted reasonably and in good faith or the fiduciary is unable to restore all losses to the plan without severe financial hardship. If the 20 percent penalty is assessed by the DOL, it will be reduced by any prohibited transaction excise tax paid to the IRS.[50]

What has been covered so far in this chapter are the rules related to fiduciary responsibility. The next section provides guidance on how to establish processes that make following these rules possible.

ESTABLISHING ROLES AND RESPONSIBILITIES

Now that we've covered the nature of a fiduciary's relationship with a 401(k) plan, let's move on to defining governance processes and assignment of roles and responsibilities. *Process,* again, is the key word and the goal is to establish procedures that will satisfy ERISA while being reasonable to follow.

A court case illustrates the importance of following sound fiduciary processes. In *Kanawi v. Bechtel*, ND Cal. 2008, the court ruled in favor of the defendant, determining that a prudent process was in place to review investment fees and related performance. The court noted, "The record show[ed] that the Committee met regularly to discuss the Plan's investments and sought the advice of [knowledgeable vendors] to ensure that it was making proper decisions." Furthermore, "the evidence showed that [the fiduciaries] regularly reviewed the performance of the Plan's investments and considered alternatives" and "the test of prudence [that the fiduciaries must live up to] is one of conduct and not performance [and that] it is easy to opine in retrospect that the Plan's managers should have made different decisions, but such 20/20 hindsight musings are not sufficient to maintain a cause of action alleging a breach of fiduciary duty."

Establishing the Benefits Committee

All 401(k) plans are required to have a plan administrator and a named fiduciary, each of whom has extensive responsibility for the operation and administration of the plans. Frequently, the employer designates a benefits committee as the plan administrator and named fiduciary. In this discussion, it is assumed that the benefits committee is serving as both the named fiduciary and plan administrator. (As we noted in Chapter 2, throughout this book there are references to committees. The words *plan, retirement, investment, benefits,* and *fiduciary* are used to describe committees. In many cases these committee names are interchangeable. The name of the committee is not as important as the committee's charter, the responsibilities they are formally given.)

Many benefits committee functions are fiduciary in nature and must be carried out in the best interests of plan participants and beneficiaries. To comply with their obligations, fiduciaries must exercise the care of a prudent person who is familiar with plan and investment issues. Plan design is normally established at the corporate level and is not a fiduciary function. However, the benefits committee may be involved in making plan design decisions.

Committee Structure   Committee structure will be dictated in large part by the terms of the company's respective plan documents and governing corporate documents (articles of incorporation, by-laws, and board of directors' actions and delegations of authority). At inception, it is important that the board of directors, or other governing body, clearly establish the authority of the committee. It is not uncommon to find that a benefits committee has authority to act on some matters, such as the selection of funds to be offered as 401(k) plan investments but needs to have other actions ratified by the board of directors (for example, amending the investment policy statement).

A single benefits committee may handle all fiduciary functions, including investment decisions and claim reviews. In other cases, given the special skills, background, or level of work required for the different issues, two committees may be formed, each with a narrower focus. For example, there may be a fiduciary investment committee whose responsibility is limited to reviewing the investments in the company's 401(k) plan. Another committee may handle matters related to administrative procedures, interpretation of plan provisions, employee appeals from benefits decisions, recommendations on plan design, and other noninvestment-related issues. It is not uncommon for committees to consider both fiduciary and nonfiduciary issues. Plan design, for example, is a nonfiduciary issue. The key is that different standards govern the committee's behavior depending on the issues it is considering.

Committee Members   Membership is often established with corporate positions in mind. For example, voting members may include positions such as the vice president for risk, the chief financial officer, the vice president of human resources, and regional operating officers. Nonvoting members may include such positions as the benefits managers and service providers. Committee membership should usually include representatives from both the HR and finance departments. The board of directors, or other governing body, generally appoints the committee members.

As fiduciary liability is personal liability, it is not appropriate for junior staff to be included as voting committee members. It is generally not recommended that a President or CEO assume a voting member role as committee members are less likely to be comfortable challenging or disagreeing with her in committee meetings.

Communication between committee members is essential for the committee to fulfill its fiduciary duties. For example, in a situation where employer stock is offered as an investment alternative under the plan, if the finance department is aware of nonconfidential issues that will likely result in share price volatility, the committee should take that into account when making decisions that affect participants' ability to change their investments.

ERISA's rules require the disclosure of information that would be material to the participants and beneficiaries. The U.S. Securities and Exchange Commission (SEC) rules, however, may be in direct conflict by prohibiting disclosure of the same information. Therefore, companies whose plans may offer employer stock as a plan investment, for example, should consider excluding the CFO and others who will have insider information, as viewed by the SEC.

As the operation of plans has become more complex, benefit committees increasingly solicit expert advice from outside providers. It is not uncommon for the committee to include fiduciary and investment consultants, who attend meetings as nonvoting members.

Operating a Benefits Committee

After the committee has been determined, the first task is to set a structure for its operations. This will include setting guidelines for frequency of meetings and investment performance reviews, a process for handling plan operations and reviewing claims and claimant appeals. Also, the benefits committee must select the plan's service providers (recordkeeper, accountant, investment advisor, directed trustee, consultant, fiduciary advisor), purchase any ERISA-required fidelity bond, and explore fiduciary liability coverage.

Once these initial tasks are complete, the following are recommended core steps to establish your fiduciary governance process:

- *Establish Committee Appointments and Acceptance*—Based upon the plan document and the plan sponsor's decision to delegate tasks to the committee, document the committee's official authority to make decisions for the plan via formal appointment, as well as each member's acceptance of their role.
- *Establish and Administer Investment Policy Statement*—The establishment of an Investment Policy Statement (IPS) is critical, as it will be the road map by which the committee selects, monitors, and replaces plan investments. Chapter 7 covers in greater detail the establishment of an investment policy statement for 401(k) plans.

- *Establish Process for Reviewing Plan Fees and Expenses*—Plan fees and expenses are an important consideration and should be evaluated periodically. Determine how to evaluate plan fees and expenses to assess if they are reasonable to plan participants (for example, internally, in conjunction with a vendor or using an independent consultant).
- *Establish a Methodology For How Fees Will Be Paid*—Consider adopting a Fee and Expense Policy Statement (much like an IPS).
- *Conduct Regular Committee Meetings*—Committees should hold regular quarterly meetings and periodically report to the board, or the other person or body that appointed the committee, to keep them informed of issues relating to plan operations. The following items would typically be reviewed during the regular quarterly meetings:
  - Investment performance
  - Classes of investments offered
  - Investment management team changes
  - Changes in a fund's investment approach
  - Level of plan participation
  - Level of participant investment diversification
  - Plan operations
  - Overall service provider activity, including review of performance guarantees
  - Government reports and disclosures to participants and beneficiaries (for example, SPD and Annual Form 5500)
  - Claims and appeals
  - Compliance with regulatory changes and changes in the benefits landscape
- *Document Actions*—Document all committee meetings and the decisions by keeping meeting minutes.

The board is the ultimate authority for delegating plan responsibilities such as adopting plan documents and appointing named fiduciaries, plan administrators, plan trustees, and plan committees. The plan committee should ensure that the delegation of roles and responsibilities by the board is clearly authorized and documented.

It is not uncommon for fiduciaries to delegate duties to other persons, or institutions, to carry out the fiduciaries' responsibilities.[51] As we covered earlier in this chapter, delegating their responsibility does not relieve fiduciaries of liability. Fiduciaries have a continuing duty to monitor the performance of those to whom they delegate authority. The plan document should permit delegation.

Another reason for following sound governance practices is to be prepared if the DOL audits the plan. If the plan sponsor and the fiduciaries have been procedurally and substantively prudent and operated the plan in accordance with the plan documents, an audit should be only an inconvenience. The IRS and the DOL have emphasized the need for plan sponsors to perform reviews of the plans to detect and correct operational defects and have established compliance policies and procedures. The advantages of these types of reviews are:

- Operational violations of the plan can be detected and corrected
- The company may avoid significant IRS and DOL penalties and participant lawsuits
- The cost of fiduciary liability coverage may be reduced

A well-organized and competent benefits committee is the key to successfully operating a 401(k) plan. A disciplined approach to the operation and supervision of a 401(k) plan will not only please risk managers, but it will also help meet many key business objectives, including attracting and retaining qualified personnel.

An important responsibility of plan fiduciaries is determining what expenses should be paid for out of plan assets. This is the topic of the next section.

USING PLAN ASSETS TO PAY EXPENSES

ERISA permits plan assets to be used for "defraying reasonable expenses of administering the plan."[52] While many plan sponsors pay the costs of operating a plan from corporate assets, it is increasingly common to pay plan expenses from plan assets. The payment of expenses from plan assets is a discretionary use of plan assets and a fiduciary act. Thus, paying expenses from plan assets must be consistent with the exclusive benefit rule and the other fiduciary requirements of ERISA.

Under ERISA, one of the fiduciaries' duties includes ensuring that fees and expenses paid from plan assets are reasonable. The key questions a fiduciary should be able to answer are:

- Does ERISA permit plan fiduciaries to pay the expenses with plan assets? The DOL has issued guidelines outlining what can and cannot be paid for by a plan. Plan fiduciaries that do not follow the guidelines, or do not know what they are, may be at risk.[53]
- Does the plan document or trust prevent the plan fiduciaries from paying the expenses with plan assets? One of the most important responsibilities for plan fiduciaries is to make sure the plan is being administered as it is written and communicated to participants. The DOL has taken the position that where a plan document is silent as to

the payment of reasonable administrative expenses, the plan may pay reasonable administrative expenses.[54]

- Have the plan fiduciaries determined the reasonableness of the expenses? Plan fiduciaries have an obligation to make sure the plan expenses are reasonable. In assessing whether a plan is paying reasonable compensation to a service provider, plan fiduciaries must determine the service provider's compensation from all sources (e.g., commissions or other payments from third parties as well as payments from the plan). Similarly, plan fiduciaries must determine whether the plan is receiving sufficient services to justify payments that the service provider is receiving from the plan. Fiduciaries should:
  - Identify all current plan expenses.
  - Benchmark the plan's expenses against the expenses of similar plans and from other providers.
  - If appropriate, meet with the vendor to negotiate the services and compensation, and if negotiations are unsatisfactory, undertake a search for a new vendor.
- Are the services being purchased necessary for the plan? The payment of expenses from plan assets is a discretionary use of plan assets and a fiduciary act. Thus, paying expenses from plan assets must be consistent with the "exclusive benefit rule" and the other fiduciary requirements of ERISA.
- Does the service pass the "but for" test? A touchstone of the DOL's application of the fiduciary rules on the payment of expenses from plan assets is that the expenses may not be paid from plan assets unless, "but for" the plan, the expense would not have been incurred. This but-for test essentially says that if there were no plan, the expense would not have been incurred.
- Is the expense the result of a settlor or administrative function? Expenses incurred in connection with plan administration activities may be paid from plan assets. However, expenses associated with settlor expenses may not be paid from plan assets. (Settlor expenses are described later in this chapter.)

Plan fiduciaries who do not follow the guidelines, including not being able to demonstrate reasonableness, could cause their plans to incur inappropriate expenses and put themselves personally at risk.

Settlor Expenses versus Plan Administration Expenses

The DOL considers the following expenses to be settlor expenses that may not be paid from plan assets:

- Plan design studies or calculations made in advance of the establishment or discretionary amendment of the plan
- Feasibility studies of plan mergers and retirement windows
- Discretionary plan amendments
- Expenses of conducting union negotiations in advance of a plan amendment

Expenses that may be paid from plan assets fall into five broad categories:

1. Communications with participants
2. Drafting plan amendments required by law
3. Maintaining tax qualifications
4. Plan administration expenses
5. Investment expenses

To the extent these expenses meet the but-for test and are otherwise reasonable, they may be paid from plan assets.

Communications required by ERISA, such as summary annual reports (SARs), summary plan descriptions (SPDs), benefit statements, and disclosures required upon the request of participants may be paid from plan assets. If reasonably necessary, the fiduciary may also pay for the cost of communications in addition to those that are legally required (such as annual benefit statements). The fiduciary will be given "substantial latitude in determining the method, form, and style of communication given to participants."[55] If appropriate, communication expenses may be paid from plan assets even though the employer may receive an incidental benefit.

The costs of drafting legally required amendments, including situations in which the plan sponsor is permitted to choose between alternatives for amending the plan, may be paid for from plan assets.[56] Plan assets may not be used, however, to pay for purely discretionary amendments, such as an amendment to change the rate of matching contributions.

The costs of maintaining the tax qualification of the plan may be paid from plan assets, including nondiscrimination testing and applying for a determination letter from the IRS.[57]

Expenses related to plan administration are payable from the plan. These include claims administration, appeals, recordkeeping, allocating employer contributions, selecting and monitoring plan investments, selecting and monitoring service providers, the annual plan financial statement audit, and complying with various other requirements of ERISA and the tax code. If plan fiduciaries retain the services of an outside administrator to perform administrative functions, the administrator's fees may be paid for from plan assets. Investment expenses are covered in detail in Chapter 7.

Evaluating Expenses for Plan Payment

When evaluating whether particular expenses may be paid for from plan assets, in addition to considering whether the expense is for an administrative or settlor function, fiduciaries must also determine whether:

- The plan document prohibits the payment of expenses
- The expenses incurred are prudent and reasonable
- The service provided was reasonable and necessary
- The amount paid from plan assets is limited to direct expenses and does not include any element of overhead or profit (for services and material provided by the employer)

Under ERISA, a fiduciary must follow the applicable plan documents to the extent they are consistent with ERISA.[58] The plan document may specify that the employer is responsible for paying the administrative expenses of the plan or that administrative expenses of the plan may be paid for from plan assets. As stated earlier, if the document does not address the payment of administrative expenses, reasonable administrative expenses may be paid for from plan assets.[59] A best practice is to clearly state in the plan document, SPD, and employee communications, the plan's intention to pay certain allowable expenses with plan assets. A plan may not pay for an amendment to permit the plan to pay expenses when the employer was previously required to pay those expenses.

Although plan sponsors can provide a number of the services necessary for the proper administration of a plan, ERISA's prohibited transaction rules would prevent the sponsor from providing them. However, ERISA exempts the "furnishing of goods, services or facilities between the plan and a party in interest" from the prohibited transaction rules. This exemption covers arrangements for office space, legal, accounting, and other services necessary for the operation of the plan, as long as the compensation paid is reasonable.[60]

A plan sponsor may be reimbursed only for its direct expenses and specifically may not be reimbursed for any overhead or profit.[61] Direct expenses include such things as photocopying, postage, stationery, and envelopes. Salaries and fringe benefit expenses of the plan sponsor's employees who provide administrative services to the plan may also be reimbursed.[62] Special care must be taken, however, when reimbursing salary expenses from plan assets.

Frequently, employees do not devote their full-time efforts to reimbursable administrative expenses. For example, an employee may spend the bulk of his time on day-to-day plan administration but occasionally be called on to provide plan design advice, such as whether the plan is competitive. Time spent on plan administration is reimbursable from the plan, but time spent on design analysis is not. If employee salary and fringe benefit expenses will be paid from plan assets, it is critical that the plan's fiduciaries adopt and follow processes to document and monitor how employees spend their time.

Fiduciaries should also ask their vendors to provide detailed billing invoices with descriptions and amounts to provide the plan with adequate documentation of the correct amounts being paid with plan assets.

Allocating Expenses to Individual Accounts

The DOL has reevaluated the issues a plan fiduciary must consider in allocating plan administration expenses to individual accounts in a 401(k) plan and has substantially reversed its earlier position. The DOL previously concluded that fees for qualified domestic relations order (QDRO) determinations could not be allocated directly to the affected participant's account because making such a determination was viewed as a plan administrator's statutory duty.[63] The DOL's position was also interpreted to mean a 401(k) plan participant could not be directly charged a fee for processing the participant's benefit distribution, but such fees had to be charged as a general plan expense and spread among all participants, if not paid by the employer.

Fiduciaries have also questioned whether it is permissible to charge reasonable plan administration expenses against the individual accounts of terminated employees while active employees are not charged (a strategy aimed at netting out small balances without cutting checks and also used to encourage terminated employees to take their plan distributions rather than leave them in the plan).

The DOL has issued a Field Assistance Bulletin (FAB) that concludes a plan fiduciary may allocate certain administration expenses incurred for a participant (for example, for hardship withdrawals, benefit calculations under different plan distribution options, benefit distribution charges, and QDRO determinations) to the individual's account. A plan fiduciary may also charge plan administration expenses to the accounts of terminated employees, but not those of active employees, in which the plan sponsor elects to cover the costs for active, but not terminated, employees.[64]

All expense allocations remain subject to general fiduciary considerations and the existence of clear plan language authorizing the allocation of these administration costs. In addition, the FAB reminds plan sponsors and fiduciaries of the requirement that plan SPDs include a statement identifying the circumstances that may result in the imposition of a fee or charge to a participant or beneficiary's account. Thus, decisions about specific expenses to be paid by the employer, by individual participants, and by the plan assets in general, need to be made and communicated to participants in the SPD.

COMMUNICATION TO PARTICIPANTS

The employer and other fiduciaries have a duty to avoid participant misunderstandings of material facts. First, fiduciaries must not make misleading statements to participants and beneficiaries. In addition, fiduciaries have a duty to communicate certain information to participants, even if it has not been requested. If there is a critical issue the fiduciaries "knew or should have known about," the fiduciaries have a duty to communicate material facts of the issue to participants. Similarly, if one fiduciary has made inaccurate statements, co-fiduciaries are obligated to communicate correct information. A basic rule of trust law is that the trustee has a duty to communicate material facts when the trustee knows the beneficiary does not know these facts and these facts are needed for the protection of the beneficiary.[65] Even without an inquiry from a participant or beneficiary, fiduciaries have a duty to disclose information when these otherwise unknown facts may have an "extreme impact" on the plan as a whole.[66]

CONCLUSION

Proper governance of a 401(k) plan requires understanding and following the fiduciary standards set forth by the laws, rules, and regulations that apply to these plans. Most of these standards are associated in some way with plan assets. When there is money involved, there is an opportunity for a fiduciary breach. The information in this chapter gives you a framework for understanding the fiduciary standards for a 401(k) plan. However, the information in this chapter and this book should not be relied upon as a substitute for proper legal counsel.

CHAPTER 6

Protecting Plan Fiduciaries

Even the most diligent plan fiduciaries can find themselves in a position in which a breach of duty has occurred. Plan fiduciaries are not without remedies for correcting breaches and protecting themselves against the consequences of a breach. Litigation against plan fiduciaries is common but one case stands out as a clear example of what can go wrong when plan fiduciaries fail in their duty. The collapse of Enron in the early 2000s sparked litigation between plan participants and fiduciaries. Out of this litigation came clear lessons that plan fiduciaries should be aware of. We begin this chapter with an overview of the impact Enron litigation has had on clarifying fiduciary standards. This chapter also covers the consequences of a fiduciary breach, the voluntary fiduciary correction program (VFCP), and fidelity bonds and fiduciary indemnification insurance. One additional way fiduciaries of 401(k) plans can protect themselves from liability is by following the rules set out by Code Section 404(c). We discuss 404(c) in greater detail in Chapter 7.

THE IMPACT OF ENRON LITIGATION

Even though it has now been many years since the collapse of Enron, the highly publicized litigation in connection with the collapse has called attention to the scope of fiduciaries' duties and liabilities. Enron sponsored a qualified 401(k) plan, a cash balance plan (a form of defined benefit plan), and an ESOP. More than 20,700 participants in Enron's 401(k) plan had nearly two-thirds of their assets invested in employer stock. About 7,600 employees participated in the company ESOP. In late 2001, Enron spiraled toward bankruptcy. However, plan participants were not told about the company's deteriorating financial condition. At the same time, Enron was making a routine change in 401(k) recordkeepers, and participants were blocked from selling their Enron stock during a blackout period that was instituted to accommodate the change of recordkeepers. Participants lost more than $1.2 billion in plan account balances through the decline in Enron's stock value when Enron collapsed. The participants claimed that Enron fiduciaries, including corporate officers and directors, breached their fiduciary duties by allowing, and even encouraging, investment in Enron stock at a time when the stock's value was plummeting.

Judge Melinda Harmon, of the U.S. District Court for the Southern District of Texas, heard the more than 20 fiduciary breach cases that were filed in connection with Enron. In the preliminary stages of that litigation, she issued a comprehensive opinion outlining her view of the law of fiduciary responsibility under ERISA that will be applied in the Enron litigation.[1] The DOL was an important commentator in the Enron case through the submission of a friend-of-the-court, or amicus curiae, brief.[2]

Together, the district court's comprehensive opinion in the Enron case and the DOL's legal brief highlight some of the issues plan fiduciaries are faced with, as well as providing measures that plan fiduciaries might consider to protect themselves from liability.

Appointment and Monitoring of Fiduciaries

Both Judge Harmon and the DOL made it clear that the act of appointing plan fiduciaries is itself a fiduciary act, carrying with it continuing fiduciary obligations. An appointing fiduciary has the duty to supervise "and take appropriate actions if the [appointed fiduciary] is not adequately protecting the interest of the Plans' participants."[3] The appointing fiduciary cannot be a passive observer and meet its obligations under ERISA "merely through the device of giving the appointed co-fiduciary primary responsibility for day-to-day management of trust investments." Rather, the appointing fiduciary has a duty to monitor the appointees, which includes making sure they have accurate information on the financial condition of the employer (in the event that employer stock is one of the investments).

Personal Liability of Fiduciaries

Enron's officers and directors argued they should not be held personally liable for breach of fiduciary duty because they were acting on behalf of Enron in its capacity as the named fiduciary under the plans. The court disagreed, noting that corporate employees, officers, and directors who serve in a fiduciary role are personally liable for their actions as fiduciaries.[4]

In its ruling, the court concurred with the DOL, observing that several other courts have previously ruled that officers who exercise fiduciary discretion are exposed to personal liability. It is important for fiduciaries to be aware that liability incurred as a result of fiduciary breaches is not dischargeable in bankruptcy.[5]

Plan Design as a Defense

In the Enron case, the plan fiduciaries argued that they were required to continue investing in Enron stock because the 401(k) plan's terms required that investment. The DOL countered that ERISA forbids plan fiduciaries from following plan documents if doing so would be imprudent or otherwise violate ERISA. Thus, if Enron stock was an imprudent investment, plan fiduciaries would be prohibited from investing plan assets in it, regardless of the plan's terms. Fiduciaries must consciously decide and monitor whether to purchase or retain employer securities. As summarized in the DOL's brief, "documents cannot excuse trustees from their duties under ERISA."[6]

Chapter 7 further discusses the implications of offering employer stock as a plan investment.

SEC Insider Trading and Confidentiality

Also in the Enron case, the plan fiduciaries said they could not have taken action to protect participants without engaging in insider trading, in violation of securities laws, because the information upon which they would have acted was not public. The court agreed with the DOL's position that ERISA's fiduciary duties and the securities laws could have been simultaneously met by:[7]

- Disclosing the information to shareholders and the public or forcing Enron to do so
- Eliminating Enron stock as a participant option and as the employer match in the 401(k) plan
- Alerting the appropriate regulatory agencies, such as the SEC and the DOL, about Enron's financial misstatements

Commentators in this complex area have not universally endorsed this view.

Directed Trustees

The Enron decision surprised many in the benefits field by concluding that a directed trustee has an obligation to independently evaluate the directions received from a plan fiduciary. It had previously been thought by many that, absent extraordinary circumstances, a directed trustee could follow the directions it receives and not be exposed to liability. In the Enron context, the directed trustee was the plan recordkeeper and asset custodian that executed orders to invest plan assets in employer stock. Judge Harmon's decision held that Enron's plan recordkeeper and asset custodian might be liable if investing in Enron stock was a fiduciary breach. Specifically, the Court said that:

> *[E]ven where the named fiduciary appears to have been granted full control, authority and/or discretion over that portion of activity of plan management and/or plan assets...and the plan trustee is directed to perform certain actions within that area, the directed trustee still retains a degree of discretion, authority, and responsibility that may expose him to liability, as reflected in the structure and language of provisions of ERISA. At least some fiduciary status and duties of a directed trustee are preserved, even though the scope of its "exclusive authority and discretion to manage and control the assets of the plan" has been substantially constricted by the directing named fiduciary's correspondingly broadened role, and breach of those duties may result in liability.*
>
> *In any ERISA retirement plan, where...the directed trustee knew or should have known from a number of significant waving red flags and/or regular reviews of the company's financial statements that the employer company was in financial danger and its stock greatly diminished in value, yet the named fiduciary, to which the plan allocated all control over investments by the plan, directed the trustee to continue purchasing the employer's stock, there is [a] factual question whether the evidence is sufficient to give rise to a fiduciary duty by the directed trustee to investigate the advisability of purchasing the company stock to insure that the action is in compliance with ERISA as well as the plan.*[8]

This Enron decision drew considerable attention to the directed trustee issue. In addition, a court dismissed claims against Merrill Lynch, the directed trustee of WorldCom's 401(k) plan.[9] WorldCom employees had sought $100 million against Merrill Lynch for violating its fiduciary duties as the plan's directed trustee in allowing participant investments in WorldCom stock. These participants suffered huge retirement savings losses after WorldCom's bankruptcy. The court held that, as a directed trustee, Merrill Lynch was required to follow WorldCom's investment orders. The court stated that Merrill Lynch would have breached its fiduciary responsibilities had it possessed information not known to the general public or should have acted differently because of publicly available information. However, the court found that Merrill Lynch did not possess any nonpublic information that would have provided it with special insight unknown to other investors.

CONSEQUENCES OF A BREACH OF FIDUCIARY DUTY

Fiduciaries are personally liable for breaching their fiduciary duties. A fiduciary is liable to the plan for the actual amount lost and any profits made through the improper use of assets. A variety of remedies address fiduciary violations. For example, criminal penalties apply to any person who willfully violates ERISA, and civil remedies are available to plan participants and the DOL in seeking to correct ERISA violations.

Section 502(a) of ERISA states that a civil action may be brought by a participant to:

- Recover benefits due under the terms of participation in the plan
- Enforce rights under the terms of the plan
- Clarify rights to future benefits under the terms of the plan

Participants and fiduciaries may also sue to:

- Enforce the provisions of ERISA and the terms of the plan
- Enjoin any act or practice that violates ERISA or the terms of the plan
- Obtain other appropriate equitable relief

The DOL is given similar authority to seek the same type of relief.

The DOL may also impose monetary fines on fiduciaries and others who violate ERISA. For example, the DOL may assess a 20 percent civil penalty against a fiduciary or any other person for breach of fiduciary duty. In addition, the courts may fashion other relief, up to and including removal of a plan fiduciary.[10]

THE VOLUNTARY FIDUCIARY CORRECTION PROGRAM (VFCP)

If a fiduciary breach occurs, fiduciaries may avoid the DOL's enforcement action and penalties by using the VFCP. The VFCP is available only if neither the plan nor the applicant is under a DOL investigation, and the application contains no evidence of potential criminal violations. Anyone who may be liable for fiduciary violations under ERISA, including plan sponsors, parties in interest, fiduciaries, and others who are in a position to correct a fiduciary breach, may use the program.

On April 19, 2006, the Department of Labor published an update to the VFCP, which simplified and expanded the original VFCP published in 2002. The VFCP is designed to encourage employers to voluntarily comply with ERISA by self-correcting certain violations of the law. The effective date of the simplified and expanded VFCP was May 19, 2006.[11]

Although the VFCP offers a complete solution for correction of certain fiduciary breaches, fiduciaries may decide not to file under the program. Even if the decision is made not to file under the VFCP, the program sets out the DOL's approach to correcting certain fiduciary breaches.[12]

In general, the VFCP has four steps:

1. Identify any violations and determine whether they fall within the transactions covered by the VFCP.
2. Follow the process for correcting specific violations.
3. Calculate and restore any losses or profits with interest, if applicable, and distribute any supplemental benefits to participants.
4. File an application with the appropriate DOL regional office that includes documentation showing evidence of corrective action taken.

Covered Transactions

The VFCP provides descriptions of 19 transactions and their method of correction. Corrective remedies are prescribed for the following fiduciary violations involving employee benefit plans:

- *Delinquent participant contributions and participant loan repayments to pension plans*
- *Delinquent participant contributions to insured welfare plans*
- *Delinquent participant contributions to welfare plan trusts*
- *Fair market interest rate loans with parties in interest*
- *Below market interest rate loans with parties in interest*
- *Below market interest rate loans with nonparties in interest*
- *Below market interest rate loans due to delay in perfecting security interest*
- *Participant loans failing to comply with plan provisions for amount, duration, or level amortization*
- *Defaulted participant loans*
- *Purchase of assets by plans from parties in interest*
- *Sale of assets by plans to parties in interest*

- *Sale and leaseback of property to sponsoring employers*
- *Purchase of assets from nonparties in interest at more than fair market value*
- *Sale of assets to nonparties in interest at less than fair market value*
- *Holding of an illiquid asset previously purchased by plan*
- *Benefit payments based on improper valuation of plan assets*
- *Payment of duplicate, excessive, or unnecessary compensation*
- *Improper payment of expenses by plan*
- *Payment of dual compensation to plan fiduciaries*

Acceptable Corrections

Applicants must completely and accurately correct the fiduciary breach, restoring the principal amount involved in the transaction, plus earnings. Generally, applicants must:

- *Conduct valuations of plan assets using generally recognized markets for the assets or obtain written appraisal reports from qualified professionals that are based on generally accepted appraisal standards.*
- *Restore to the plan the principal amount involved, plus the greater of lost earnings, starting on the date of the loss and extending to the recovery date, or profits resulting from the use of the principal amount, starting on the date of the loss and extending to the date the profit is realized.*
- *Pay the expenses associated with correcting transactions, such as appraisal costs or fees associated with recalculating participant account balances.*
- *Make supplemental distributions to former employees, beneficiaries, or alternate payees when appropriate, and provide proof of the payments.*

The VFCP details the calculation of earnings, and in no case will this calculation result in a loss to the plan or a participant. Therefore, even if there would have been losses to participants if the breach had not occurred, the correction must include the payment of either actual earnings or an assumed rate of earnings. The VFCP also provides that the cost of any correction must be borne by the fiduciary, plan sponsor, or other plan official and the plan may not pay for any portion of the correction.

The VFCP now includes an online calculator to assist applicants by automatically calculating correction amounts that must be paid to the plan.

The online calculator is available on the DOL's web site at: www.dol.gov/ebsa/calculator/main.html. While the DOL anticipates that most applicants will use the online calculator, applicants also may perform manual calculations.

Once the correction is made, plans must then file, when necessary, amended returns to reflect corrected transactions or violations. Applicants must also provide proof of payment to participants and beneficiaries or properly segregate the affected assets in cases in which the plan is unable to identify the location of missing individuals. A *de minimis* exception applies when correction involves distributions to certain former employees, beneficiaries, or alternate payees. If the amount of the corrective distribution would be less than $20, the distribution may not be required. However, if the applicant uses the *de minimis* rule, the full value of the correction must be paid to the plan.

Application Process

To use the VFCP, a plan official or her authorized representative (for example, benefit consultant, attorney, accountant, or other service provider) prepares a detailed application for submission to the DOL. The application is a narrative describing the breach and the corrective action to be taken and requires plan officials to provide supporting documentation to the DOL's appropriate regional office, such as:

- *A copy of relevant portions of the plan and related documents*
- *Documents supporting transactions, such as leases and loan documents, and applicable corrections*
- *Documentation of lost earnings amounts*
- *Documentation of restored profits, if applicable*
- *Proof of payment of required amounts*
- *Specific documents required for relevant transactions*
- *A signed checklist*
- *A penalty of perjury statement*

The VFCP provides a model application form. While use of the model application form is entirely voluntary, the DOL encourages its use to avoid common application errors that frequently result in processing delays or rejections. The DOL says that the use of the model form will enable their regional offices to provide a more expedient and consistent review of program applications. The model includes the VFCP's mandatory checklist.

Effect of Using the VFCP

Upon making proper corrections and filing the application, plan officials will receive a "no action" letter from the DOL, indicating that there will be no enforcement action by the DOL on the corrected transaction and no civil penalties. However, the DOL reserves the right to conduct an investigation at any time to determine the accuracy of the facts set out in the application and that the corrective action is properly taken. If the correction falls short of a complete and acceptable correction, the DOL may reject the application and pursue enforcement, including assessment of a 20 percent penalty.[13]

Using the VFCP does not necessarily protect plan fiduciaries from all possible consequences of a fiduciary breach.[14] Compliance with the program does not preclude:

- *Any governmental agency from conducting a criminal investigation of the transaction identified in the application*
- *DOL's assistance to such other agency*
- *DOL making the appropriate referrals of criminal violations as required by section 506(b) of ERISA*
- *DOL seeking removal from positions of responsibility with respect to a plan or other nonmonetary injunctive relief against any person responsible for the transaction*
- *Referring information regarding the transaction to the IRS as required by section 303(c) of ERISA, or*
- *Imposing civil penalties based on the failure to file a timely, complete, and accurate Form 5500*

To encourage use of the VFCP and to address plan sponsor concerns about the possible imposition of excise taxes, the DOL has released a prohibited transaction class exemption. Under the exemption, the DOL has provided limited excise tax relief for the correction of four transactions provided under the VFCP.[15] Transactions covered under the exemption include:

- *Late transmittal of participant contributions and participant loan repayments to a pension plan*
- *Loans between a plan and party in interest at less than a fair market interest rate*
- *Purchase or sale of an asset, including real property, between a plan and a party in interest at fair market value*
- *Sale and leaseback of real property between a plan and employer at fair market value and fair market rental value*

Illustrations of eligible transactions are provided in the exemption. The DOL also included an exemption to cover the purchase of an asset by a plan when the asset has been determined to be illiquid (including real property) from a party in interest at no greater than fair market value at that time, and the subsequent sale of such asset to a party in interest, provided the plan receives the correction amount as described in the VFCP.[16]

The IRS has also said that it will not impose excise taxes on transactions covered by the VFCP.[17] The DOL further noted that applicants who would not otherwise be liable for excise taxes under the Code, but who are in a position to correct a breach, are not made liable for excise taxes solely by virtue of their participation in the VFCP. The relief from excise taxes applies to the four transactions included in the VFCP, if plan officials comply with the conditions of the exemption. To take advantage of the excise tax relief, interested persons, such as participants and beneficiaries, must be given formal notice of the voluntary fiduciary correction filing. One consideration for plan fiduciaries is whether the excise tax relief warrants possible participant concerns from providing formal notice of the voluntary fiduciary correction filing.

FIDELITY BONDS VERSUS FIDUCIARY LIABILITY INSURANCE

Under ERISA, in general, every fiduciary of a 401(k) plan and every person who handles plan funds or assets must be bonded.[18] These so-called ERISA fidelity bonds provide protection to the plan in the event the employees of the plan sponsor cause losses to the plan through dishonest or fraudulent acts. Fidelity bonds are often attached to the employer's crime insurance policy or provided on a stand-alone basis if: the employer does not purchase corporate crime insurance or the fiduciary is managing third-party plans and is required to be bonded. ERISA fidelity bonds do not protect against losses arising from breaches of fiduciary duty or errors in plan administration. Protection for such losses requires the purchase of fiduciary liability insurance.

Fidelity Bonds

ERISA requires that every administrator, officer, and employee of an ERISA-covered pension or welfare plan who handles funds or other property[19] of a plan must be bonded.[20] The bond, commonly known as a fidelity bond, protects the plan against losses from fraud or dishonesty.[21] Each individual who could create a loss to the plan through fraud or dishonesty by manipulating or disposing of plan assets is considered to be "handling" plan funds and, therefore, is required to be bonded. Investment advisors, who do not handle funds, are not required to be bonded.[24]

Fidelity bonds are usually written to cover all individuals associated with a particular plan without identifying them by name or position. The amount of the bond must equal 10 percent of the funds handled, but it should be no less than $1,000 and no more than $500,000 unless required by the DOL.[23] To compute the value of the bond, the amount of plan assets handled for the previous year should be used or, in the case of a new plan, the estimated value of plan funds that will be handled.[24] This coverage may be paid from plan assets[25] or by the employer. Fidelity bond coverage may be issued for more than one year; the amount may have to be adjusted each year, however, to ensure coverage at the minimum amount.[26] The bond must also include a clause that extends coverage through a period of no less than one year after termination or cancellation of the bond if a violation is discovered during that period.[27]

ERISA provides limited exceptions to its bonding requirements. For example, a bond is not required for totally unfunded plans[28] and insured plans whose premiums are paid out of the employer's general assets, except to the extent funds (such as dividends) returned by the insurer belong to the plan and are subject to handling.[29] Additionally, no bond is required of any fiduciary (or any director, officer, or employee thereof) if:

- Banks that are subject to federal regulation and are federally insured
- Savings and loan associations subject to federal regulation, if they are the plan administrator
- Qualified insurance companies[30]

Fiduciary Liability Insurance and Indemnification

In contrast to ERISA's bonding requirements, ERISA does not require the purchase of fiduciary liability insurance. Because of the increased frequency and severity of ERISA lawsuits, however, many employers, both large and small, secure this protection. Generally speaking, fiduciary liability insurance is designed to protect the sponsoring organization, the plans, and certain individuals (including the sponsor's directors, officers, and employees in their capacity as plan fiduciaries or administrators) against liability arising from violations of fiduciary obligations, responsibilities, or duties under ERISA, including the selection and monitoring of investments. Coverage also extends to liability arising from certain acts, errors, and omissions in the administration of the plans. Fiduciary liability insurance policies typically cover the following costs: damages, judgments, settlements, defense costs, civil penalties of up to 5 percent imposed under ERISA §502(i) and up to 20 percent under §502(l), and certain settlements, fines, and penalties pursuant to various voluntary compliance and correction programs. Unlike ERISA fidelity bonds, fiduciary liability insurance policies generally exclude (among other things) losses arising from dishonest or fraudulent acts.

ERISA fiduciaries are personally responsible for their errors or omissions and may be personally liable for a co-fiduciary's breach.[31] Provisions in a plan or other agreement that excuse a fiduciary from liability are invalid because they violate public policy. However, fiduciaries may either purchase insurance or may be indemnified by the plan sponsor, but they may not be indemnified by the plan.[32]

As stated earlier, a plan may purchase insurance to cover losses resulting from a breach of fiduciary responsibility.[33] Additionally, a fiduciary may purchase insurance to cover his own liability, or an employer or union may purchase liability insurance for plan fiduciaries. Whether the fiduciary will be subject to recourse by the insurance carrier will depend on to whom the policy is issued. If the policy is issued to the plan, the insurer will likely have recourse against the fiduciary. On the other hand, if the policy is issued directly to the fiduciary, there will likely be no recourse against the fiduciary.

Some employers have a fiduciary compliance audit completed by an independent party and use favorable audit results to negotiate lower premiums. Many policies cover the defense costs and damages for breaches, but there are exclusions and limitations. For example, policies often do not cover claims arising out of profit-taking, fines and penalties, and deliberate or fraudulent acts.

A supplement or alternative to purchasing liability insurance is for the plan sponsor to indemnify the fiduciary. Under an indemnification agreement, the plan sponsor will agree to pay any losses or claims suffered by the fiduciary or any portion of their expenses not covered by a fiduciary liability policy. Indemnification usually provides that the plan sponsor will not bring suit against a fiduciary, except for willful misconduct or criminal actions. Fiduciaries and plan sponsors should be certain they have a written indemnification agreement that addresses the broad range of issues that may arise if a claim is made against the fiduciary. Fiduciaries must bear in mind that the indemnification they receive is only as valuable as the plan sponsor's willingness and ability to pay any liability the fiduciary may incur. Indemnification parameters are governed by state law. Legal counsel should be involved in drafting an appropriate indemnification agreement.

CONCLUSION

401(k) plan fiduciaries can avoid breaching their duties by understanding their responsibilities, setting up sound governance processes, and following those processes diligently. When a breach does occur, the Voluntary Fiduciary Correction Program is available as a possible corrective remedy. To protect plan participants, fidelity bonds are required. To protect plan sponsors and individual fiduciaries, fiduciary liability insurance is a good idea. As with all of the technical topics covered in this book, our intent is to provide an overview of the issues. This information is not intended to be legal advice.

Establishing and Managing Plan Investments

The core of any retirement program is its assets. In 401(k) plans, how the assets are invested over time has a significant impact on the ultimate benefit to plan participants and beneficiaries. 401(k) plans have a unique challenge; they are by their nature largely made up of participant-directed accounts. The participants in the plan choose where their accounts will be invested. Plan sponsors, however, select the options from which plan participants are allowed to choose. Plan sponsors have a fiduciary duty to do this with care, skill, prudence, and diligence. The purpose of this chapter is to provide plan sponsors with information to help them meet this duty. We cover here constructing an investment policy statement and the plan's investment menu, selecting and monitoring investment managers, understanding investment-related expenses, complying with 404(c) rules, selecting a default investment in the plan, evaluating education and advice options, and dealing with special situations such as employer stock, brokerage accounts, and mutual fund windows.

THE INVESTMENT POLICY STATEMENT

Every 401(k) plan should have an investment policy statement (IPS). This is different from a funding policy required by ERISA for DB plans. The IPS is a critical component in managing a 401(k) plan's investments. While ERISA does not specifically require a written IPS, the DOL has said that maintaining a written IPS is prudent.[1]

The IPS defines the specific criteria that will be used by the plan fiduciaries in selecting, monitoring, and replacing investment managers or funds for the plan. It delineates the plan's investment strategy and ongoing review process. In a defined benefit plan, in which the trustee or an investment committee will make investment and asset allocation decisions (known as a trustee-directed plan), the IPS establishes the plan's asset allocation strategy. In a typical 401(k) plan, in which participants make their own investment or asset allocation decisions (known as a participant-directed plan), the IPS establishes the types of investments and asset classes that will be offered and describes the risk-and-return characteristics of each investment. We make a distinction here between investment types and asset classes. Examples of investment types are target date funds versus single asset class funds such as a U.S. large cap equity fund. Examples of asset classes are cash, bonds, large cap equity (large companies), mid cap equity (midsize companies), small cap equity (small companies), and international equity, among others.

An IPS for a participant-directed plan will typically include an introduction and sections on investment options, investment guidelines, and performance evaluation. In some instances, a section on communications will be included. Following is a list of sections and what each covers.

Introduction
- Provides an overview or executive summary of the investment policy
- Includes background information relating to the plan and the purpose of the trust
- States the purpose of the IPS (for example, to establish investment objectives and sets standards for evaluating the performance of investment managers)
- Lists the individuals responsible for making decisions relating to investments (typically members of a retirement or investment committee) and delineates their specific tasks
- Typically contains a statement that the plan is intended to comply with ERISA, if the plan is subject to ERISA

Investment Options
- Contains information relating to the plan's investment objectives and philosophies.
- Identifies the specific investment types and asset classes of funds to be included in the plan, including specific fund objectives
- Includes information relating to return expectations, relative to specified benchmarks or indexes
- Sets categories or types of funds that will be excluded from consideration as investment vehicles for the plan

Investment Guidelines
- Includes information relating to quality standards applicable to funds or securities held in the trust
- Provides details regarding prohibited fund practices, proxy voting, and any additional criteria (for example, requirements relating to assets

under management, manager tenure, portfolio turnover, beta, expense ratio, loads) relating to a fund's inclusion as an investment option

Performance Evaluation

- The market cycle or other period over which investment funds will be evaluated
- The frequency of performance reviews to be conducted by the plan sponsor (typically members of the retirement or investment committee)
- Specific benchmarks that will be used to evaluate the performance of each investment fund
- Specific guidelines and procedures applicable to the potential replacement of investment funds or managers

In some instances, it may be appropriate for the IPS to provide a summary of specific investment-related materials that will be provided or made available to plan participants. Participant communications typically include:

- Description of each investment alternative available under the plan
- Details of investment fund-related fees and expenses
- Description of procedures relating to participant-directed investment instructions
- Copy of the most recent prospectus for each investment fund

At the time this chapter was written, new laws and regulations were being contemplated related to what information participants must receive, how they must receive it, and when it must be made available. All plan documentation, including the plan's IPS, should be reviewed and amended if necessary as new rules become effective.

THE INVESTMENT MENU

We mentioned earlier that the IPS should prescribe the types of investment options to be offered in the plan. A 401(k) plan's investment menu should therefore be the direct result of following the plan's investment policy statement. In the early days of participant-directed 401(k) plans, participants were given very few options. It was not uncommon for a plan to have a stock fund, a bond fund, and a cash option as the entire investment menu. As plans evolved, the number and types of investment choices ballooned dramatically. Participants faced with large numbers of investment options struggle with choice overload, which often leads to suboptimal investment outcomes.[2] Insights from the field of behavioral finance along with real-life observations of participant behavior have led to more sensible investment menus in 401(k) plans.

What is emerging is a three-tiered structure to 401(k) investment menus. The first tier is represented by a set of prediversified funds or portfolios that the participant can choose as a single option. The most popular form of this type of fund today is the target date fund. The second tier is represented by single asset class funds. These single asset class funds are the building blocks participants can use to build their own portfolio. The number and type of funds in this tier should be enough for a participant to be able to build a well-diversified portfolio that matches their investment objectives and risk tolerance. Care should be given not to include so many funds in this tier that the number of options causes confusion or anxiety. The third tier is represented by a broader selection of funds for those participants who want and can use appropriately a wide range of funds. This tier is often satisfied by offering a brokerage account or mutual fund window. Participants should be aware that plan sponsors are not performing due diligence on every investment offered in the *window* and as such should perform their own due diligence on any investment they choose.

The content in the next two sections covers prediversified portfolios and portfolio construction in greater detail.

PREDIVERSIFIED PORTFOLIOS

The term *prediversified portfolios* refers to any investment option a participant can select as a single option that has within it a mix of asset classes, such as stocks, bonds, and cash. There are three broad categories of prediversified portfolios: target date funds (which are also known as lifecycle funds), lifestyle funds (sometimes referred to as target risk funds), and balanced funds. The key difference between these types of funds is the way the asset allocation within the fund is determined and managed over time.

Target date funds typically have an asset allocation that becomes more conservative over time, which makes the asset allocation dynamic. The formula for how the target date fund becomes more conservative over time is usually predescribed by the fund manager so the investor has an idea of how much risk the fund is taking at any given time. This predetermined asset allocation is often referred to as the fund's glide path. The reason it is called a glide path is because a chart of the allocation between the more risky assets (stocks) and less risky assets (bonds) within the fund over time looks like a downward sloping line from left to right. This line looks like the path of an airplane landing, or its glide path. These funds typically specify a target date, often in their name, that signifies the projected retirement date of the individuals for which the fund is designed. Each fund's equity allocation is gradually reduced as the years pass and the retirement target date comes closer. For example, a fund named "the 2040 fund" would be primarily invested in equities in the year 2010 and would shift the equity allocation toward fixed income securities as the year 2040 approaches. The premise of these funds is that participants need simply to select the fund that is closest to their targeted retirement year and make no further investment decisions prior to retirement.

In contast, lifestyle and balanced funds typically have an asset allocation that remains constant based on a predetermined risk profile, which makes the asset allocation static. In some cases, the fund managers reserve the right to adjust their asset allocation as they see fit. Even so, they typically keep their asset allocation within a predescribed band of risk, which is reflected in the investment objective of the fund. Balanced funds have been around for decades and are a form of a lifestyle fund, the difference being that balanced funds are often just a single fund in a family of funds whereas lifestyle funds often come in a series of funds, each with a different level of risk. The premise of lifestyle or balanced funds is that participants only need to determine what overall level of risk they want and then choose the fund that corresponds to that level of risk. The fund manager does all of the work behind the scenes to manage the portfolio to the predescribed risk objective.

When evaluating target date, lifestyle, or balanced funds, plan fiduciary due diligence efforts typically include a determination of the following:

- Investment performance versus peer groups and benchmarks
- Quality and type of the underlying funds used in the portfolios
- Investment and other operating expenses
- The appropriateness of the approach (target date versus lifestyle) given the demographics and financial sophistication of the plan participants

However, since most target date, lifestyle and balanced funds are "fund of funds" products, more in-depth analysis may be warranted. In addition to these factors, the fund's portfolio construction methodology, use of tactical asset allocation methods, rebalancing policy, and guiding principles concerning the overall allocation between equities and fixed income should be considered.

Custom designed funds are alternatives to prepackaged target date, lifestyle or balanced funds. Larger plans may consider creating customized funds constructed from the plan's underlying single asset class investment options. This practice may be more cost-effective than prepackaged funds and offers control over determining the fund's underlying investment options and asset allocation. The custom mix can also enhance diversification by including managers from a variety of fund families. This approach automatically takes advantage of the ongoing due diligence being performed on the plan's single asset class or lifestyle investment options.

A less expensive alternative is to create these funds as model portfolios or as a single choice option that automatically implements a model portfolio for the participant when selected. Most recordkeepers today offer automatic rebalancing of portfolios, making this concept relatively easy to implement and maintain.

PORTFOLIO CONSTRUCTION

Portfolio construction is the process for determining both the asset allocation (the percentage to be invested in various asset classes) and the funds to be used for the asset class assignments within a portfolio. Whether participants construct their own portfolio, using the funds available in the plan, or they delegate this function to a professional through the use of prediversified portfolios such as target date funds, portfolio construction is a key determinant of their investment returns over time. We discuss in this section the basics of asset allocation, the difference between strategic and tactical asset allocation, and style diversification.

Asset Allocation

A key component of any investment portfolio is its asset allocation, or mix of asset classes. Asset classes are groups of securities that have similar characteristics and behave similarly in the marketplace. Equities (stocks) can be considered an asset class; the definition of asset class in practice, however, has evolved to describe more specific groups of securities. Today, instead of just defining "stocks" as an asset class, a portfolio manager might define specific allocations to U.S. large cap stocks, U.S. mid cap stocks, and U.S. small cap stocks. They may have specific allocations to foreign stocks as well. Further refinement of asset class definitions has also occurred with fixed income securities (bonds) as well. It is beyond the scope of this book to list all of the asset classes and subclasses that are currently in use, but it is important to be aware of these refinements when considering the asset allocation of a portfolio.

Strategic versus Tactical Asset Allocation

An asset allocation can be considered strategic or tactical. Strategic asset allocations are intended to remain constant, given a specific investment objective regardless of external temporary factors such as the most recent movements of capital markets. Tactical asset allocations on the other hand may change on the basis of external factors or the portfolio manager's opinion regarding the short-term return potential of specific asset classes. Therefore, two portfolios, one using strategic asset allocation and one using tactical asset allocation, may have identical investment objectives, yet very different allocations to stocks, bonds, and cash.

Success factors for a strategic asset allocation portfolio are: the portfolio manager's ability to develop accurate long-term assumptions regarding how specific asset classes will perform, the mix of these asset classes in the portfolio, and the selection of funds or securities within each asset class.

Success factors for a tactical asset allocation portfolio are: the portfolio manager's ability to accurately predict which asset classes will perform well for the window of time they have set their tactical allocation, the mix of these asset classes in the portfolio, and the selection of funds or securities within each asset class.

It is not uncommon for portfolios to use a mix of both approaches. For example, a portfolio manager may wish to keep the equity allocation in a portfolio constant (strategic) yet allow some of the managers of the funds within the equity allocation to make tactical decisions regarding style, market capitalization, or geography of the equities they select.

The most popular type of prediversified portfolio in 401(k) plans today is the target date fund. The asset allocation in target date funds intentionally changes over time. Generally, target date funds become more conservative as they move closer to the retirement date for which they are named (for example, a 2040 target date fund is intended for people who want to retire in the year 2040). So, given that target date funds' asset allocation changes over time, are they considered strategically or tactically asset allocated? It depends. Target date funds that prescribe in advance the asset allocation they will have each year in the future are considered to be strategically asset allocated because the allocations are determined in advance. Other target date funds may only prescribe general guidelines or bands of asset allocations for dates in the future. These funds are likely using some tactical asset allocation in their portfolio management.

Style Diversification

An asset *style* is different from an asset *class*. We described what an asset class is earlier in this chapter. An asset style is a further refinement of a group of securities. For example, within all of the U.S. large cap stocks that exist, some of these stocks are considered to be growth stocks and others value stocks. Growth stocks are shares of a company whose earnings are expected to grow more rapidly than the market in general. Value stocks are companies whose shares tend to trade at values below what their fundamental metrics would suggest they are worth. Therefore, portfolio managers may have specific allocations to large cap growth and large cap value stocks. This is only one example of style variations within asset classes.

Why would a portfolio manager be concerned about style diversification within asset classes? Based on analysis of historic returns, we can observe that there are times when one style outperforms another within an asset class. Unfortunately, it is extremely difficult, if not impossible to determine prospectively which style will perform best in the future. Therefore, a portfolio manager may wish to stay diversified across the various styles to reduce volatility and increase return potential of the portfolio.

This section covered asset allocation, strategic versus tactical asset allocation, and style diversification. The next section discusses the selection of investments and managers.

SELECTION OF INVESTMENTS AND MANAGERS

Under ERISA, plan fiduciaries are judged against the care, skill, prudence, and diligence that people familiar with such matters would use, which is sometimes referred to as the "prudent expert" standard. When selecting investment funds and investment managers for a plan, a fiduciary must follow this prudent expert rule. This requirement is met if the fiduciary has given appropriate consideration to those facts and circumstances relevant to each investment and has acted accordingly.[3]

If fiduciaries are not investment experts, they have an obligation to seek expert advice to assist them in selecting and monitoring plan investment funds and investment managers. Fiduciaries may limit their liability by hiring investment managers to manage, acquire, and dispose of plan assets.[4] If an investment manager is properly appointed and monitored, trustees are relieved of potential liability in connection with assets invested by the manager.[5] The investment manager should be prudently selected by the fiduciary, acknowledge its fiduciary responsibilities regarding the investment of plan assets in writing (usually in the investment management agreement), and be carefully monitored once selected.

The IPS will often provide criteria for the selection of investment managers. Factors to consider when choosing and reviewing the performance of an investment manager include:

- *Historical Investment Performance.*   Investment performance should be reviewed for various periods of time (for example, current year-to-date, one-year, three-year, five-year, and 10-year results). These time periods should include both bull and bear markets. Performance numbers should be carefully scrutinized to determine whether they are reported on a net or gross-of-fees basis. For example, publicly traded fund returns are typically reported net of fees, while institutional and separate account fund returns are reported on a gross-of-fees basis.

- *Performance Relative to Assumed Risk.* Also known as risk-adjusted performance, this attribute of an investment fund or manager is of great importance, particularly in the context of retirement plan investments. This, in effect, gives an indication of the "pain required for the gain," or the relative degree of volatility the portfolio experiences compared to its performance outcome. Certain statistical measures, such as the Sharpe ratio, can help determine and benchmark an investment portfolio's or manager's risk-adjusted return profile.

- *Adherence to Stated Asset Allocation Guidelines.* Some fund types (for example, target date, lifestyle or balanced funds) use multiple asset classes in varying proportions corresponding to their stated investment objectives. Ranges for the proportions of the included asset classes are typically stated in the fund objectives or other related materials. Deviation from these ranges for any material length of time can be a cause for concern because it is a violation of the fund's stated guidelines.

- *Adherence to Stated Investment Style.* Plan fiduciaries that specify asset classes based upon investment style in their plan menus should review their plans' investment options for style adherence and take note of deviations. Plan investments should also be evaluated against style specific benchmarks.

- *Performance Evaluation.* Prudent performance evaluation requires that investments be measured against appropriate benchmarks and investment manager universes. The benchmark index must contain securities similar in nature to those used by the manager, and the universe (or peer group) must contain managers applying a similar investment approach.

- *Fund Expenses.* Expenses related to investment management, marketing, and the ongoing operation of the fund should be examined to ensure they are reasonable.

- *Manager Tenure and Performance of Key Decision Makers.* The length of time a manager or management team has been in place determines the extent to which the fund's historic track record is attributable to the manager or team. Therefore, management tenure, or lack thereof, is important in determining the relevance of an investment portfolio's past performance.

- *Investment Firm Organizational Stability.* Investment management is both a cyclical and volatile enterprise. Changes in ownership and management are frequent and can have meaningful implications for the investment firms affected. Investment firms should proactively communicate organizational changes to plan sponsors.

- *Subjective Review.* In many instances, a personal interview may be appropriate in the evaluation of a particular manager.

MONITORING INVESTMENTS

To mitigate fiduciary liability, it is important that investment managers, mutual funds, and other pooled investment funds be monitored on an ongoing basis. With a formal review process, fiduciaries will determine whether the investment manager or fund is meeting the criteria set forth in the IPS. If the manager or fund is not meeting these criteria, fiduciaries must take appropriate action.

The IPS should establish guidelines and procedures for terminating and replacing investment managers and funds. Manager termination is one of the most challenging responsibilities of plan fiduciaries. It requires both objective and subjective assessment of facts and the potential implications for plan participants. It is important that fiduciaries not set too rigid standards that would require them to proceed to termination when otherwise compelling reasons remain for retaining an investment fund or manager.

The termination and replacement process will usually be triggered by a manager or fund's failure to meet key criteria listed in the IPS over a pre-established period. Poor short-term investment performance may not be grounds for terminating an investment manager or fund. In this context, poor performance means performance that is worse than that of benchmarks or similar funds. The duration of underperformance that will trigger a change in funds or managers depends on the nature of the fund. For example, only a short duration of underperformance would likely be tolerated in a money market or indexed fund. For actively managed equity funds, however, underperformance of three to five years may warrant consideration of a change. The metrics and timeframes for measuring performance should be included in the IPS.

An important aspect of selecting and monitoring investments is the evaluation of investment fees. The next section discusses in greater detail aspects of investment-related expenses.

Understanding Investment-Related Expenses

Investment fees are typically deducted from the return of the funds, as such they are often considered indirect plan expenses. Indirect expenses usually take at least one of the following forms:

1. Fund management fees
2. 12b-1 fees
3. Revenue sharing
4. Sub-transfer agent fees
5. Wrap fees

Plan fiduciaries must understand and evaluate the reasonableness of indirect expenses. Indirect expenses are considered to be a payment from plan assets just as if the plan's fiduciaries had written a check from the plan.[6]

Fund Management Fees Whether the funds in the plan are mutual funds, collective investment trusts, separate accounts, or some other type of fund, returns reported by the fund are reduced by the costs of running the fund (unless the plan sponsor has made arrangements to pay these fees themselves outside the plan). In most instances, the plan sponsor is not paying for fund expenses outside the plan, so in these cases the fund management fee is embedded in the return of the fund. The expense of operating a fund is established and reported as a percentage of the value of the assets in the fund. For example, an expense ratio of 125 basis points is 1.25 percent of the value of the assets in the fund. Therefore, if a fund had gross earnings of 9 percent, it would report a return of 7.75 percent. Expense ratios comprise the cost of operating the fund as well as other costs such as 12b-1 fees and sub-transfer agent fees (also discussed in this section). It is essential that plan fiduciaries understand the level of these fees and determine whether the fees are reasonable compensation for the services delivered to the plan and its participants.

The costs of operating a fund include all expenses of the management and administration of the fund. Passively managed index funds are less expensive to operate, therefore index fund fees are generally lower than actively managed funds.

12b-1 Fees 12b-1 fees are included in the expense ratios reported by mutual fund managers. 12b-1 fees are assessed to provide money for mutual funds to pay distribution fees (that is, commissions) to brokers to sell the funds. 12b-1 fees can also be used to pay for other services such as advertising, marketing, sales materials, and administrative services provided by third parties. A fund is required to disclose its maximum 12b-1 fee in its prospectus. Although funds do not have to charge the maximum 12b-1 fee in its 12b-1 plan, many funds charge the maximum, or close to that amount, each year.

The SEC authorized mutual funds to charge 12b-1 fees starting in 1980 to provide incentives for brokers to sell and service mutual funds so they could increase the assets under management by mutual funds, spread fixed costs over more assets, and reduce expense ratios for the benefit of existing shareholders. Although the original rationale for 12b-1 fees rested upon the stated purpose of lowering overall investment management fees and expenses, it is unclear whether in practice, funds using 12b-1 fees have lower fees than they would have had if they had not had a 12b-1 plan in place.

Revenue Sharing   In the 401(k) marketplace, revenue sharing describes money transferred from an investment manager (or mutual fund company) to a third party providing recordkeeping and/or administrative services. Like expense ratios, these expenses are usually expressed as a percentage of plan assets. For example, a fund or manager may pay 30 basis points (0.3 percent) revenue sharing to the plan's recordkeeper. Revenue sharing reduces a fund's returns, is considered to be a payment from plan assets, and must follow ERISA's rules on the use of plan assets.

The DOL has issued two opinion letters describing the conditions under which a 401(k) plan recordkeeper can accept revenue sharing payments from mutual funds offered to plan participants without violating ERISA's conflict of interest rules. In both cases, the sources of the mutual fund payments are 12b-1 fees or similar asset-based fees[7] imposed by the mutual fund on investors (that is, plan participants) within its funds.

The first advisory opinion says that recordkeepers have no ERISA conflict of interest problem if the recordkeeper's compensation remains the same regardless of which mutual funds are selected.[8] In this case, the recordkeeper uses the revenue sharing payments to pay recordkeeping fees it would have otherwise charged to the plans.

The second advisory opinion indicates that recordkeepers have no ERISA conflict of interest problem if the recordkeeper is not acting as a fiduciary with regard to the selection or retention of the mutual funds as plan investment options.[9] As a result, the recordkeeper could accept the payments from the mutual fund, even though the recordkeeper's compensation would depend on the funds in which the plan assets are invested.

In both opinion letters, the DOL reminded plan sponsors of their fiduciary duty to decide whether the total compensation paid to the recordkeepers is reasonable and to obtain sufficient information about the recordkeeping fees and mutual fund payments to make informed decisions.[10]

Sub-Transfer Agent Fees   A transfer agent is employed by a mutual fund to maintain records of shareholder accounts, disburse dividends, and send shareholder account statements, federal income tax information, and other shareholder notices. Transfer agents, usually banks or trust companies, can delegate certain recordkeeping and administrative tasks to a sub-transfer agent for a fee. For example, a 401(k) plan recordkeeper could receive sub-transfer agency fees for handling record keeping and administrative tasks that would otherwise be performed by the transfer agent. An issue for a fiduciary committee to consider is whether the sub-transfer agency fees are being paid solely for recordkeeping services or to also influence the record-keeper to keep the mutual fund in the recordkeeper's mutual fund lineup.

Wrap Fees   In some cases, recordkeepers charge a so-called wrap fee. These fees are not customarily referred to as wrap fees in formal documents. Functionally, wrap fees are an additional charge to plan assets and must be understood and evaluated by plan fiduciaries. For example, a service provider may charge a 1.25 percent fee in addition to the fund expense ratios. The plan fiduciaries must determine whether the additional 1.25 percent fee is appropriate and necessary for the plan.

COMPLYING WITH SECTION 404(C)

Section 404(c) of ERISA provides fiduciaries of participant-directed individual account plans with limited relief from fiduciary liability for participants' investment losses. It states:

> *In the case of a pension plan which provides for individual accounts and permits a participant or beneficiary to exercise control over assets in his account, if a participant or beneficiary exercises control over the assets in his account....[N]o person who is otherwise a fiduciary shall be liable under this part for any loss, or by reason of any breach, which results from such participant's or beneficiary's exercise of control....*

To exercise control, participants must be given the opportunity to direct investment of their plan accounts and receive written confirmation that the direction was followed.[11] They must also be furnished specific information relating to the investment alternatives available under the plan.[12] The participant must be able to choose from a broad range of investment alternatives that consist of at least three choices.[13] These three investment alternatives must be internally diversified and permit overall diversification, have materially different risk-and-return characteristics, and permit investment selections with risk and return characteristics normally appropriate for plan participants.[14] Participants must be allowed to change investment elections no less frequently than once within a three-month period.[15] In practice, plans might allow participants to change more often than any three months depending on the volatility of the investment.

To fall within 404(c) protection, securities offered to participants must be traded on a national exchange or other generally recognized market and traded with sufficient frequency and in sufficient volume to ensure prompt execution of trades.[16] Participants holding these securities must also receive all information provided to other stockholders, and voting and tender rights must be passed through to participants.

For a plan to meet the 404(c) requirements, the following information must be provided to participants:

- *An explanation that the plan is a 404(c) plan*
- *A general description of all investment alternatives*
- *Identification of any designated investment managers*
- *An explanation of all investment procedures and description of fees and expenses that affect account balances*
- *A description of additional information to be provided upon request, including the name, address, and phone number of the fiduciary who will provide this information*
- *A description of procedures relating to the purchase and sale of company stock*
- *Immediately following a participant's initial investment in a fund, a copy of the most recent prospectus[17]*

Additional information to be provided upon participant request includes:

- *Descriptions of annual operating expenses that affect each fund's rate of return*
- *Copies of prospectuses, financial statements, or other reports provided to the plan*
- *A list of the underlying securities held in each fund (including market value)*
- *Current and historical performance data for each fund*
- *Current value of shares or units held in a participant's account[18]*

Although the plan fiduciaries may be relieved from liability associated with investment losses attributable to participant investment elections, the DOL takes the position that compliance with 404(c) does not afford protection from liability associated with imprudently selecting and monitoring the funds made available for investment. Plan fiduciaries should carefully consider whether they can rely on 404(c) protection in plans with employer securities, and self-directed brokerage options.

EMPLOYER STOCK IN 401(K) PLANS

Employer stock has been, and continues to be, a popular investment for some retirement plan sponsors and fiduciaries. However, this investment when included in a 401(k) plan presents unique fiduciary and business issues and warrants special consideration. The rules and best practices for holding employer stock are, in some respects, quite different from those applicable for other investments.

Fundamentally, fiduciaries want answers to the following questions:

- Is it prudent, under ERISA, to offer employer stock in a 401(k) plan?
- If employer stock is offered, what opportunities should participants be given to diversify (convert employer stock to other investments)?
- If employer stock will be offered, how can fiduciary exposure be managed?

Employer stock may be held in 401(k) plans as well as in DB plans. The issues faced by plan fiduciaries are more complex when employer stock is held in 401(k) plans than when held in DB plans. In DB plans, there is relatively little risk of participant losses as a result of investing in employer stock. In DB plans, the plan participant (employee, former employee, or beneficiary) is promised a particular benefit at a particular time, which is paid from a trust account that holds all of the plan's assets. Except in rare circumstances, the performance of plan investments has no bearing on what benefit the participant will receive.

In contrast, 401(k) plan assets are held in individual accounts for each participant, and the benefit received by a participant directly depends on the performance of the investments in which those assets are held. The business failures of Enron and WorldCom, among others, have demonstrated the risk to participants of investing in employer stock.

Regulatory Environment

As mentioned earlier, under ERISA, plan fiduciaries are judged against a "prudent expert" standard. ERISA's prudence standard applies equally to employer stock and other investments offered in a defined contribution plan. The objectives of all plan investments are to avoid the risk of large losses and produce a reasonable rate of return. In practice, this requires diversification of plan investments and ongoing monitoring of investments to assure they continue to be appropriate investment alternatives. The performance and ongoing appropriateness of employer stock must be monitored just as other plan investments are monitored.

It is worth repeating the point from previous chapters that fiduciaries are also required to act exclusively in the best interests of plan participants and beneficiaries. That is, when acting in their fiduciary role, plan fiduciaries cannot put their personal interests or the employer's interests ahead of the interests of plan participants. For example, if employer stock ceased to be a prudent investment, and liquidating the employer stock would be seen as a failure of the company's management, continuing to offer employer stock to avoid executive embarrassment would violate the "exclusive benefit rule." The interest in fiduciary issues under ERISA is brought into sharp focus because plan fiduciaries are personally liable for breaches of their fiduciary responsibilities, and that liability is not dischargeable in bankruptcy.[19]

Generally, ERISA limits the amount that pension plans may invest in qualifying employer stock to no more than 10 percent of the total plan assets—at cost.[20] The 10 percent limit, however, is not a safe harbor. If employer stock is or becomes an unacceptable investment, then plan fiduciaries are required to reduce or eliminate the investment in employer stock.

In most cases, 401(k) plans are not subject to the 10 percent limit.[21] Although there is no ERISA-imposed limit on the amount that may be invested in employer stock, the amount that participants are permitted to invest in employer stock and the degree of participants' opportunity to diversify, are questions under current consideration by many plan sponsors and fiduciaries. In many cases plans have self-imposed plan limits (such as 25%) to help avoid diversification issues.

Best Practices

When including employer stock as a 401(k) plan investment, there are fiduciary best practices for corporate and fiduciary committee governance, monitoring the employer stock investment, and other operational considerations.

Corporate/Committee Structure and Function
- Committee members should be prudently selected to assure that ERISA's prudence requirement can be met. That is, does the committee have the talent to act as a prudent expert on investment matters?
- Committee members must be able to reconcile their fiduciary duties under ERISA with the insider trading rules of section 16(b) of the Securities Exchange Act of 1934. In this regard, it is common to exclude corporate insiders from fiduciary committees. However, in some situations, eliminating this talent from the committee creates the need to augment the committee with outside advisers, such as an independent investment adviser.

- The person or group that appointed the committee should monitor its activities and document that effort.
- The committee should have in place an investment policy statement to guide their activities in the selection and monitoring of investments—including the monitoring of employer stock.
- The investment policy statement should include provisions to trigger the committee's formal consideration of retaining an independent fiduciary to take over trading of employer stock. This occurs most frequently in corporate transaction and distress situations, where share price volatility is likely. Triggers for the selection of an independent fiduciary may include such things as an impending event, a particular bond rating or a degree of change in bond ratings, share price fluctuation, and share trading volume, among others.

Monitoring the Employer Stock Investment

- Monitor daily trading volumes, price fluctuations, news, and events affecting the plan sponsor and its industry. Daily monitoring is intended to identify acute situations that may require immediate action. This is similar to the ongoing review provided by independent investment advisory firms.
- Review analyst input regarding such items as peer group companies; analyst reports, including information from at least one buy-side analyst; and bond ratings from the major rating firms.
- Attend and participate in analysts' calls.
- Review the plan sponsor's government filings with the SEC.
- Monitor and assess quarterly:
  - The employer's stock performance relative to that of selected peers
  - The employer's stock performance relative to that of a selected benchmark
  - Financial metrics of the plan sponsor, such as price/earnings ratio price/book ratio, earnings per share, earnings estimates, and debt ratios
  - Risk adjusted returns of the employer's stock
  - Critical personnel changes that may affect the plan sponsor's performance
  - Any other factor that may affect the plan sponsor's performance
- Perform the preceding analysis more frequently than quarterly if circumstances warrant.
- Monitor the process for determining the amount of cash to be held in a unitized employer stock account to optimize exposure to employer stock through market cycles.
- Take action consistent with the results of monitoring activities.
- Document monitoring activities and any actions taken.

Other Operational Considerations
- Plan fiduciaries may want to consider holding the employer securities in an ESOP to reduce fiduciary risk.
- Evaluate whether, and to what extent, to permit participants to diversify their employer stock into other investments or to limit participants' ability to invest in employer stock.
- Verify that the plan complies with SEC S-8 registration statement requirements.
- Special requirements under ERISA 404(c) apply if a plan offers employer stock as an investment alternative and wishes to obtain 404(c) protection.[22] Among other rules, the stock must be publicly traded, and plan participants must have the right to vote employer stock held in a retirement plan.
- Educate employees on the inherent risk of holding a nondiversified investment such as employer stock.
- Provide targeted education to employees holding large amounts of employer stock to emphasize the risks associated with nondiversified investments.
- Secure fiduciary insurance in the appropriate amount, with retentions and other terms that will meet the plan fiduciaries' needs.
- Track insider trading and report trades under the Sarbanes-Oxley Act as appropriate.

Including employer stock in a 401(k) plan creates many challenges for both plan fiduciaries and plan participants. The purpose of this section was to provide you with a framework for understanding and dealing with these challenges.

DEFAULT INVESTMENT OPTION AND MAPPING

There are a couple of situations that arise in which a participant's account in a 401(k) plan might be invested without the participant making an affirmative election of the fund into which they are being invested. First, when a participant is enrolled in a plan yet makes no investment election, their account is invested in the plan's default fund. Second, when a fund within a plan is being replaced by a new fund and all of the assets in the old fund are mapped over to the new fund, the participant ends up with an investment she did not affirmatively elect. This section discussed both of these situations in detail.

Default Investment Option

When participants fail to direct the investment of their accounts, fiduciaries must direct the contributions to a default investment option.[23] One of the most common instances for which this applies is automatic enrollment. When a plan sponsor automatically enrolls employees into its 401(k) plan, the employee's contributions are deposited in the plan's default investment option.[24]

Ordinarily, ERISA 404(c) protection does not apply if participants do not make their own investment decisions. The DOL has taken the position that a participant has not exercised investment control when the participant is merely apprised of investments that will be made in the absence of contrary instructions.[25] PPA, however, provides the plan sponsor with some fiduciary relief if the default investment option in the plan meets the definition of a qualified default investment alternative (QDIA). DOL regulations describe three long-term types of investment options that meet the QDIA standard of PPA: age-based funds or models (such as target date funds), balanced funds or models (such as risk-based lifestyle funds), and managed accounts.[26]

The DOL final regulation defining QDIAs conditions fiduciary relief on the following:[27]

- Assets must be invested in a QDIA.
- Participants must have been given the opportunity to direct the investment of their accounts, but failed to do so.
- A notice must be given to participants and beneficiaries in advance of the first investment in the QDIA and annually thereafter. The notice must contain the information outlined in the regulation.
- Materials provided to the plan for the QDIA must be provided to the participants.
- Participants must have the opportunity to direct investments out of the QDIA as frequently as afforded to participants who affirmatively invested in the QDIA, but no less frequently than once in any three-month period.
- Transfer fees, redemption fees, or restrictions cannot be imposed upon a defaulted participant who opts out of the QDIA within 90 days of the first investment in the QDIA. After the 90-days, the default investment may be subject to the same transfer fees and restrictions that generally apply to all participants.
- The plan must offer a "broad range of investment alternatives" as defined under section 404(c) of ERISA.

When choosing a default option, fiduciaries are under no ERISA obligation to choose the most conservative investment vehicle available. According to the DOL's prudent investment rules, fiduciaries generally should select investments "reasonably designed...to further the purposes of the plan, taking into consideration the risk of loss and the opportunity for gain (or other return)."[28]

Mapping

Mapping refers to the process of moving participants' accounts from one investment to another that is similar to the original investment in terms of objective, style, risk-and-return profile, and other characteristics, without action or input from the participants. Mapping occurs most frequently when a plan changes recordkeepers and there is a corresponding wholesale change in the funds offered in the plan or, when a fund is terminated and replaced with a new fund. While the mapping process offers convenience and ease of administration, ERISA 404(c) protection may be lost because plan participants did not exercise control over their investment choices. When accounts are mapped from one investment to another, participants are usually given advance notice of the mapping and considerable time and opportunity to move their account to whatever investment they would like before the mapping takes place.

Prior to PPA, the DOL's position was that mapping would result in the loss of 404(c) protection.[29] PPA allows plan sponsors 404(c) protection when participant accounts are mapped from one investment to another so long as certain requirements are met. PPA describes mapping as a *qualified change in investment options*, and prescribes the requirements which must be met in order for plan sponsors to be afforded the protection.[30] A summary of the requirements are that the participant investments must be mapped to an investment that is reasonably similar in risk and rate of return to that of the investment from which they were mapped, the participant must receive written notice of the change at least 30, but not more than 60 days before the change, the notice must include a comparison of the old and new investments and explain that unless the participant makes an affirmative election to the contrary their account will be mapped to the new investment. In addition, the plan must have satisfied the conditions of 404(c) prior to the mapping. Meeting these requirements may not always be easy. For instance, the determination of "reasonably similar in risk and rate of return" can be a somewhat subjective decision. Therefore, plan fiduciaries must carefully consider the effects of their mapping decisions and conclude that any action they take is in the best interests of plan participants and beneficiaries.

ADVICE AND EDUCATION FOR PLAN PARTICIPANTS

Given the level of reliance workers now place on their 401(k) accounts for retirement security, providing investment advice to plan participants has become increasingly important. Providing specific investment advice to participants has significant fiduciary implications. The selection of service providers, including outside investment advisors, is a fiduciary act. A fiduciary that imprudently selects or fails to monitor the advisor could be liable for the consequences of a poor selection (for example, participant losses).

There have been times over the past several decades when it seemed like any investment strategy would return positive, and in some cases, largely positive returns. But in more recent times, investors have learned that risk is real from their experiences ranging from the bursting of the tech bubble to the economic meltdown of 2008–2009. Today many employees are anxious for help in managing their retirement accounts. Employers are equally anxious to help employees, but many are concerned about the fiduciary liability that may be associated with giving investment advice or are baffled by the myriad of advice products in the marketplace. This section will help employers to develop an effective approach to participant advice and education by examining:

- The differences between investment advice and education
- Types of education and advice solutions available today
- Appropriate amount of due diligence required when selecting an education or advice provider

Education versus Advice

Employers have historically provided information and education to participants but have stopped short of providing investment advice (advice being defined as telling participants how they should invest). While education has been helpful to some employees, it failed to help others make appropriate savings and investment decisions. Employers have been reluctant to provide advice for several reasons, including:

- Concerns about liability for advice that may result in a loss
- Challenges in selecting a competent advice provider
- The ability to properly monitor the advice provider on an ongoing basis

In light of participant demands and interest, fiduciaries are increasingly considering the provision of investment advice programs.

What is the difference between education and advice? Under ERISA, a person is considered to be a plan fiduciary to the extent that he "renders investment advice for a fee or other compensation."[31] Investment education does not specifically tell an employee which funds to use, whereas investment advice does. In June 1996, the DOL issued Interpretive Bulletin 96–1[32] to clarify that providing the following kinds of investment information to participants does not constitute investment advice:

- *Plan Information.* Information about the advantages of plan participation emphasizing that participants should participate in available plans as soon as they are eligible and make the maximum contribution possible to the plan.
- *General Information.* Information about general financial and investment concepts, such as risk and return, diversification, dollar-cost averaging, compounded return, and tax-deferred investment.
- *Allocation Models.* Pie charts, graphs, and case studies illustrating model investment allocations for hypothetical individuals with different time horizons and risk profiles.
- *Interactive Materials.* Questionnaires, worksheets, software, and so on that allow a participant to estimate future retirement income needs and assess the impact of different investment allocations on retirement income.

The rationale behind asset allocation and interactive material safe harbors described previously is that they require plan participants to draw their own conclusions.

Advice goes beyond education by making a recommendation to the participant to invest in specific funds. Investment advisors are governed by the Investment Advisers Act of 1940, which requires the investment advisor to make a reasonable determination that the investment advice provided is suitable based on the participant's financial situation and investment objectives. A proper suitability analysis requires that the advisor glean the participant's investment objectives, risk tolerance, financial needs, and long-term plans to better make a suitable recommendation for the participant.[33] Investment advisors who give advice to plan participants are fiduciaries.

Regulatory and Proposed Legislative Initiatives

The DOL has issued an advisory opinion approving an investment manager providing asset allocation advice to 401(k) plan participants, even though the investment manager would receive additional compensation if participants allocate their investments to the advisor's products instead of the investment products of other vendors.[34] The DOL was satisfied that the investment manager had addressed the potential conflict of interest through a set of independent controls. In particular, the investment manager would hire an independent financial expert to develop an asset allocation advice program under an arrangement that insulated the advice from the investment manager's influence.[35] The financial expert would retain independence from the investment manager under an arrangement that would allow it to develop the asset allocation advice program solely in the interest of the plan participants without being influenced by the investment manager.[36]

The DOL has also sanctioned the development of a new form of advice, the professionally managed account, whereby the participant selects a manager to manage the participant's account in accordance with ongoing allocation advice provided by an independent third party.[37]

More recently, PPA contained regulatory developments related to investment advice. PPA amended ERISA to create a new statutory exemption from the prohibited transaction rules to expand the availability of investment advice to participants in 401(k) plans. Since the passage of PPA the DOL has taken several actions related to this issue including issuing a request for information from the public in December 2006, publishing a proposed regulation in August 2008, holding a public hearing in October 2008, and publishing a final rule in January 2009. However, the final rule from January 2009 was withdrawn by the DOL in November of 2009 in response to public concern over the ability of the final rule to mitigate the potential for investment adviser self-dealing.

On February 26, 2010 the DOL issued a new proposed regulation. The new proposal allows investment advice to be given under the statutory exemption in two ways. One way is through the use of a computer model certified as unbiased. A second way is through an adviser who is compensated on a level-fee basis. At the time of writing this chapter, the DOL was accepting public comment on this proposed regulation.[38] In a final development, (also mentioned in Chapter 5) the DOL announced in December 2009 their plans to publish a proposed regulation sometime in 2010 to amend the regulatory definition of "fiduciary" to include more persons, such as pension consultants. At the time of this writing, the proposed regulation had not been issued. It is anticipated that the proposed regulation will include clarification regarding the fiduciary status of individuals and organizations who deliver advice to 401(k) plan participants.

Today's Tools

A description follows of common guidance and advice tools provided by mutual fund sponsors, insurance companies, brokers, accounting firms, banks, financial planning firms, and independent investment advisors.

Internet-Based Online Tools Retirement calculators offering general asset allocation guidance have been available for quite some time. Some service providers offer interactive programs (populated in part by data from the plan's recordkeeping system) that offer specific investment recommendations. If set-up costs are not significant, online advice may be a reasonably inexpensive way to help participants make investment decisions. However, many investors have been reluctant to use these programs because they perceive them to be confusing, time-consuming, or too impersonal, preferring instead to obtain advice from a live person.

Employee Education Group Meetings Most recordkeepers offer a menu of meetings, some of which may be included in the plan's baseline annual service fees. Third-party advisors also offer educational meetings. Meetings have been shown to be among the best ways to provide general financial education, either as a stand-alone activity or as the first step in an advice program. Research has shown that education sessions are effective at changing people's intentions with regard to their participation or investments in 401(k) plans. The longer the individual waits to act on her intentions, however, the less likely she is to act at all.

One-on-One Financial Counseling Many employees highly value the opportunity to meet with a financial counselor once or twice a year to chart an investment plan. The majority of modern 401(k) programs offer some level of investment education service as part of their baseline fee but do not have additional fees built in to pay for one-on-one investment advice. Accordingly, a plan or employee may incur additional costs to obtain these services. Alternatively, a commission-based broker may agree to provide the service at a substantially lower cost but with the provision that the broker is given the opportunity to sell additional products to plan participants, such as IRAs, personal life insurance, and broader financial planning services. Plan sponsors must ensure that they understand all of the ways in which the advice provider can be compensated to avoid any potential conflicts of interest involving plan assets.

Managed Accounts The term *managed accounts* has a specific meaning in the context of 401(k) plans. Plan sponsors contract with a managed account firm to provide asset allocation services to plan participants. The level of involvement a plan participant has with the managed account process varies according to the plan and the managed account provider. In some cases, the participant merely signs up for the service and the account management (asset allocation) is done for him on the basis of the information the plan sponsor has provided to the managed account provider about the participant (this information could include information such as age, salary, account balance). In other cases, the managed account provider allows the participant to provide additional input into the process such as taking a risk tolerance quiz or otherwise modifying his investment objective. In either case, the managed account provider takes responsibility for setting and managing the participant's asset allocation.

FINRA's web site provides the following description of managed accounts:

> *With a managed account, your 401(k) will be invested in a portfolio of various mutual funds or possibly individual securities that are chosen by a professional investment manager. The way the account is structured will depend on the plan provider your employer chooses.*
>
> *Managed accounts are similar to actively managed mutual funds, as both have managers who follow a specific investment style—ranging from conservative to aggressive—and who select securities to meet a particular objective, such as long-term growth or income for retirement. Unlike a mutual fund manager, the account's investment manager oversees many similar but not necessarily identical accounts simultaneously, and will typically make the same transaction for most or all of the accounts.*[39]

Managed accounts typically have a fee associated with them. A fee is charged to the participant's account to pay for the managed account provider's time and effort. When choosing to include managed accounts as part of the plan it is important to consider the fees involved and analyze whether the additional fees are worth the benefit derived from the managed account service.

Outside Vendors   Selecting an advisor to provide investment advice to plan participants is a fiduciary decision. Plan fiduciaries should approach the due diligence process for selecting an advice vendor with the same level of prudence that applies to other plan fiduciary activities. Plan sponsors should consider using a formal request for proposal (RFP) to ensure they evaluate a representative group of vendors on a consistent basis and follow and document a prudent process. Although the plan's recordkeeping vendor may already have an established relationship with an advice vendor, that vendor might not offer the sponsor the best solution. Suggested topics to address in an RFP may include the following:

- Organization overview
- Program objectives and structure
- Respondent's background, qualifications, and general information
- Overall advice methodology
- Questions on specific services and delivery systems to be provided
- Ability and process for monitoring advice given
- Fees and service guarantees
- Anything unique to the plan, participants, and plan sponsor that may affect the services to be delivered
- Instructions for responding to the RFP

In addition to selecting a vendor, fiduciaries must prudently monitor the selected advice provider. At a minimum, monitoring would involve evaluating the quality of the services provided to plan participants and the cost of those services. Monitoring activity should be documented in the fiduciaries' records.

BROKERAGE ACCOUNTS AND MUTUAL FUND WINDOWS

Some 401(k) plans give participants the option of opening a self-directed brokerage account within the plan. These accounts give plan participants a vast array of investment options. According to Vanguard, approximately 17 percent of 401(k) participants are offered these types of accounts.[40] Usually, brokerage accounts are little used. Vanguard reports that of the participants who are offered a brokerage account option, only about 1 percent actually use this option.

Some employers and fiduciaries fear they may be held liable if participants make poor investment choices. However, these brokerage accounts may fall within ERISA's limited 404(c) protection if the 404(c) requirements are met for the plan. Nevertheless, to meet ERISA's fiduciary requirements, brokerage accounts should be selected in a prudent manner and monitored to ensure participants can diversify their investment through the brokerage accounts and that the brokerage accounts are operated properly. In addition, employees should be educated about the risks and costs of these accounts.

Some further considerations for fiduciaries are:

- Some plans limit the types of funds (for example, mutual funds) or securities (for example, only NYSE-listed stock) available through these accounts. Other limits include a minimum balance to open the account[41] or a percentage limit on how much can be put into a self-directed account. Caution should be exercised if this option is considered. It could be argued that any limit to investing through the brokerage window increases the fiduciaries' exposure.

- A fiduciary must be careful that all of the investments offered through the brokerage account are permitted under the plan and trust documents and would not give rise to a prohibited transaction under ERISA.
- Accounts should be monitored for risky behavior, such as inappropriate market timing.
- Procedures should be implemented to make it less likely that unsophisticated investors would make the choice to have this type of account. For example, establishing a multistep process for employees to select this option that clearly explains the costs and risks involved.

Finally, fiduciaries should consider the potential for low participant usage and the other factors mentioned earlier when considering whether to offer brokerage accounts.

As was just mentioned, some employers have elected to limit the investments allowed in the brokerage accounts. A variation on this theme is the mutual fund window. A mutual fund window allows the participant to exit the plan's finite investment lineup by "going out a window" and having access to a broad selection of mutual funds. The difference between a mutual fund window and a brokerage account is that the mutual fund window is limited to the mutual funds the plan sponsor has chosen to give participants access to. In some cases, plan sponsors allow any mutual fund that the window provider has on its platform; in other cases, the plan sponsor has limited the list of mutual funds to a smaller universe. In either case, the plan sponsor rarely provides due diligence and oversight to each and every fund offered in the window. This fact should be clearly communicated to participants electing to invest their account through this option.

SOCIALLY RESPONSIBLE INVESTING

Some fiduciaries may wish to align the plan's investment choices with their core values by incorporating social, ethical, moral, and religious criteria into their investment strategy. The DOL has said that selecting a socially responsible fund as a plan investment option is not, in itself, inconsistent with ERISA's fiduciary standards.[42] However, above all else, plan fiduciaries must act prudently and solely in the interests of participants and beneficiaries. Therefore, to invest in a socially responsible fund, they must determine that the fund is reasonably expected to provide an investment return, expenses, stability, and other relevant factors comparable to other investments with similar risks. In essence, a socially responsible fund may be used if it is also a sound investment, based on traditional investment criteria.

For example, a socially responsible mutual fund may be designed to achieve an investment goal by using traditional investment processes and by investing in enterprises that the fund managers believe make a significant contribution to society through their products and services or by the way they do business. When selecting investments, the fund managers will evaluate investments for financial soundness, as well as the fund's social criteria.

The DOL has also commented on so-called economically targeted investments (ETIs).[43] ETIs are investments that may generate favorable economic effects in addition to investment returns and can include the creation of jobs, affordable housing, or address environmental concerns. According to the DOL, a plan fiduciary may not subordinate the economic interests of the plan to economic interests outside the plan. Their first obligation is to examine investments on such factors as risk and return. However, if two investments have comparable characteristics, the fiduciary may choose the ETI. In essence, both socially responsible mutual funds and ETIs are subject to the same standards as any other investment offered by ERISA-covered plans.

CONCLUSION

Investments are the heart of any retirement program and can be a challenge to manage. Establishing and managing the investments of a 401(k) plan is even more challenging because of plan participant involvement in directing their accounts. Plan fiduciaries can meet these challenges and help their plan participants reach their retirement goals by following prudent governance processes.

CHAPTER 8

Managing Your Plan's Operations

We discussed in Chapter 2 the evolution of 401(k) plan stewardship. One of the points we emphasized is that plan sponsors are becoming more proactive in the management of their plans. No longer is it the standard to relinquish plan operations to the recordkeeper. The standard is evolving to one of plan sponsors as empowered plan managers. We cover in this chapter the information you need to be an empowered plan manager, including how to manage your service providers, what services to expect from them, elements of a service agreement and standards that should be included in the service agreement, and activities related to operational and regulatory compliance.

MONITORING YOUR SERVICE PROVIDER

One of the keys to successful plan operations is the optimal performance of your service provider. The term *service provider* may be used to refer to a variety of entities such as a recordkeeper, an investment consultant, a communications provider, a defined contribution consultant, or even an ERISA attorney. This chapter focuses on record keeping, administration, and related services. For the purposes of this chapter, we also refer to your recordkeeper and administration service provider as your *vendor*.

As a plan fiduciary you have the responsibility to ensure that the services your vendor is providing are accurate, timely, and for the exclusive benefit of the participants and beneficiaries. In many cases, some or all of the fees that your vendor is receiving are paid, either directly or indirectly, by your plan participants. If this is the case for your plan, you have a fiduciary responsibility to ensure their money is being spent on valuable and prudent services. Even if your organization pays the entire cost of plan administration and record keeping directly, it still makes sense to be sure you're getting your money's worth from your vendor.

VENDOR SERVICES

There are many services your vendor provides that can and should be measured and evaluated. There are basic services, such as accurate recordkeeping and transaction processing; client-facing services such as the call center and employee communication and education materials; and subjective services, such as being responsive to you, the plan sponsor. We focus here on the following six service categories:

1. Recordkeeping
2. Compliance
3. Vendor responsiveness
4. Call center
5. Education and communications
6. Participant behavior

Recordkeeping

The recordkeeping category covers administration, transactions, and reporting functions. For example, in the area of administration, is your vendor calculating your company contribution accurately and on time? What about the vesting calculation? Or initial plan eligibility? In the area of transactions, accuracy and timing are the key items for loans, withdrawals, distributions, transfers, and so forth. And for reporting, you'll want to look at the participant statements as well as the reporting your vendor provides to you and your auditor.

You want to establish clear guidelines with your vendor around responsibility, timing, and data required. Once these guidelines or parameters have been identified, you can monitor your vendor's performance against the agreed-upon procedures and timing.

Monitoring your vendor in this service area is especially important when it comes to managing your cost as well as your risk. If you have service level agreements with fees at risk in the contract with your vendor, then you want to be sure you recognize when those levels have not been met and your fees should be discounted. In addition, having agreed-upon procedures in place can help minimize mistakes that could affect your plan's qualification status, or necessitate a corrective action, which could be costly.

Compliance

Compliance refers to tasks such as nondiscrimination testing, Form 5500 filing, contribution limitations and timing, and required participant notices.

Similar to recordkeeping, you must establish clear guidelines with your vendor about responsibility, timing, and data required to effectively monitor your vendor's performance related to compliance activities.

It is particularly important to monitor your vendor's ability to perform the compliance activities both accurately and on a timely basis. The accuracy and timeliness requirements are not open for debate, and missing them or providing incorrect information can put your plan and participants at risk. This can also be costly, resulting in penalties or correction measures.

Vendor Responsiveness

Assessing the responsiveness of your vendor is a mostly subjective undertaking. A part of your vendor's effectiveness will depend on how well your team and their team work together—how well the individuals' styles fit. However, there are several objective measures that can be looked at as well to help you quantify the level of responsiveness.

You want to look at how long it takes to return phone calls or e-mails, and how long it takes to get issues resolved. In addition, does your vendor meet with you on a regular basis to review plan operations, and does the relationship manager proactively suggest plan features or newly developed products that you and your participants could benefit from? Many plan sponsors find it frustrating that new clients are offered the most recently developed tools and features of the vendor, but existing clients are sometimes not given these options until much later.

Monitoring your vendor's responsiveness can have an impact on your costs and your risk, as described earlier, but it also is likely a big indicator of your overall satisfaction with the relationship. If your vendor is measuring up in the quantitative areas, but you are not comfortable with the people you are dealing with, you can certainly ask for a new team or individual to serve your plan. Vendors will gladly make staffing changes rather than risk losing your business.

Call Center

The call center is a critical, participant-facing service. For many plan participants, this is their primary connection to the plan. Participants call to get advice, discuss their investments, perform transactions, and gather information in general. You want to be sure that your participants' experience is a positive and productive one when they speak to the call center representatives.

Some of the important call center metrics include:

- Maximum and average call abandonment rates (what percentage of calls are not answered before participants hang up)
- Maximum and average wait times (how long does it take before a call is picked up)
- Percentage of calls completed without needing additional research or follow-up (sometimes referred to as the "one and done" rate)
- Length of time for additional research to be completed

Note that many call centers measure the average call length as a productivity measure. You'll want to ensure that call center representatives are not encouraged to end their calls quickly, as this could result in participants feeling rushed or answers not fully explained.

It is common for vendors to have pre-established goals in place for their call center metrics. You'll want to review the metrics against published standards and negotiate with the vendor any metric that does not meet your standard. This can be particularly effective if you have a dedicated set of call center representatives that work on your plan.

Monitoring your vendor's call center metrics can have an impact on the benefit adequacy of your plan. Access to timely and convenient advice and information can help participants stay more involved with their retirement and make good decisions when managing their accounts. A bad experience can cause frustration and make a participant feel disconnected. Managing their retirement accounts can easily fall to the bottom of their to-do lists.

There is also a cost component related to the call center. Call center metrics are very common items in service-level agreements with fees at risk. Review your vendor contract for this type of arrangement, and be sure to monitor your vendor's performance.

Participant Education and Communications

Participant education and communication services are an area in which your vendor will interact directly or indirectly with your employees—directly through group and individual meetings, and indirectly with enrollment packages, print communications, and electronic tools. You should first determine the level of interaction you want your vendor to have with your participants. Will you have group meetings, or offer one-on-one meetings? Will your vendor provide investment education or actual advice? (See Chapter 7 for a discussion on investment education versus advice.)

You should determine the type of communication campaign you want your vendor to execute; for example, a personalized or a targeted campaign (Chapter 11 covers participant communications in more detail). After you have determined and implemented the communication and education campaigns, you can also track the effectiveness of those campaigns. Information such as how many meetings are conducted at each of your locations and how many employees attend those meetings is useful. You can also monitor participant activity right after the campaign to see if employees are acting on the messages you are giving them. Are employees increasing their deferral rates? Are they diversifying their investments? Depending on the type of campaign, you can see if the participants are reacting in the desired way. This should be reviewed and modified each year as your plan and participant behavior evolve.

This service area can have a great impact on the benefit adequacy of your plan. An effective communication plan can help participants stay involved in managing their plan accounts. Alternatively, if the communication and education plan is not proving to be effective, it is important to understand why and to make necessary adjustments. Every company is different, so a campaign that worked for one company may not work for your employee demographics. Understanding your employees and their education needs is a key part of developing an effective communication strategy.

Communication materials can be very expensive to print and mail, and the time spent by employee education professionals to conduct meetings can also be very expensive. Vendors often have communication budgets for these services built into the fees you and your participants are paying for. A best practice is to meet with your vendor and establish an annual communications plan to make the best use of the campaigns they offer and to ensure you are spending your budget wisely.

Participant Behavior

Monitoring the behavior of your participants ultimately ties all of the previously discussed service areas together. Key metrics to consider are:

- *Participation Rate*—What percentage of your participants are participating in the plan?
- *Deferral Rate*—What is the average rate of deferral for the employees who are participating in the plan?
- *Diversification Rate*—What percentage of employees are invested in more than one fund, or have all their assets invested in a target date fund?
- *Match Maximization Rate*—What percentage of your participants contribute enough to get the maximum match?
- *Loan and Hardship Withdrawal Usage*—What percentage of your participants are eroding their account balance through loans and hardship withdrawals?

The review of this information on a regular basis (at minimum annually) can provide you with a better understanding of how your participants are using the plan, and how they are evolving over time.

COLLECTING AND USING VENDOR METRICS

There are two ways to collect this information from your vendor—work with them directly to obtain the data, or use a consultant to collect it for you. Some vendors have much of this information readily available, and some will need to collect it manually for you. The advantage of using a consultant is that he likely collects these metrics for many clients, so they have experience collecting this information from the vendors.

Once you have the information to assess the performance of your vendor, you may be pleased with their performance, and assured that your participants' or your company's money is being spent wisely. If you find that your vendor is not meeting your expectations, you have several options:

- *Negotiate Service Levels.* Have a frank conversation with your vendor and discuss your expectations of them and goals for the plan. Work with them to agree upon service levels and write them into your contract. Ideally, you can negotiate financial penalties if the service levels are not met.
- *Negotiate Fees.* You may look at your plan metrics and decide that you are satisfied with the service levels in general, but that they do not warrant the fees you and your participants are paying. In that case, you can negotiate the recordkeeping and administration fees associated with your plan.
- *Conduct a Vendor Search.* If you are left unsatisfied by your attempts to work with your current vendor, you may decide to market your plan to other vendors. Conducting a vendor search does not necessarily mean you will ultimately decide to change vendors, but it will give you a true picture of the services available for your specific plan, and the associated fees. This may lead you to change to a vendor with a better fit to your plan, or it may reaffirm that you are receiving a good value for the fees spent with your current vendor.

Monitoring your service provider by tracking its performance sends a message that you are paying attention and you take its performance seriously. We look next at service agreements and the service standards that should be part of these agreements.

SERVICE AGREEMENTS AND STANDARDS

A service agreement is a legal document that vendors will request plan sponsors to execute as part of the conversion or implementation process. Even if you have not changed service providers, from time to time, your current service provider may amend or change some of the terms included in this legal document. As this is a contract that delineates responsibilities between the vendor and the plan sponsor, this document should be carefully reviewed by the plan sponsor and legal counsel before executing the agreement or amendment. Like any other contract, it is important to note that there are provisions in the service agreement that are negotiable, so be sure to review, question, and investigate your service agreement.

Having a comprehensive service agreement with agreed-upon service standards in place with your vendor is a vital component of the plan sponsor–vendor relationship. Once you have executed this agreement, you have an ongoing responsibility as a fiduciary to ensure that the terms of the agreement are being met. Thus, you should monitor and review the terms included in your agreement on a periodic basis.

The following are some of the typical components in many recordkeeping service agreements.

- *Effective Date and Length of Contract.* The contract should specify when the contract terms become effective, and when they cease. In some cases, the contract might indicate a fixed time period, and in other cases, it might be a continuous contract with a minimum notice period to terminate the contract.
- *Termination Requirements.* Know the termination provisions, such as what will it cost to terminate the contract and switch to another recordkeeper. If it is not clear, request that it is clearly stated what costs or expenses will apply if the contract is terminated. Understand how and when you, or the vendor, may terminate the contract and the notice requirements involved with such a decision.
- *Administrative Responsibility.* The contract should indicate who is responsible for the basic tasks in administering the plan. This can include specific recordkeeping functions, providing data, compliance activities, communications, employee notices, investing funds, and so forth. It is extremely important that the responsibilities described in the contract match the vendor's proposal (if it is a new vendor) or the current practice (if it is an existing vendor). Vendors frequently require plan sponsors to complete tasks that the vendor could be doing, such as vesting calculations and eligibility determination. Be sure that you

review the administrative responsibilities carefully and are in agreement
with the allocation of responsibility.

- *Pricing.*   It might seem obvious, but the contract should contain all of
  the pricing information. This includes any per-participant charges,
  asset-based administration fees, fees for specific functions (such as
  compliance testing, mailings, and so forth), employee transaction fees
  (loans, withdrawals) as well as the revenue sharing amounts collected
  from each of the investment funds (see Chapter 5 for more information
  about revenue sharing).
- *Investment Information.*   The contract should list the investments
  included in the plan, the fund ticker symbols and share classes, as well
  as the default investment fund if one is selected (this is sometimes a
  separate agreement, but it should be specified somewhere in writing).
- *Authorized Signatures.*   The contract should specify who at your organization is authorized to sign for various approvals and instructions,
  and what format is required (for example, e-mail, hard copy, oral, and
  so on). The designated people will typically have different levels of
  authorization. For example, you may want a day-to-day person at your
  organization to be able to approve employee transactions, but only
  members of the investment committee to authorize investment fund
  changes.
- *Paperless Policy.*   Your contract should indicate which transactions
  will be processed on a paperless basis using electronic authorizations
  instead of hard copy signatures. This typically includes loan and certain
  withdrawal transactions.
- *Confidentiality Agreement.*   In today's environment of security and
  identity theft, this is a crucial clause to ensure that the plan and participant information are properly protected. Ensure that there is a
  confidentiality agreement included in the contract to ensure the vendor
  is contractually obligated to take all steps necessary to protect the
  confidentiality of the plan and participant information.
- *Trust Agreement.*   In a bundled recordkeeping arrangement, the trust
  agreement will be a part of your service agreement, but if you are using
  an outside trustee, it will be separate.
- *Legal Business Terms.*   The contract will include certain business terms
  such as limitations on liability, indemnity clauses, data retention policy,
  and so forth. These terms should be reviewed by your legal counsel.

Negotiating service standards into your service agreement is a great
way to ensure that the vendor maintains the appropriate level of servicing
of your plan. These standards should be very specific, and tied to a financial

penalty for the vendor if they are not met. The standards typically revolve around the time it will take for the vendor to perform certain tasks, such as:

- Sending out employee statements
- Processing employee transactions
- Sending distribution payments
- Depositing contributions
- Delivery of call center services, including wait time and abandonment rate
- Completing compliance testing, including possible refunds
- Completing audit packages
- Completing Form 5500
- Sending out required employee notices
- Completing communication campaigns
- Conducting employee education meetings

One often-overlooked aspect of service standards is ensuring that the vendor is held accountable for not meeting the service standards. Ensure that your contract explicitly states how and when the results of the standards will be disclosed to you, the plan sponsor. It is easy to place standards in a contract, but meeting them is more important.

In addition to the measurable timing standards, you may want to consider incorporating some employee behavioral standards. For example, if your plan participation rate is low, and increasing participation is a goal for you, you could consider negotiating a target participation rate that you and your vendor agree to. Then the vendor will conduct communication campaigns and meetings that are targeted to increasing the participation rate. Some examples of these types of goals are included in the "Monitoring Your Service Provider" section under "Participant Behavior" discussed earlier.

As you can see, the service agreement is a living document that you, the plan sponsor, should continually review and discuss with your vendor. The review and negotiation of a service agreement can be time-consuming and you may decide to use the expertise of a consultant who, along with your legal counsel, can advise you and work with the vendor on obtaining the appropriate service agreement for your plan and your participants. Vendors often want to use the same standard service agreement for all of their clients, but not all plans are the same and most are not standard, so it is important to ensure your service agreement is tailored to your plan.

OPERATIONAL COMPLIANCE

To maintain your plan in operational compliance, it is important to understand what is meant by this term. Operational compliance is a broad topic and covers just about every aspect of the administration of your plan. We will define operational compliance and discuss some key topics and areas that are of significant importance.

For purposes of this chapter, the term *operational compliance* is defined as following the terms outlined within your written plan document. As was discussed in Chapter 4, one of the basic fundamental regulatory requirements is maintaining a written document that will identify the provisions of the plan. Operational compliance is the process by which you are ensuring that the plan is following the provisions outlined in the written plan document.

Many plan sponsors believe that since they have a recordkeeper who is responsible for operating the plan, they do not need to worry about this topic. As you have already learned in Chapter 5, as a fiduciary to the plan, you are ultimately responsible for ensuring that those functions that are being completed by the recordkeeper are in fact being completed in a timely and correct manner and in compliance with your plan document. You will also learn that there are items considered operational compliance tasks that you are completing on a regular basis.

We look next at five major topics of operational compliance, which are as follows:

1. Enrollment and eligibility
2. Contributions and forfeitures
3. Vesting
4. Loans and withdrawals
5. Testing compliance

We also look at options for correcting operational failures and methods for preventing future failures.

Enrollment and Eligibility

When looking at the operation of your plan from an enrollment perspective, you need to understand the eligibility requirements of your plan and how they pertain to all employees. It is not uncommon to have two different eligibility requirements, one to contribute employee money and one (typically stricter) to receive employer contributions. Based on your company demographics and plan eligibility requirements, this can be a complex and

and difficult administrative task. Timely enrollment of new employees and their eligibility determination are important operational functions of the plan. If an employee is enrolled late to the plan, you have, in essence, prevented an employee from an opportunity to contribute to the plan.

When determining eligibility requirements for the plan, it is advisable to take into account the operational aspects of the design. This will assist you in mitigating risk, as the inability to effectively and efficiently manage these processes can ultimately result in an operational failure of the plan.

Here are some questions that can assist you in determining whether you are effectively managing the operational requirements of your plan in the area of eligibility and enrollment.

- Have employees been entering the plan on a date other than the entry date or a date specified in the plan document?
- If you have automatic enrollment, are employees receiving the proper notification before being auto-enrolled in the plan?
- Who is tracking eligibility for your plan?
- Who is determining eligibility when a terminated participant is rehired?
- Who is responsible for mailing the enrollment materials and SPD to any newly eligible employees? (The SPD is often a missed item that is not provided to new participants. We discuss the SPD in more detail later in this chapter.)
- If you include an hour's requirement in the plan, are you tracking the hours or providing this information to the recordkeeper for proper tracking and determination?
- If you have different eligibility requirements for different aspects of the plan, who is tracking this to ensure individuals are being timely entered for each aspect?
- Have you ever prohibited an employee from entering the plan on the appropriate entry date? If so, did you correct this?

If you have encountered one of these operational failures, the next step is to correct the failure and ensure that procedures are developed and documented to avoid a future occurrence.

Contributions and Forfeitures

Once you have successfully managed the eligibility and enrollment process, your next step is to ensure that all of the appropriate rules are being followed in relation to the allocation of contributions and the use of any potential plan forfeitures.

Depending on your plan document, you may have several types of contributions, but for our purposes we will distinguish these between employee-contributed and employer-contributed. For employee-contributed amounts (including loan repayments), the DOL aggressively enforces the timeliness of these amounts to the plan. From a best practice perspective, these amounts should ideally be contributed to the plan at the same time that payroll is issued, since the employee could have elected to receive these amounts in a paycheck rather than contribute to the plan.

The rules relating to employee deposit timing states that these amounts must be deposited as soon as administratively feasible, but not later than the fifteenth business day following the month in which they were withheld. The IRS and DOL have focused on the first part of this definition "administratively feasible." There wasn't a consistent definition of this time frame by the DOL, however, until February 2008 when they released a proposed regulation that defined administratively feasible as *seven business days* following each payday. This regulation was finalized in early 2010.[1] It is important to note that the final regulation is intended for plans with fewer than 100 participants as of the first day of the plan year. For larger plans, we recommend these deposits be made at the same time they would have been available to participants, had they elected to receive the amounts in their paychecks, or no later than when payroll taxes are due.

As we mentioned earlier, it is not uncommon to have a different eligibility requirement for any employer contribution. In addition to having a different eligibility requirement, the plan may also impose an allocation requirement. This additional requirement is put in place so that only the employees who meet this requirement will receive the employer contribution. A typical allocation requirement is for an employee to work 1,000 hours and be employed on the last day of the plan year. A mistake that is frequently made with this plan option is the employer making contributions throughout the year rather than all at once at year end. This may not sound like a problem, but when employees are terminated during the year, under the allocation requirements, they will not be eligible for an employer contribution. If the employer contributions are deposited during the year and an employee terminates, you must have a process to correct these contributions before the account is distributed to the participant, or else the participant will be overpaid from the plan.

The document will also specify how any forfeitures (nonvested amounts) can be used within the plan. There are several options plan sponsors can choose from when designing their plan. They can reallocate forfeitures to participants, to use them to offset future employer contributions, or use them to pay plan expenses.

Depending on your plan document provisions, you may be able to use forfeiture balances to pay for the ongoing administrative costs of the plan or to reduce your employer contributions. This is an important consideration, specifically in recent economic times. Some employers have terminated their plans or suspended their company contributions because of the downturn of the economy and cutting back where possible on expenses. If these plans maintained forfeiture balances, and the document permitted, these employers could have used the pending forfeitures to help reduce their overall costs.

Here are some questions that can assist you in determining whether you are effectively managing the contributions and forfeitures in your plan.

- Are you depositing employee contributions in accordance with the DOL requirements?
- Do you reconcile the employee contribution amounts from your payroll records to the amounts posted by the recordkeeper and spot check individuals to ensure contributions are posted properly on an ongoing basis? This is an important step and is a recommended best practice. Plan sponsors have a responsibility to ensure that the contributions are allocated correctly to the plan, and by establishing a procedure to verify plan totals and a spot check on a percentage of participants, you are taking prudent steps to ensure the contributions are allocated appropriately. Your recordkeeper may be able to provide on-line access to assist with reconciliation.
- Are you calculating any employer contributions consistent with the document (including any potential true-up)?
- Are your employer contributions deposited in accordance with the deductibility rules?
- Do you reconcile the employer contribution amounts to the amounts posted by the recordkeeper on an ongoing basis?
- Are you using the correct compensation, as defined in your plan document, to calculate contributions?
- Is the proper compensation for new participants being used (full plan year or partial plan year) as specified by the document?
- Are you limiting compensation and contributions in accordance with the proper IRS limits?
- Are you using forfeitures in accordance with the provisions of the plan document?
- Are the correct employees receiving the employer contribution?
- Are you reviewing employee contribution amounts and percentages to ensure they are not exceeding either a plan limit (percentage limit) or the annual 402(g) limit?[2]
- Where are forfeitures invested in your plan? (Some recordkeepers will deposit these amounts in the funds which the employee was invested to ease the administrative burden of moving the funds. From a best

practice perspective, however, you should consider having a process by which these amounts are deposited to the fixed income or money market fund so as to avoid exposure to market fluctuation.)

Understanding your plan design is critical in operating the plan and establishing procedures that will avoid any operational failures. A very minor issue such as using incorrect compensation amounts can result in an operational failure to the plan.

Vesting

Depending on the size and design of your plan, this may be an area that you spend a good deal of time and effort on when managing your plan. Vesting determination ultimately depends on the quality of the information being provided to calculate the vesting, so, making sure you are providing the right information to your recordkeeper is a vital step to proper vesting.

Administering vesting properly can be very challenging. The first step is to answer two key questions: "What is your plan's vesting schedule?" and "How does an employee become vested?"

There are two terms that are frequently used in the retirement world that relate to vesting—*graded* and *cliff*. Graded means that an employee will vest in a portion of her company account balance for each year of service that she completes. A typical vesting schedule is a five-year graded schedule during which an employee becomes 20 percent vested for Year 1 and 20 percent for each subsequent year until she becomes 100 percent vested in Year 5. Cliff vesting is an all or nothing situation. The most common cliff vesting for matching contributions is 100 percent after three years of service. Therefore, if an employee terminates with two years of service, she gets zero percent of the employer money, and if she terminates with three years or more, she gets 100 percent of the employer account. Vesting schedules are discussed further in Chapter 9.

The next aspect of vesting is to understand what constitutes a year of service. This is an item that should be specifically defined within your plan document. The two typical definitions of a year of service are 1) completing 1,000 hours of service within the plan year, or 2) the elapsed time since the employee's hire date.

Here are some questions that can assist you in determining whether you are effectively managing the operational requirements of your plan on the subject of vesting.

- Do you know who is responsible for calculating vesting for distributions? Are you completing the calculations or is your recordkeeper?

- Does your plan use actual hours determining a year of service for vesting? If so, do you provide this information to your recordkeeper regularly?
- Do you have a process by which rehired employee vesting is properly calculated, in accordance with your plan document?
- Do you have more than one type of employer contributions (that is, match or profit sharing)? If so, do they have the same vesting definitions and requirements? If not, is vesting being determined correctly for each contribution type?
- Do you verify vesting before any distribution is made from the plan?
- Do you verify that the nonvested amounts are deposited to the forfeiture accounts?

Loans and Withdrawals

From an operational perspective, recordkeepers process loans and distributions, but understanding the requirements of your plan and the responsible parties for each step is key to monitoring for any potential problems.

Loans have become rather commonplace in 401(k) plans, and provide a participant with the opportunity to access some of his funds should the need arise. Loans can be difficult to monitor, depending on the requirements in your loan policy. For example, do you allow participants to make loan repayments by means other than payroll deduction? Payroll deduction of all loan repayments is a recommended best practice because this allows you, as the plan sponsor, to maintain oversight over the activity relating to the loan. You want to be sure that your loan program and policy are structured in a way that you can effectively and efficiently manage the program, but also maintain oversight relating to the program.

Here are some questions that can assist you in determining whether you are effectively managing the loans and distributions in your plan.

- If your plan allows for hardships, has the proper documentation been supplied for the request and has the employee suspended her contributions?
- Must the plan sponsor sign off on all distributions before they are processed?
- Do you have a force-out provision in your plan document and do you force out small vested balances? (This is an item that can lead to additional cost savings to the plan or plan sponsor, because administrative fees are typically charged per participant account.)
- Are required minimum distribution rules being met?
- Do you have a loan policy?

- Are loans being administered in accordance with the loan policy?
- Do you limit loans to one outstanding at a time?
- If loans are not being repaid, are they being defaulted?
- Who is responsible for making the determination of whether a loan is in default?

Testing Compliance

The more complex the plan design, the more complex the testing that needs to be completed. Please note, however, that operational issues do affect test results and issues can be minimized by developing and implementing best practices and procedures. A complete list and explanation of the compliance tests a 401(k) must pass is beyond the scope of this book. The tests listed in this section are intended to give you an idea of the extent to which 401(k) plans must pass various compliance tests.

We earlier mentioned the important role that compensation plays in the calculation of contributions. Did you know that your plan can have a different definition of compensation for testing purposes? For example, you may allocate your employer contribution based on total compensation as defined by the IRS but for testing purposes you do not include bonus amounts. If you use the wrong compensation, the test results would be incorrect and any potential corrections would be calculated incorrectly. Compensation is a key component to meeting a number of operational requirements.

The following questions will help you identify some of the common operational hurdles involved with testing.

- Does the plan complete the actual deferral percentage (ADP) and actual contribution percentage (ACP) testing requirements annually?
- Do you have union employees, and are these employees being tested separately?
- Are any corrective distributions processed on a timely basis?
- If your plan has had refunds, has Form 5330 been filed, if applicable?
- Is the correct population included in your testing?
- Are you using the correct definition of compensation?
- If your plan has an allocation requirement for the match, are those employees who did not satisfy the allocation requirement excluded from the ACP test?
- If your plan is top heavy, have you provided a contribution to *all* of the employees required to receive a minimum contribution? This may include employees who were excluded for a last day rule or another provision.

Correcting an Operational Failure

If you find that your plan is not operationally compliant, the IRS has developed methods for correcting items that fall into the IRS definition of an operational failure if certain criteria are satisfied. These methods have been established because of a growing number of operational failures. The number of operational failures may not be increasing so much, but rather plan sponsors have become more educated and informed on the proper operation of their plans and are now seeking guidance and assistance on correcting these failures. In any event, the IRS has provided guidance on acceptable ways that these failures can be corrected. The methods that can be used to correct an operational failure are outlined by the IRS in Revenue Procedure 2006–27. A brief summary of the methods available follows.

■ *Self-Correction Program (SCP)*—As the name indicates, this simply requires the plan to correct the failure based on available guidance. There is no formal filing with the IRS, no fee, and no reporting requirements. Please note that although there is no formal filing or reporting requirement, you should maintain proper documentation in your files of the operational failure and the correction.
■ *Voluntary Correction Program (VCP)*—Unlike the SCP program, this program requires a formal filing with the IRS, which will review the submission and proposed correction action and issue an approval. There are program fees associated with this type of correction.
■ *Audit Closing Agreement Program (Audit CAP)*—If your plan is currently under audit and an operational failure is discovered, you may correct this failure under this program. Higher fees are charged under this program, as they are intended to be a sanction for the failure. The fees charged under this program are typically open to some negotiation.
■ *Voluntary Fiduciary Correction Program (VFCP)*—The VFCP is designed to encourage employers to voluntarily comply with ERISA by self-correcting certain violations of the law. In May 2006, the DOL updated the VFCP to cover 19 categories of transactions.[3] (Please refer to Chapter 6 for a more detailed description of the VFCP.)

Depending on the type of failure the plan has incurred and whether you have satisfied the criteria outlined under the program, your particular situation will dictate whether you are eligible for one of these programs and which program should be used. It is advisable that you confer with your legal counsel or consultant when determining the appropriate correction method.

Preventing Future Occurrences

If you are not sure if the plan has been following all of the terms of the plan document, the IRS recommends that you have an independent review of the plan and its operations. The IRS also suggests a complete annual independent review of the operation of the plan.[4] One step that we recommend relating to this review is the creation of an administrative manual that outlines and describes the operation of your plan and identifies all of the responsible parties. This document provides a blueprint for the ongoing operation of the plan and a detailed set of procedures to be followed. This document is very useful in a situation where the individual responsible for handling a portion of the day-to-day responsibilities for the plan leaves the company or you decide to reallocate the workload.

Equally important to establishing such a document is the ongoing review and maintenance. As the plan design, vendor, or organization changes, so will the procedures, so its maintenance is vital to the continuity of best practices for operational compliance. The IRS understands the complexity involved with the daily responsibilities of the plan and has created methods for correcting these issues. It has also commented that "Setting up operating procedures for the plan is an important first step. If you need help, a benefits professional can help you set up a system that works for you and your retirement plan."[5]

REGULATORY COMPLIANCE

If you are managing a 401(k) plan, you will likely be familiar with a number of the topics discussed in this section. What you may not be familiar with are the steps that can be taken to assist in mitigating risk and in turn successfully manage the administrative costs of the plan.

Regulatory compliance, simply stated, is following the rules and regulations outlined by the DOL and IRS. Following the rules and regulations may sound like an easy task, but you will learn that this can be a complex and time-consuming responsibility with costly penalties and ramifications for noncompliance.

As we begin to discuss the specifics relating to specific areas of regulatory compliance, it is important to note that most 401(k) plans have engaged a recordkeeper or vendor to complete the everyday administrative tasks for the plan. Most plan vendors provide tools to assist you in the area of regulatory compliance. The plan sponsor as a fiduciary, however, will ultimately be held accountable for any noncompliance with regulatory requirements. You must therefore be actively engaged in the process to ensure that the appropriate requirements are being satisfied on an ongoing basis.

For our purposes, regulatory requirements are broken down into three main topics. We briefly discuss the requirements of each topic and the steps you should consider as you manage your 401(k) plan. The topics are as follows:

1. Plan document compliance
2. Participant notifications
3. Reporting and disclosure

Plan Document Compliance

The plan document is the road map for the operation of the plan. As this is a governing instrument, this document must be in compliance with all current rules and regulations. When we discuss plan document compliance, we break it down into two components that are intertwined, but have different requirements and audiences. These components are plan sponsor documentation requirements and participant documentation requirements.

Plan Sponsor Documentation Requirements   A fundamental requirement under ERISA is that the terms of an employee benefit plan must have a formal written plan document that details the plan requirements and operation.[6] In today's marketplace, we have seen a trend away from the traditional defined benefit plan to an employee-funded 401(k) plan, and as a result, 401(k) plan designs have become increasingly more complex. Recent regulatory and legislative changes have also added to the complexity. Depending on your specific plan design, there are several options available to you to satisfy the written plan document requirement.

Master/Prototype (M and P) and Volume Submitter (VS) Documents. This document option, which is often referred to as a prototype document, is typically a cost effective way for plans with limited complexity to meet the written document requirement. This type of plan is a preapproved plan, which means the firm sponsoring this document has submitted the document to the IRS and the IRS has issued an approval letter (in the case of an M and P plan) or an advisory letter (for a VS plan), which approves the provisions contained in the document. Because these plans are preapproved by the IRS, they typically provide limited flexibility. Generally, you would not need to submit this plan to the IRS for a determination letter as long as you stay within the normal provisions of the document. In certain cases, though, changes you may make to these documents can cause a plan document to lose its preapproved status and thus make the plan an individually designed plan. Most recordkeeping vendors, insurance companies, and even investment firms sponsor these types of documents. These can range in complexity from very basic to somewhat flexible.

Individually Designed Plan (IDP) Document. This document option provides the most flexibility and can be designed to meet your specific plan needs and objectives. There are significantly higher costs involved with the creation, approval, and maintenance of this type of document. This document is typically drafted by an attorney, consultant, or other benefit specialist. Unlike the M and P and VS document options described earlier, an IDP document is not preapproved. If the document is submitted to the IRS for approval, this results in additional costs charged by the IRS to review the document and issue a determination letter specific to the plan.

Depending on the complexity of your plan design and the flexibility that you desire in the plan, you may need to use an IDP. If you believe that an IDP is the only option to achieve your desired plan design results, you should carefully evaluate whether the benefit structure in your plan justifies the additional costs (and risks) of maintaining the IDP.

Now that you have met the fundamental requirement of having a formal written plan document, you must continue to maintain the document and update the document with all changes and amendments either required by law or as a result of any design changes you may make. If you do not have an ERISA attorney or a consultant engaged with the ongoing administration of your plan, a prototype document can be beneficial to you. The prototype sponsor is responsible for updating the document for all required legislative and regulatory changes and must provide you with any necessary amendments for you to keep the plan in compliance.

Important Note: Although the prototype sponsor will provide the necessary amendments to the document, some amendments may require a signature to execute these amendments by a certain date for the document to be updated accordingly. Please be sure to review carefully all the correspondence you receive relating to the plan document.

Participant Documentation Requirements   Equally important to the written document requirement is the necessity for you to communicate the terms of the plan to participants. This is accomplished through an SPD. The SPD must satisfy content and format requirements that are outlined under ERISA. ERISA also requires that the SPD be furnished to all employees and beneficiaries that are covered under the plan within 90 days of becoming covered.[7] You must supply an updated SPD no later than five years plus 210 days after the end of the plan year in which the SPD was last updated. This requirement can be delayed for 10 years plus 210 days if, during the five-year period, changes to the plan did not affect information in the SPD.[8]

If an amendment is made to the plan document that changes any of the information that is required to be in the SPD, rather than update and distribute a new SPD, you may complete and distribute a summary of material modifications (SMM), which must be provided to participants and beneficiaries of the plan. An SMM, similar to the SPD, must be written in a way the participant can understand and must contain an explanation of the modifications made to the plan. The SMM must be distributed to all participants and beneficiaries of the plan within 210 days after the plan year in which the change was adopted.

There are three areas that present typical pitfalls for plan sponsors when it comes to satisfying the plan documentation requirements, as follows:

1. Timely amendments to the plan document for legislative and regulatory changes
2. Completion and distribution of any required SMM
3. Timely distribution of the SPD to new employees

The following are steps a plan sponsor can take to avoid these potential pitfalls and mitigate risk of any potential penalties.

1. *Timely Amendments.* If you are using an M and P or VS document, the document sponsor will amend the document as required by new legislation and regulations; your role, however, is to ensure that the necessary amendments are executed in a timely manner. If you use an IDP, this can create some challenges if you do not have an ongoing relationship with the drafter, which may result in hiring legal counsel to complete the necessary amendments.
2. *Completion and Distribution of the SMM.* When you make any amendment to your plan, make it a standard procedure to provide an SMM or an updated SPD to all plan participants. This will alleviate any potential issues with disclosure to the participants. It is better to give too much information to your participants than too little.
3. *Timely Distribution of the SPD to New Employees.* Does your recordkeeper assist with this today? If not, talk to your recordkeeper about including a copy of the SPD in the enrollment materials that are mailed to new employees.

You should review your plan and participant documentation on an annual basis to ensure that both you and your recordkeeper have the most up-to-date documentation executed and on file.

Participant Notifications

Over the past several years, there has been an increase in the amount of required participant notifications. This is a result of the number of changes that have taken place in the landscape of 401(k) plans, some as a result of litigation in the aftermath of the Enron collapse and the impact that has had on employer stock and others as a result of legislative changes in available options for 401(k) plans. Thus, you need to ensure that proper processes are in place to meet both your current notice requirements, and the potential for additional notice requirements in the future.

There are a large number of notice requirements, including the recent addition of Qualified Default Investment Alternatives (QDIA), Qualified Automatic Contribution Arrangements (QACA), and Eligible Automatic Contribution Arrangements (EACA). We will not delve into the specific requirements of every notice but rather provide insight for how you can establish best practices for ensuring your plan is satisfying all of the notice requirements. Do you know if any of the following notices are required to be provided for your plan?

- Safe-harbor notice
- QDIA
- QACA
- EACA
- 404(c)
- Notice of right to divest employer securities

If you answered yes to any of these notices, do you know who is completing and distributing these notices to the participants in a timely manner?

In most cases, the person responsible for administering the plan for the plan sponsor has various other functions within the organization and the management of the 401(k) plan is one of many responsibilities she has.

With the constantly changing environment, it can be extremely difficult for any individual to stay abreast of the changing rules and requirements. The first part of being able to meet the notice requirements is to understand what notices your plan must provide and then resolve the question of who is fulfilling this requirement.

The assumption that the plan recordkeeper is fulfilling the notice requirements is one of the most common causes of missing or late participant notifications. In most cases, recordkeepers will provide sample notices or language that can be used by the plan sponsor to meet the notice requirements, but the recordkeeper may not be actually assuming the responsibility of completing and managing the process.

You must ensure that you are having ongoing conversations with your recordkeeper on this topic. Be sure to refer to your service agreement to determine who has agreed to perform notice requirement tasks. If the recordkeeper will not complete this task for you, discuss what he can provide to assist you in meeting the notice requirements specific for your plan. Can he provide sample notices? Can he provide a listing of employees who may need to receive the notice?

You, the plan sponsor, are ultimately responsible for ensuring that these requirements are satisfied, so being educated in the requirements, understanding how they affect your plan and seeking assistance from your recordkeeper or other professional would be a prudent course of action.

Reporting and Disclosure

The overall reporting and disclosure requirements are rather straightforward as they relate to a 401(k) plan. The complexity and confusion typically come from a lack of clear delineation of responsibilities. Your recordkeeper should be able to help you meet most of the following requirements, but you will need to be involved in some areas, so it is crucial that you have an understanding of the roles and responsibilities of each party.

Form 5500   401(k) plans are required to file an annual report each year with the DOL. This annual report is typically completed by your recordkeeper; it must be signed, however, by the plan administrator and submitted prior to the filing date. The annual report that is required to be filed is a Form 5500. This annual report includes information relating to the plan sponsor, plan participation, and financial information regarding the assets of the plan, and is required to be filed within seven months after the end of the plan year. For example, a plan that has a December 31 year-end, must file Form 5500 by July 31 of the following year.

There are two types of extensions that are available to extend the deadline for the filing of this form.

The first is the corporate extension. This is only available if the following conditions are met:

- The plan year and the corporate tax year are identical.
- The corporation applied for and received an approved extension from the IRS for their corporate tax return.

- A copy of the approved corporate extension is attached to the Form 5500 filing.

If all three of these criteria are met, the filing date of the Form 5500 can be extended to the extended due date of the corporate return. This is a commonly missed opportunity for plan sponsors to extend the filing of the 5500 if they did not complete Form 5558, discussed next.

The second, and most common, extension for Form 5500 is to file a Form 5558 "Application for Extension of Time to File Certain Employee Returns." If Form 5558 is filed by the original filing due date of the Form 5500, a one-time extension to the filing deadline of two and a half months is added. For example, Form 5500 for a plan with a December 31st year end is due on July 31st; this extension would extend the final filing deadline to October 15.

A plan that is determined to be a large plan, generally greater than 100 participants as of the beginning of the plan year, is also required to attach an independent qualified accountant's opinion with the Form 5500. In some situations, a plan may be able to benefit from what is commonly referred to as the 80–120 rule. This rule typically helps plans that have roughly 100 participants delay or even avoid the necessity for a few years of filing a qualified accountant's opinion. Plans that are able to use this rule even once can find themselves saving thousands of dollars on audit expenses. In general, the rule, simply stated, allows a plan that has between 80 and 120 participants as of the first day of the plan year to elect to file in the same manner as the previous year. For example, if a plan filed as a small plan for 2008 and as of January 1, 2009, had 119 participants it can elect to continue to file as a small plan and not require an audit for 2009. However, if the plan filed as a large plan for 2008 and had 119 participants on January 1, 2009, it would be required to file as a large plan.

It is important to understand where your plan falls in the reporting requirements relating to Form 5500. If your plan has roughly 100 participants, will you need an audit this year?

Another area to consider is if your organization has gone through some downsizing. Do you have a number of terminated participants in the plan who have less than $5,000? If so, you may be able to force these participants out of the plan and reduce your participant count so that you may be able to avoid an audit in future years. Please refer to Chapter 9 relating to distributions on how you may be able to reduce your participant count for some terminated participants.

Summary Annual Report   Each year, the participants and beneficiaries of the 401(k) plan are required to receive a summary annual report (SAR).

This document contains various components of the information filed on Form 5500 and is meant to provide the participants with a report of the plan's financial activity.

The SAR is generally required to be provided to participants and beneficiaries within nine months after the end of the plan year. However, as this document contains information from the annual Form 5500, which can be filed up to nine and a half months (including extensions) later, the SAR can be provided to participants and beneficiaries up to two months after the extended 5500 deadline.

This, similar to participant notices, raises the question "Do you know who is providing this notice and how it is being supplied to participants?" You should ensure that you determine the responsible party for the distribution of this document and a process for handling any potential requests for this information. This is a document that participants may request at any time. If you do not provide them with the latest version within 30 days of the request, a civil penalty of $110 a day may be imposed.[9]

Annual Form 1099-R   Every distribution that is made from the 401(k) plan must be reported to the IRS on Form 1099-R: distributions from pensions, annuities, retirement or profit-sharing plans, IRAs, insurance contracts, and so on. This is typically a function that recordkeepers or the trust company will provide to the plan. You should verify who the responsible party is for completing these forms and ensure they are being completed in a timely way.

A copy of this form is required to be provided to the affected participant as well as to the IRS. All distributions, whether a taxable lump sum distribution or a direct rollover to an IRA or another qualified plan are reported on these forms and distributed annually.

One common mistake made relating to 1099-Rs involves plans that provide life insurance within the plan. Most 401(k) plans do not provide life insurance as an option, but nonetheless it is a noteworthy issue. These plans will have amounts called PS-58 costs. These amounts represent an amount calculated by a government table that represents the taxable amount provided to an employee for the death benefit provided under a qualified retirement plan. These amounts are required to be reported annually on Form 1099-R. In most cases, the insurance carrier does not prepare the 1099-Rs so you must be sure to coordinate with your recordkeeper or tax professional that these amounts are being reported properly.

Regulatory compliance is an important area that requires ongoing education of the constantly changing landscape in regulatory and legislative rules. One way you can manage these various responsibilities and deadlines is to develop a tracking mechanism or calendar that outlines all of the appropriate deadlines and regulatory requirements that must be met during the upcoming year. This calendar should be reviewed on an ongoing basis to ensure the appropriate deadlines and deliverables are being satisfied by the appropriate party.

With the high visibility of recent legal actions, it is becoming a common trend for plan sponsors to seek the expertise of outside professionals to assist with the management of this process. Although this process may seem overwhelming, you can be effective at managing your regulatory responsibilities with the appropriate tools and diligence.

CHANGING RECORDKEEPERS

This process is typically known as a plan conversion. If you are considering going through a change or are about to implement a change in your recordkeeping vendor, this section will provide you with insight into the key areas of the process and items to watch out for along the way.

There are two rules to remember when deciding to initiate a plan conversion:

1. Everything will *not* go perfectly. However, with proper support and resources from the plan sponsor, a dedicated conversion team at your new recordkeeper, and possibly help from an outside consultant, it can be a success.
2. You, as the plan sponsor, must be engaged in the process or have representatives that can assist in managing the process on behalf of the plan sponsor.

After selecting your new vendor, you will need to communicate with your current vendor that you will be terminating your contract. However, before you contact your current vendor make sure you have thoroughly reviewed your existing contract to identify any costs and time requirements contained within your existing agreement. Also, it is possible that some plan investments may also contain exit charges, so you must ensure that all of these factors have been reviewed with the appropriate individuals so that you have a full understanding of the implications of changing your vendor.

Once you have reviewed your contract and investments, you are ready to notify your current vendor that you will be terminating your recordkeeping service agreement with them. This notification should be in writing, clear, and to the point, and include the following information:

- Inform them of the date of the conversion to the new vendor.
- Provide authorization for them to speak to and release information to the new recordkeeper.
- Request any appropriate paperwork or documentation required to initiate the process.
- Request the name and contact information of the deconversion specialist who will be assigned to handle your plan's deconversion (producing the data files, control totals, and other information that the new vendor will need).

Similar to any other project, a timeline and project plan are useful documents and tools that can assist in making the conversion process as smooth as possible. Your new vendor should provide both a timeline and project plan that clearly illustrates all of the steps of the conversion from start to finish. These documents should identify both target dates and task owners. As part of the conversion process, the vendor will likely conduct ongoing conference calls during the project. These calls are typically held biweekly in the very early stages and then transition to weekly as the conversion gets more involved. During these conference calls, the timeline and project plan should be reviewed and updated for the current week's tasks and any previous tasks that remain open. This will help ensure that all parties are aware of where the process stands, if it is on schedule, and if there is any risk of the conversion date being missed.

One topic that you will discuss with both your new and existing vendor is what type of a conversion will take place. There are three types of common conversions:

Re-Enrollment Conversion—This option creates the most administrative work and requires a great deal of coordination. This is an option that is being used less and less, but still remains as an alternative. Historically, under this option all of the investments in the plan are liquidated and transferred to a default investment at the new vendor. The current trend relating to this option, when it is used, is to use the plan's current default fund (typically an asset allocation fund) rather than a money market fund. Plan participants and beneficiaries must submit an enrollment form directing how their account balance should be allocated at the new vendor. Without participant instruction, the money will remain in the default investment option. This type of conversion requires a significant amount of effort, as new enrollment forms must be received for all employees and beneficiaries in order to allocate their balances to the new fund lineup. Also, assets can be out of the market for a longer period of time than under the next two options.

Mapped Conversion—With the aid of an investment professional, you can select a new array of funds that are similar to those in the current plan. The investment professional can assist you with developing a mapping strategy, whereby the funds at the old vendor will move into similar style investments at the new vendor. It is important to note that under this option, there is still a liquidation of the assets and then a repurchase into the new funds, but the repurchase happens very quickly after the sale, and the new fund will have a very similar risk-and-reward profile. Once the conversion date arrives, the funds in the old investments will be liquidated and used to purchase shares in the new funds in accordance with the mapping strategy. Chapter 7 discusses fiduciary aspects related to mapping of plan assets.

Reregistration of Existing Assets—This option is usually the least requested, but if you are satisfied with the investment options under the plan and are only making a change for service reasons, this may be an option for you. For this option to be available you will need to check with your new vendor to ensure they can offer the investments that you would like to maintain in the plan. Under this option, the plan assets are not liquidated, but are rather reregistered from the previous trustee to the new trustee. Thus under this option, there are no buy or sell transactions completed.

Once you determine the type of conversion that will be taking place, it is time to work with your new recordkeeping firm to see what communication materials they have available for plan participants. One often overlooked item, yet one of the most important, is communicating the conversion to participants and what they should expect. A conversion is oftentimes completed successfully from a transactional perspective, but not successful from a communications perspective. This may lead employees to be skeptical of why a decision was made and even dissatisfied with the plan and employer. If this is the case, your human resources department may spend time and energy defusing a problem that could have been avoided.

In most cases, a change to a new vendor is completed solely for the benefit of the participants. Some key reasons for changes are reduced fees, enhanced services and education, enhanced technology, or access to better investment funds. These benefits should thus be communicated early on to the participants so they understand the reasons the change is being made. In the end, if the employees are informed, they are more likely to become advocates for the change and assist in eliminating any potential human resource issues or questions.

When it comes to the communication of the changes, you must determine if the materials your vendor will provide are appropriate for your employee population. If this is not the case, you should consult with an outside communications specialist who can assist in properly tailoring an informative message specific to your needs.

Depending on the type of conversion you select, your plan may be subject to a blackout period.

Blackout Period Requirements

The section explains what blackout periods are, their purpose, and the operational requirements that go along with them.

What Is a Blackout Period?   A blackout period is a period of time when participants are not able to complete transactions relating to their accounts. In many cases, an upcoming blackout period must be communicated to participants in advance (see the following). In any event, whether your plan is subject to the advance notice or not, we believe you should always communicate blackout period to all participants.

What Is the Purpose of a Blackout Notice and Why Is It Required?   The blackout notice has evolved as a result of the Sarbanes-Oxley Act (SOA) of 2002, which included provisions designed to prevent plan participants and beneficiaries from suffering losses similar to those involved in the Enron collapse.

The advance notice to participants is intended to inform participants and beneficiaries of the restriction on their ability to conduct certain transactions within the plan, such as loans, transfers, and distributions. It is important to note that both the DOL and Securities and Exchange Commission (SEC) have issued rules relating to the application of the SOA blackout notice requirement.

When Is a Blackout Notice Required?   Generally, a blackout notice is required to be provided to all plan participants and beneficiaries whenever the blackout period will last for three consecutive business days or longer.

When Must the Notice Be Supplied to Participants?   The notice must be supplied 30 days before the blackout period begins. It is important to note that this notice may *not* be issued more than 60 days before the blackout.

There are numerous special circumstances that affect whether a notice is needed, so please consult with your professionals for your specific requirements. The potential penalties for not satisfying this requirement are $100 per day of the blackout, per participant. For example if your plan has 50 employees and your blackout is five days, your potential penalty is $25,000 ((50 × $100) × 5 days).

What Must Be in the Notice?   The notice must explain the purpose for the blackout and clearly identify what participant rights will be suspended for this period. The notice must indicate when the blackout will take place as well as contact information if a participant or beneficiary has any questions.

CONCLUSION

Operating a 401(k) plan properly is a complex job. Rarely does a plan sponsor actually perform all of the tasks related to operating the plan. Most operational tasks are outsourced to service providers such as recordkeepers and payroll providers. To get the most out of your service providers, you need to demonstrate that you are paying attention to their performance and you are an informed consumer of their services. This chapter hopefully provides you with the information you need to become an empowered plan manager.

CHAPTER 9

Design and Management of Distribution Options

The previous chapters of this book have set the foundation for establishing and governing a 401(k) plan and how assets accumulate under 401(k) plans. Now let's explore the required features as well as voluntary options available for distributing assets from a 401(k) plan.

When designing a 401(k) plan, sponsors should understand the vesting rules, requirements for paying distributions upon the occurrence of certain distributable events, corrective measures related to nondiscrimination test failures, and the forms of these distributions can take. In addition to these factors, this chapter covers optional design features related to plan distributions as well as tax considerations and other distribution-related issues.

VESTING RULES

Many employers today offer a 401(k) plan as their only retirement plan. In addition, employers often supplement employee savings in 401(k) plans by adding employer contributions to help employees accumulate wealth for retirement. As previously discussed, the employer contributions can be in the form of a discretionary profit-sharing contribution, employer match, or non-elective contribution. While employers with 401(k) plans generally want to help employees save for retirement, many are not willing to just give away these contributions. Employers want something in return for the additional contributions, such as the ability to attract and retain a productive workforce. These goals, as well as the cost of providing an employer contribution in a 401(k) plan can be addressed by the addition of a vesting schedule designed.

The term *vesting*, in its simplest form, is the percentage of a participant's account balance that is owned by the participant at a particular time. In other words, it is the process by which a participant accumulates ownership in the employer funded portion of his account. An employee's right to receive benefits vests when it is no longer contingent upon remaining in the service of the employer.[1] Employees are always 100 percent vested in their salary deferral, rollover, Roth, after-tax and catch-up contribution accounts in a 401(k) plan. If a vesting schedule exists in a plan, it will apply only to the employer contribution account.

While 401(k) plans are not required to have a vesting schedule, there are rules that apply if a vesting schedule is incorporated into a plan. Code Section 411 describes the minimum vesting standards for 401(k) plans. A plan can satisfy the requirement of Code Section 411 by allowing an employee who has completed at least three years of service to have a right to 100 percent of the employee's derived benefit from employer contributions.[2] This is sometimes referred to as *cliff vesting*. Figures 9.1a and 9.1b show two examples of the minimum cliff vesting standard.

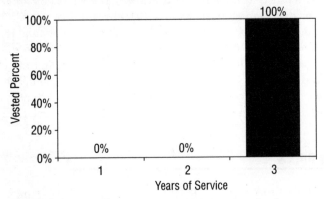

FIGURE 9.1a   Cliff Vesting: IRC Minimum Standard

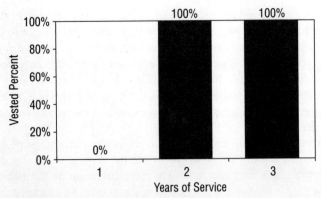

FIGURE 9.1b   Cliff Vesting: Alternative

TABLE 9.1 Two- to Six-Year Vesting: IRC
Minimum Standard

Years of Service	Nonforfeitable %
2	20
3	40
4	60
5	80
6 or more	100

Another minimum standard vesting scheduled allowed by Code Section 411 is "Two- to Six-Year Vesting." Under this vesting schedule, a plan will satisfy Code Section 411 if an employee has a nonforfeitable right to a percentage of the employee's accrued benefit derived from employer contributions determined under Table 9.1.[3]

Figures 9.2a and 9.2b show two examples of schedules that satisfy the two- to six-year vesting requirement.

Figure 9.2a shows the minimum vesting required under Code Section 411 Two- to Six-Year Vesting schedule. Figure 9.2b shows an acceptable alternative whereby as long as the participant is fully vested by Year 6, and meets or exceeds the minimum vesting rates in Table 9.1, the plan will meet the minimum vesting requirements of the Code.

Vesting schedules may vary by type of employer contribution. For example, a profit sharing contributions could be subject to a graded vesting schedule while the employer match could be 100 percent vested immediately. Because of this flexibility, vesting schedules are an important issue to evaluate when establishing a 401(k) plan. Depending upon the sponsor's industry and the types of employer contributions permitted in the plan, vesting schedules may help retain talent and offset plan expenses.

The use of vesting schedules may help employee retention by providing an incentive not to leave until fully vested. From a cash flow and plan cost perspective, an employer can use the unvested portions of a terminated employee's account, called forfeitures, to offset plan expenses or fund future employer contributions. According to a recent survey of plan sponsors, most matching contribution forfeitures are used to reduce future employer contributions. Other uses included offsetting plan expenses and reallocating to participants. Forfeitures of profit-sharing contributions are also widely used to reduce employer contribution funding.[4] Another survey found that 44 percent of plan sponsors provide immediate full vesting for matching contributions.[5] The prevalence of employers' use of immediate vesting of matching contributions versus those who have vesting schedules may be

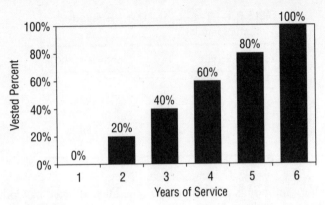

FIGURE 9.2a   Two- to Six-Year Vesting: IRC Minimum Standard

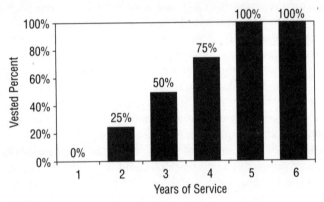

FIGURE 9.2b   Two- to Six-Year Vesting: Alternative

explained by sponsors electing to have a safe harbor plan or to use automatic enrollment in their plan. Many employers want to provide incentives for low-paid employees to immediately participate in plans both for the employee's benefit as well as to help pass the required discrimination testing. An employer can control costs and affect employee retention by varying vesting schedules among the types of employer contributions.

Vesting schedules generally go hand-in-hand with an employer's overall benefit philosophy. A survey by the Profit Sharing/401k Council of America (PSCA) found that over 72 percent of employers surveyed allow employees the ability to immediately participate (that is, requiring less than 3 months of service) and begin deferring money into a 401(k) plan. The survey also found that the larger the employer is, the more likely they are to offer a shorter eligibility period.[6]

DISTRIBUTABLE EVENTS

Now that we have discussed vesting, let's explore the required 401(k) plan design features that govern when assets are distributed. A plan document should outline what happens upon the occurrence of the following distributable events: normal retirement, termination of employment, non-discrimination testing failures, required minimum distributions (RMDs), disability, and death. The plan document also determines the timing and form of distributions.

401(k) elective deferrals cannot be distributed earlier than the date of the employee's separation from service with the employer, death, disability, attainment of age 59½, a hardship event, or the termination of the plan. However, plan sponsors have the flexibility to establish certain other distribution dates. If such language is not included in the plan, then the 401(k) plan must follow the rules outlined in the Code.

The primary benefit of a 401(k) plan is to help employees save for retirement. The earliest age at which a terminated employee can first access an unreduced benefit is called the normal retirement age. The most common normal retirement age is 65.[7] 401(k) plan sponsors do not have to specify a normal retirement age in the plan document. If they do not specify a normal retirement age, the Code states that a qualified plan may delay benefit payment until 60 days after the end of the plan year in which the later of the following events occurs: the attainment of age 65, the tenth anniversary of the date on which the participant commenced participation in the plan, the termination of the participant's service, or the participant's election of a future date provided you design your plan to allow that feature.[8] The biggest impact the plan's normal retirement age has on a 401(k) plan is how it affects the vesting of matching and nonelective discretionary contributions. All plans must fully vest participants when they attain normal retirement age.

401(k) plan sponsors should also consider the impact of allowing immediate distributions upon employee termination at any age. Code Section 401(a)(31) requires plans to allow participants the option to elect a rollover distribution directly to an IRA or other eligible plan. When a participant elects a cash distribution rather than a direct rollover, the plan administrator is required to withhold 20 percent of the otherwise taxable amount for income taxes. If the same participant is not yet age 59½, the participant will generally incur a 10 percent tax penalty for taking a distribution. Exceptions to the 10 percent tax penalty are discussed later. Although a plan sponsor may have reasons to delay distributions beyond the employee's termination date, most employers allow terminated employees to take a distribution from the 401(k) plan at any time. This reduces administrative costs for the plan and minimizes fiduciary liability for the sponsor. Plan sponsors also realize that vested funds in a 401(k) plan are the participant's money, and that he should have a right to manage and consolidate his account with his personal IRA or another employer 401(k) account.

Although most 401(k) plans allow employees to roll over their accounts after they terminate, many employees will keep their account balances in the plan even after they retire. Downturns in the economy resulting in large losses in 401(k) accounts may spur older Americans to return to work. Many of these same participants will either not take a withdrawal or may even suspend payments that had previously commenced. Terminated and retired employees are allowed to do this until they attain age 70½, while employees still working beyond age 70½ are permitted to defer distributions later than age 70½, provided the plan document allows. Code Section 401(a)(9)(C) states that, in general, a participant must start receiving distributions from a tax-qualified plan by April 1 of the calendar year following the later of the calendar year they attain age 70½ or, if later, the calendar year in which the employee retires. This distribution is called a required minimum distribution (RMD). If the individual is not a 5 percent owner of the company that sponsored the plan and is still working for the employer after age 70½, then the RMD can be postponed until the participant retires from the current employer. If the participant is at least a 5 percent owner, he must start receiving the RMD by age 70½, although some exceptions exist. A rare 5 percent owner exception available in long-established 401(k) plans, called a TEFRA 242(b) election, also exists that allows participants to defer the distribution until after 70½, based on the employee's election.

The Code provides specific guidelines for paying RMDs, and the amount required to be paid annually. RMDs are not eligible to be rolled over into another tax-deferred retirement account. The amount distributed each year must be amortized over a period not to exceed the life expectancy of the participant or joint life expectancy with the designated beneficiary[9] The intent of RMD rules is to have participant's take their account balances systematically and entirely over the participant's remaining lifespan.

If the RMD is not made, there is a substantial penalty to the participant for not taking the money out of the plan. *Note:* The Worker, Retiree, and Employer Recovery Act of 2008 waived the RMD requirement to take a distribution for the 2009 tax year for 401(k) plans. This was enacted by Congress to allow participants in defined contribution plans to potentially recover some losses incurred because of the recent market downturn instead of locking in those losses with a distribution. At the time this chapter was written, it was not known if this would be extended and applied to 2010

RMDs. Even if it is extended, do not expect this to last much longer, because as Ben Franklin said, "Nothing can be said to be certain except death and taxes." This brings us to the topic; distributions as the result of a participant's death.

Upon the death of an active participant, plans are not required to fully vest any unvested employer contributions in the participant's accounts, but normally do. If a participant dies before the RMDs have begun, the required start date for post-death benefits depends on whether the plan allows for either the five-year rule or the life expectancy rule.

The five-year rule states that plans must distribute the employee's entire account within five years after the date of the participant's death, regardless of who receives the benefit distribution, if there is no designated beneficiary.[10] Many plan documents require the account balance to be paid as soon as administratively practical. There are several exceptions to the five-year rule. If the beneficiary is a participant's spouse, distributions must commence no later than the end of the calendar year following the calendar year in which the participant died, or the end of the calendar year the participant would have attained age 70½.[11]

The life expectancy rule is a rule by which payments must begin within one year of the participant's death and be distributed over the life of the beneficiary, beginning within one year of the participant's death.[12] In the case of a nonspousal beneficiary, payments must commence no later than December 31 of the calendar year following the calendar year in which the participant died.[13] The rule requires that the participant's account be distributed over a period not to exceed the beneficiary's life expectancy determined using the beneficiary's age in the year following the calendar year in which the participant dies.[14] PPA made it possible for nonspousal beneficiaries to roll the distribution into a qualified plan or IRA provided the plan document allows this.

Finally, if a participant dies after the RMDs have begun, the RMDs must be distributed at least as rapidly as the method of distributions used before the participant's death.[15]

NONDISCRIMINATION TESTING FAILURES AND REGULATORY LIMITATIONS

There are times when a distribution is not requested but is required to be made due to contributions that either exceed regulatory limits or fail discrimination testing. Individuals and companies are limited in the amounts they can contribute to a 401(k) plan. The first limit to the amount a participant can electively contribute on a pre-tax basis to a 401(k) plan in a calendar year is the Code Section 402(g) limit. The 402(g) limit is a dollar amount that is adjusted every year by the IRS. Employees attaining age 50 can contribute an additional amount called a "catch-up contribution." If a participant's contributions exceed either of these limits, a correction must be made by refunding the excess amount, including allocable earnings by the participant's tax filing deadline in April. The excess deferrals and earnings are reported as ordinary income to the IRS.

In addition to the limit on a participant's elective contributions, an overall limit applies to the sum of employer and employee pre-tax as well as after-tax contributions made to 401(k) plans. This limit is described in Code Section 415(c)(1)(A). In contrast to the 402(g) limit, the 415 limit is based on the limitation year defined in the plan document. It can either be a calendar year or other consecutive 12-month period the sponsor chooses, although it is generally easier to apply the limit on a calendar-year basis. The 415 limit is the lesser of 100 percent of compensation or the applicable dollar limit for the year. Both the 402(g) and 415 limits may be adjusted annually by the IRS.

As previously discussed, 401(k) plans are required by the Code to ensure they are not discriminatory in favor of highly compensated employees (HCEs). An HCE for the testing year is generally defined as a 5% or more owner or anyone who earned more than a certain dollar amount in the prior calendar year. There are several tests used to determine if employee deferrals, employee after-tax, or employer contributions are nondiscriminatory. One set of tests is used to examine the minimum coverage requirements as described in Code Section 410 (for example, ratio percentage test and average benefit test) and another set of tests for the nondiscrimination in amount of contributions (for example, average deferral percentage test (ADP) and average contribution percentage test (ACP)).

The mechanics of these tests, as well as the ways of configuring participant data to pass the tests, are not within the scope of this book. Corrections needed due to the failure of the minimum coverage test do not result in distributions and therefore are not discussed here. However, corrections involving the ADP and ACP tests may result in a distribution from a plan. The ADP test is used to determine whether participant deferrals, on average, are discriminatory in favor of highly compensated employees. The ACP test is used to determine whether employer matching contributions along with employee after-tax contributions are discriminatory in favor of highly compensated employees.

When a plan fails the ADP test, a plan sponsor has two options to correct the failure and pass the test. The plan sponsor can either return excess deferrals to the highly compensated group or give the non-highly compensated group an additional amount called a qualified nonelective contribution (QNEC). The QNEC is treated like an employee deferral for testing purposes. It is allocated to the non-highly compensated group in an amount that allows the plan to pass the ADP test. If corrections are made using distributions, then deferred contributions made by the highly compensated group are reduced until the test is passed. These distributions are taxed as ordinary income to the participants receiving the distributions.

Similarly, if the plan fails the ACP test, after-tax contributions are usually first returned to the highly compensated group until the plan passes the test. If the test still does not pass, then amounts are forfeited from the employer match account and associated deferrals are returned. The plan document must describe the methodology for correcting testing failures.

Nondiscrimination failures and the resulting corrective measures can be aggravating to both employees and plan sponsors but are more common than you might think.

We next discuss the forms of distributions that can be offered from a 401(k) plan.

FORMS OF DISTRIBUTIONS

Plan sponsors must clearly state in their 401(k) plan document the forms of distribution available to participants.[16] Plan sponsors can allow participants the ability to elect their form of distribution or make the form of distribution mandatory. Depending on how the 401(k) plan is designed, it can offer nonperiodic distributions such as lump sum distributions or periodic payments such as annuity or installment payments. If annuities are chosen as the form of payment, the 401(k) plan is not permitted to pay the annuity directly from the plan. Annuities are guaranteed periodic payments over the remaining life span of a participant or some other long period of time. Therefore, when an annuity is chosen as the form of distribution for a participant, the 401(k) plan must purchase an annuity from an insurance company. In doing so the plan sponsor must perform the appropriate due diligence on the insurance company to ensure they will be able to meet the obligations of the annuity contract for the time frame of the purchased annuity.

One form of annuity that may be required in a 401(k) plan is a Qualified Joint and Survivor Annuity (QJSA). A QJSA is required unless the plan provides that a participant's benefit is payable in full to the spouse on the death of the participant, or if there is no spouse, to a designated beneficiary.[17]

OPTIONAL DESIGN FEATURES

We have covered the distributable events that must be addressed in a plan document to assure the plan's qualified status. There are many other features, however, that sponsors may want to consider offering as part of their plan. These optional features have become popular and often expected by employees and therefore have become necessary to keep the plan competitive in the marketplace.

For Terminated Employees

The topics in this section are organized based on those that apply to terminated employees versus those that apply to employees who are still actively employed. This subsection covers the issues related to employees taking early retirement, those who have become disabled, employees terminating before they qualify for early or normal retirement, and involuntary distributions to terminated employees.

Early Retirement   Once an employee satisfies the requirements for normal retirement, they can apply for a distribution of their entire account balance, including the employer money that may be subject to a vesting schedule. Satisfaction of the normal retirement eligibility requirement allows for all accounts held by the employee under the plan to become fully vested.

Similarly, if the plan offers an early retirement option, the employee becomes fully vested in all accounts upon satisfaction of the eligibility requirements for early retirement. The typical early retirement age requirement is 55. The plan may also impose a service requirement to meet early retirement eligibility.

You may not need this feature in your plan if it only allows for only employee deferral contributions, as they are already fully vested and may be withdrawn without penalty anytime after age 59½. However, with an early retirement feature, the 10 percent federal tax penalty is also waived for distributions occurring as early as age 55.

Advantages of Offering an Early Retirement Feature
- *Attract New Employees*—Employees closer to the early retirement age may be more likely to take a job with an employer who provides this feature knowing they will fully vest in the employer's money at an earlier date.
- *Employee Cost Savings*—As long as the employee is at least age 55, the premature distribution penalty will not apply.

Disadvantages of Offering an Early Retirement Feature
- *Employee Retention*—You may want to consider the potential loss of employees who will consider retiring early if the funds are available to make retirement financially feasible.
- *Employer Cost*—The determination of eligibility and approval of this distribution must be made by either the plan sponsor, requiring a significant time commitment, or by a service provider, who must be compensated for this service.

Disability   Plans have the option to define the occurrence of disability as another event that allows for a distribution before reaching the retirement. While early retirement may depend on the attainment of a certain age or years of service, disability retirement is instead triggered by a determination that the employee has become totally and permanently disabled. Similar to the early retirement feature, disability guarantees that an employee becomes fully vested in all accounts held under the plan.

Advantages of Allowing Disability Distributions
- *Benefit Adequacy*—If you do not provide disability benefits under another retirement or welfare plan, this may be an appropriate option to offer as a way to supplement the employee's income received through the Social Security program.
- *Employee Tax*—Disability is another distributable event which, when it occurs before age 59½, qualifies for the exemption from the premature distribution penalty.

Disadvantages of Allowing Disability Distributions
- *Benefit Adequacy*—Anytime assets are withdrawn from the account before retirement jeopardizes the participant's ability to accumulate the wealth necessary for a secure retirement.
- *Employer Cost*—There must be a determination made as to whether the employee's condition meets the eligibility requirements to be considered for disability. The administrative time involved by either the employer's staff or a service provider may result in increased operational costs.

Termination Before Reaching Retirement   Employees who, upon termination of employment, want to take a distribution before meeting either the early or normal retirement eligibility requirements may do so immediately if permitted under the plan document. All vested accounts will generally be available for distribution. The unvested portion of the accounts will be forfeited in accordance with the terms of the plan as was covered previously. Alternatively, the plan may require the employee to wait until he has reached the normal retirement age before becoming eligible for a distribution.

Advantages of Allowing Distributions to Terminated Employees Prior to Retirement

- *Employer Cost Savings*—The distribution of terminated employee accounts will reduce the employer's costs for maintaining records and delivering plan communications, including required notices. Maintaining current addresses of terminated employees can be costly and time-consuming. If this group of participants has on average relatively low account balances, allowing them to take distributions will favorably affect the average account balance of the plan, thus making the plan more attractive to recordkeeping service providers should the plan go out to bid for services at a future date.
- *Additional Employer Cost Savings*—Short-term employees will likely leave nonvested employer money behind that can then be used (as forfeitures) to pay fees or offset the funding of future employer contributions.
- *Employee Portability*—For employees who are changing jobs and have the opportunity to participate in their new employer's plan, this feature gives them the opportunity to consolidate accounts, making it easier to monitor and make investment decisions.

Disadvantages of Allowing Distributions to Terminated Employees Prior to Retirement

- *Benefit Adequacy*—Often with small account balances, the employee will immediately spend the money rather than allowing it to continue to grow.[18]
- *Employee Cost*—Cash distributions that are not rolled over will be immediately taxable, and may be subject to a premature withdrawal penalty.

Involuntary Distributions If you experience a high rate of turnover with your employee population, the plan may end up maintaining records for a large number of accounts with small balances. Since the maintenance of these accounts contributes to the overall cost of services for the plan, you may want to consider adding a mandatory cash-out feature. This feature gives the plan administrator the ability to distribute the account balances of former employees without their consent.

There is some flexibility with this feature. To require a mandatory distribution without the participant's consent, the following must be true:

- The value of the account does not exceed $1,000.
- The distribution is made in the form of a single payment.

- The payment is made before the later of the participant's normal retirement age or age 62.

For accounts that are over $1,000 but do not exceed $5,000:

- The employer must automatically roll over the balances to an IRA established for the individual
- The funds must be invested in a vehicle that intends to preserve capital and have a reasonable rate of return.

When determining whether the account may be distributed without employee consent, any amounts attributable to a rollover may be disregarded. This feature does not apply to distributions payable to surviving spouses and alternate payees.

Advantages of Making Involuntary Distributions
- *Employer and Employee Cost Savings*—Plan administrative expenses are directly linked to the number of accounts maintained and as the number of accounts decreases, so should fees. Furthermore, administrative fees are generally affected by the average account balance of the plan. Cashing-out small account balances of terminated participants helps maintain a higher average account balance for the plan.

Disadvantages of Making Involuntary Distributions
- *Employer Risk*—Automatic rollover accounts with reasonable rates of return and low fees may be hard to find. Establishing an individual plan and selecting the investment for these accounts is a fiduciary responsibility not to be taken lightly.
- *Benefit Adequacy*—As mentioned earlier, it is often the case with small account balances that the employee will immediately spend the money rather than allowing it to continue to grow.[19] Once the opportunity, within 60 days, has expired to roll over the distribution proceeds, the individual has lost forever the opportunity for those funds to grow on a tax-deferred basis.

For Active Employees

Not all plan distributions are made to employees who have terminated employment. In some cases employees who are still actively working may receive distributions from the plan. In this subsection, we cover in-service withdrawals, participant loans, hardship distributions, and phased retirement distributions.

In-Service Withdrawals In-service withdrawals are a category of distributions made to participants while they are still employed yet the distribution is not a loan, financial hardship distribution or the result of the participant reaching retirement age. Essentially, participants who have reached age 59½ can withdraw all or part of their account without incurring the normal 10% federal tax penalty. Prior to age 59½, in-service withdrawals are generally limited to amounts in a participant's rollover account or their after-tax contributions. It is beyond the scope of this book to describe all of the requirements that must be met for a proper in-service withdrawal. The point here is to make you aware that it is possible to allow participants access to their accounts through in-service withdrawals prior to one of the events mentioned at the beginning of this paragraph.

The increased use of automatic enrollment in 401(k) plans has resulted in the need for a special type of in-service withdrawal. If your plan qualifies as an eligible automatic contribution arrangement (EACA), you have the option of allowing for a distribution of employee deferrals that were automatically made. These distribution requests must be made within 90 days of the employee's first contribution. Without this special withdrawal feature, the employee has the option to cease her contributions but may not withdraw the contributions previously made until there is a distributable event.

Advantages of Offering In-Service Withdrawals
- *Employee Cost*—New employees who have qualified accounts with a prior employer may be more willing to roll over these funds into your plan if they know they will have access to them should there be a financial need. Rollovers increase the value of your plan assets and may allow you access to lower fees from investment managers and recordkeeping service providers. Lower fees benefit all participants.
- *Employer Cost*—For plans with an auto-enrollment feature, there are often accounts established for employees who cannot afford to participate and will immediately suspend their contributions. The ability to distribute these accounts can help keep your recordkeeping servicing cost down.

Disadvantages of Offering In-Service Withdrawals
- *Employer and Employee Cost*—This feature is often highly used by employees, leading to a greater number of transactions for the recordkeeping service provider to process. This can lead to higher administrative fees for employer, employee, or both.
- *Benefit Adequacy*—There is a risk that participants will take in-service withdrawals and use the funds for purposes other than retirement. This can jeopardize their ability to accumulate sufficient wealth at retirement. In addition, allowing in-service withdrawals may send the wrong message to participants, particularly if the 401(k) plan is the only retirement plan of the employer.

Loans   Another distribution option for active employees is to take a loan from their account. 401(k) plans may allow participants to borrow from their 401(k) account if certain requirements are met. A distribution that is taken as a loan is not a taxable event. A loan program requires the establishment of firm guidelines for determining eligibility and the terms of the loan including rate of interest, payment period, frequency of payment, minimum amount of loan request, and maximum number of outstanding loans and procedures for defaulting loans. Most 401(k) plans allow loan repayments only through payroll deduction.

A plan loan would normally be considered a prohibited transaction were it not for an exemption provided by the DOL. To qualify for the exemption, loans must be made available to all participants on a reasonably equivalent basis, be granted under specific terms contained in a plan document, bear a reasonable rate of interest, and be adequately secured.[20]

The loan program document, which can be part of the plan document or a separate document, must contain the following:

- The name of the person who administers the program
- The procedure for requesting a loan
- The standards used in the approval process
- The limits on the minimum or maximum amounts allowed
- The types of loans permitted
- The procedure for determining a reasonable rate of interest
- The types of collateral allowed to secure the loan
- When a loan is in default and what steps are then taken

You may place a limit on the minimum loan amount of up to $1,000, as approved by the IRS.[21] A reasonable rate of interest is one that is comparable to the rates charged by commercial lenders for a similar loan. Likewise, the type and amount of collateral should be similar to that required in a commercial setting. However, most plans use the guidance provided by the DOL and establish that up to 50 percent of the participant's account balance can be used as collateral. There must be an intent to pay back the loan and therefore, most employers require that the payments be made through payroll deductions.

The following IRS rules[22] must also be met to avoid taxation on the loan.

- The duration of the loan cannot exceed five years, with a permissible exception for loans made to acquire a principal residence.
- Payment frequency must be no less than quarterly with payments in substantially level amounts.

- There must be a legal agreement in place with the loan amount limited to the lesser of:
  - $50,000 reduced by the difference between the highest outstanding balance of loans during the prior 12 months and the current loan balance
  - The greater of $10,000 or 50 percent of the vested account balance

Advantages of Offering Participant Loans

- *Benefit Adequacy*—A loan provision will reduce the need to take a hardship withdrawal for some participants, thus allowing them to pay back the amount to their retirement account so that it can continue to grow on a tax-deferred basis. Also, a loan is not a taxable event to the participant unlike a hardship withdrawal.

Disadvantages of Offering Participant Loans

- *Benefit Adequacy*—Even though the intent is to pay back the entire amount to the participant's account, some participants default on their loans resulting in a taxable event and the loss of that portion of their account balance.
- *Employer Risk*—Plan fiduciaries must ensure that the administration of the loan program adheres to DOL and IRS standards. Failure to meet these standards can result in the loans becoming prohibited transactions whereby the fiduciaries responsible for the plan can be held personally liable.
- *Employee Cost*—It is common for special administrative charges to be levied by the service provider against the participant's account that covers the cost of approving and setting up the loan as well as ongoing charges for servicing the loan.

Hardship Withdrawals   Before age 59½, active employees may be given the opportunity to make a withdrawal from their pre-tax contributions account if they can prove they have a financial hardship. It is important to know whether the plan will be using the IRS standard safe harbor definitions for what constitutes a financial hardship or if the plan will have a customized set of rules. For ease in administration, many plans use the IRS-provided safe harbor rules. This also allows for the hardship approval process to be outsourced without the recordkeeping vendor taking on a fiduciary role.

The approval process following the safe harbor rules must determine whether the reason for the request meets one of the required definitions of a hardship event and whether all other sources of income to meet the need have been exhausted.

The events that qualify as financial hardships under the IRS safe harbor[23] are as follows:

- Medical bills that would be deductible under Code Section 213(d)
- Costs related to the purchase of a principal residence
- Payments needed to prevent eviction or foreclosure on the principal residence
- Tuition for post-secondary education along with other related expenses for the next 12 months
- Expenses to repair damages to the principal residence that would qualify for the casualty deduction under Code Section 165
- Funeral expenses for the participant's deceased parent, spouse, child, or dependent

Once you have determined that the hardship satisfies one of these categories, you must then determine that the participant has exhausted all other means to satisfy their financial hardship. The safe harbor rules require that the participant has received all distributions and loans available under all plans provided by the employer. In addition, the employee is prevented from making employee contributions to the plan for at least six months.

The amount available for a hardship withdrawal is limited to the December 31, 1988 pre-tax account balance plus any contributions made after that date minus any prior hardship withdrawals received.

Advantages of Offering Hardship Distributions
- *Higher Employee Participation*—Employees are more likely to participate in the plan knowing they have access to their accounts in the case of an emergency.

Disadvantages of Offering Hardship Distributions
- *Benefit Adequacy*—Employees who take hardship distributions are reducing their retirement account thereby putting at risk their future financial security. Furthermore, if the safe harbor rules are used, the six-month suspension on employee contributions can result in a cessation of participation in the plan that can last beyond the required six months.
- *Employer Cost*—Whether the plan sponsor manages the hardship approval process in-house or outsources the process to their record-keeping vendor, there is a cost to managing hardship distributions.
- *Employee Cost*—Employees who take hardship distributions experience an immediate tax liability and often a premature distribution penalty.

Phased Retirement   In a down market, many times employees nearing their planned retirement date will either opt to remain on the job for several more years or look to continue on a part-time basis. A popular option we see, especially with higher education institutions, is a phased retirement program. Provided to allow older workers the opportunity to delay retirement, this option has advantages for both the employer and employee. The employer is able to retain workers who may represent a significant store of the organization's intellectual capital while allowing the employee to ease out of work life gradually with a part-time work schedule and income supplemented by partial payouts from the retirement program.

Advantages of Offering Phased Retirement

- *Employee Retention*—An aging workforce is often looking for a way to ease into retirement. This feature allows the employee to do that financially while remaining in a highly productive capacity on the job.
- *Employer Cost*—If employees who take advantage of this feature are in a higher wage bracket, moving them into a part-time position eases the employer's expenses relating to payroll and other benefits that are based on compensation levels.

Disadvantages of Offering Phased Retirement

- *Employee Risk*—The premature drawing down of the retirement account can lead to insufficient funds available when the employee retires permanently.
- *Benefit Adequacy*—Since the employee is still considered actively employed, she may not be eligible to withdraw from certain accounts such as employer money. Furthermore, depending on the employee's age and level of income, continued employment may reduce the employee's Social Security payments.
- *Employer Risk*—This is a benefit rights feature that if not offered to all employees will need to be tested for nondiscrimination purposes. If eligibility rules are not clearly defined, the approval process may become burdensome with noncompliance issues arising.

TAXATION CONSIDERATIONS

Nearly all distributions from a 401(k) plan have some tax implications that must be considered. This sections discusses the tax implications of various distribution situations.

Depending on how a distribution is taken, any or all of the following may occur:

- An increase in taxable income for the year
- A requirement for tax withholding at the time of distribution
- The payment of an excise tax

Certain eligible distributions may be rolled over into another qualified plan or to an IRA. By rolling over the amount to another tax deferred account the distribution avoids current taxation. For employees who have terminated their service with the employer, rolling their account into another plan or IRA may allow them to broaden their investment options. The requirement for tax withholding is similarly avoided by making a direct rollover within 60 days of distribution.

For a distribution that would otherwise be eligible for tax-free rollover but is taken directly by the participant, there must be federal tax withholding at the rate of 20 percent of the taxable portion. This rule does not apply if:

- The distribution is a nonperiodic payment under $200.
- The distribution amount satisfies the required minimum distribution rules that apply after age 70½.
- The entire distribution is made up of employer securities (even though the cost basis of the securities is reportable as taxable income).

A distribution that does not qualify for a tax-free rollover is not subject to the mandatory 20 percent withholding. These distributions are generally subject to 10 percent federal tax withholding unless an election is made otherwise to withhold at a different rate or not at all. Examples of distributions that do not qualify for a rollover:

- QDRO payments to someone other than a former spouse[24]
- Part of a series of substantially equal payments made at least annually
- Required minimum distributions
- Loans
- Corrective distributions made due to excess contributions or deferrals

Withdrawals Taken While Actively Employed

The main purpose of 401(k) plans is to provide income for retirement. Therefore, depending on the type, withdrawals that occur while an individual is still actively employed may have special tax considerations attached to them. This section discusses the tax considerations associated with withdrawals taken by individuals while still actively employed.

- Withdrawal of an after-tax account will require taxes be withheld on the earnings portion at a 20 percent withholding rate. For partial withdrawals of an after-tax account, the amounts contributed before

January 1, 1987, may first be withdrawn as nontaxable, then any amount after that must be a pro-rata portion of after-tax contributions made after 1988 and taxable earnings.

- Withdrawal of any portion of the pre-tax contribution account once age 59½ is attained is generally taxable and requires mandatory federal tax withholding as well as state tax withholding where required.
- Withdrawal of any portion of the pre-tax contribution account before age 59½, as in the case of a hardship distribution, is generally taxable subject to the tax withholding requirements. In addition, these amounts are generally subject to a 10 percent federal excise tax. While the actual withdrawal amount for a hardship may not exceed the actual amount needed to cover the hardship, it may be increased by the amount required for tax withholding purposes.
- Amounts withdrawn from vested employer accounts and rollover accounts are generally taxable and require a mandatory federal tax withholding as well as state taxes where required.
- Loans are not taxed when taken as provided for in Code Section 72(p). However, once a loan is deemed to be defaulted, it is immediately taxable as ordinary income. This taxable event does not eliminate the need to pay back the loan with accrued interest. Additionally, anytime a loan fails to meet the requirements set forth under Code Section 72(p), it becomes immediately taxable.
- For participants who have had deferrals made on their behalf as the result of an automatic enrollment feature and elect to take a distribution of these deferrals within the allowed 90 day timeframe, these amounts are subject to taxation.
- Refunds of excess deferrals, contributions that exceed the dollar limit under Code Section 402(g), must be distributed by April 15 following the year in which they are made. The distribution is taxable in the year distributed and must also include the attributable income earned on the deferrals. The distribution may not be rolled over and is subject to neither the mandatory federal withholding nor the 10 percent penalty tax.
- Refunds and associated earnings as a result of failed nondiscrimination testing are taxed in the year of distribution and must be made by March 15 of the following year to avoid an employer excise tax of 10 percent.

We next look at tax considerations that apply specifically to situations in which the individual has left employment or has reached an age or service level that classifies him as being retired.

Distributions Taken Upon Termination of Employment or Retirement

Once an employee terminates employment or meets the qualifications of early or normal retirement they become eligible for a distribution from the plan. This section discusses the forms of distributions that may be available in a 401(k) plan for these employees.

- Lump sum distributions:
  - If taken as cash and not rolled over into another qualified plan or IRA, lump sum distributions are reported as ordinary income net of any after-tax basis. They require mandatory federal tax withholding as well as state tax withholding where required at the time of payout and are reported as taxable income in the year in which they are received.
  - If directly rolled over to an IRA or eligible employer plan, they are not subject to the tax withholding and are considered tax-deferred distributions. They are not reported as ordinary income until such time as they are distributed in the future.
  - If taken in cash but then rolled over within 60 days, mandatory tax withholding will apply to the distribution. The entire amount of the distribution is still allowable as a rollover and the participant may use outside funds to make up for the taxes withheld.
  - If your plan allows for in-kind distributions of employer securities, then the participant will be taxed on the lesser of the market value of the securities on the distribution date or the cost basis of the securities. The unrealized appreciation will not be subject to taxation until the securities are sold. There is no mandatory withholding required if the entire distribution is taken in the form of company stock.
- Periodic payments that are not considered eligible rollover distributions are generally taxed when made and are not subject to mandatory federal tax withholding
- Outstanding loans that are not paid off when the employee terminates service will generally be considered in default and are immediately reported as ordinary income.

MISCELLANEOUS

Participant accounts in 401(k) plans are protected from creditors and may not otherwise be assigned or alienated. There are, however, a few instances when a distribution from a participant's account is permitted above and beyond the occurrence of a common distributable event or participant withdrawal request.

Qualified Domestic Relations Orders

In a divorce proceeding, the division of the couple's assets usually takes into consideration retirement plan benefits accrued to date. A judge may award a spouse of a participant (soon to be an ex-spouse) all or a portion of the participant's 401(k) account as part of a divorce settlement. This is done through a decree contained in a Domestic Relations Order (DRO).

Once a plan administrator has received a DRO, a determination must be made as to its qualified status. The rules established in 1984 state what is required to qualify the decree. Many times, the employer outsources this function to the recordkeeping vendor servicing the plan.

The DRO must contain all of the following to be deemed a Qualified Domestic Relations Order (QDRO):

- Name and last known mailing address of the participant as well as that of each alternate payee
- The name of the plan
- The amount or percentage of assets to be established in an account for the alternate payee or the methodology for determining the amount
- Number of payments or form of payment and the effective date

Once the QDRO is approved, the alternate payee account is established in the plan and assets are transferred to it from the participant's account. Alternate payees remain a beneficiary in the plan until such time as they request a distribution. The form of the distribution is limited to those provided for in the plan document for all participants. There can be a special provision in the plan document allowing for an accelerated date for payments to begin for alternate payees.

Operational Errors

There are instances when impermissible contributions are made to the plan. Reliance on faulty payroll data, operational flaws, and a lack of procedures are just a few of the reasons that cause these errors.

It is imperative for plan fiduciaries to monitor the operations and procedures of the plan so they can uncover these mistakes and correct them as soon as possible. The IRS has provided for the ability in some cases to correct these errors by making distributions under already established correction programs. Chapter 8 outlined the four correction programs available to plan sponsors, the Self-Correction Program (SCP), Voluntary Correction Program (VCP), Audit Closing Agreement Program (Audit CAP), and the Voluntary Fiduciary Correction Program (VFCP). Depending on the type of error, the magnitude of the correction required, duration over which the errors were made, and whether the plan is currently under audit, plan sponsors may be able to use one of these programs to make corrections to ensure the continued compliance of the plan.

Plan Termination

If an employer decides to terminate the plan, provided there are no other defined contribution plans sponsored by the employer, a plan termination and full distribution of benefits is permitted. If there is another defined contribution plan in place anytime within 12 months of the plan termination date, then distributions are not permitted. In this case, the plan is frozen rather than terminated.

Upon a permissible plan termination, all accounts under the plan are immediately made 100 percent vested on the date of termination. Since no assets of the plan may revert back to the employer, any forfeiture amounts that would ordinarily be used to offset the funding of employer contributions are required to be reallocated across participant accounts.

Annual reporting requirements (such as filing a Form 5500) continue until all assets have been distributed. This can sometimes be problematic when there are participants who cannot be located to make a distribution to. Reasonable steps must be taken to locate missing participants. Once all options have been exhausted, alternative distribution methods may be considered such as:

- Automatic rollover to an IRA
- 100 percent tax withholding
- Establishment of a federally insured bank account
- Escheat to the state as unclaimed funds

CONCLUSION

The ultimate goal of a 401(k) plan is to distribute the accumulated account balances to the participants. Ideally, these distributions occur once the individual has reached retirement age and is able to take her distributions in a manner that supports a sensible spending plan. As you've seen in this chapter, there are many other instances when distributions can or must be made from the plan. Plan sponsors should be aware of these situations and be prepared to deal with them through proper plan design and operations.

CHAPTER 10

How Business Transactions Affect 401(k) Plans

When confronted with or planning a change in your business structure, a myriad of employment and labor issues must be considered. Whether dealing with a business merger or acquisition, divestiture, downsizing, or distress situation, retirement benefit issues cannot be minimized. Of key importance, and the focus of this chapter, are managing the legal, fiduciary, and financial requirements of your 401(k) retirement program while continuing to support the attendant business and human resource objectives.

Managing an efficient and effective 401(k) plan is an objective in stable times as well as in times of change. Best practices include effective use of the total compensation or benefits budget, plan design aligned with business needs, and appropriate governance over fiduciary and compliance risk.

As with many matters governed by the IRS and DOL, the devil is in the details. Included in this discussion is a road map of options and considerations, as well as ideas to best manage your organization's opportunities and limit your exposure to risk.

WHY IT MATTERS

In an ideal world, any foreseen changes in the employer's business structure or conditions trigger prompt discussions as to the potential impact on the 401(k) plan. In reality, benefits and finance team members are often brought in after decisions and timelines are determined. However, it's never too late to turn the ship around and make the adjustments to the business restructure plan, the 401(k) plan, or both so that all turn out well in the end.

The worst case consequences of plan mismanagement can result in IRS disqualification and significant unexpected taxes for your organization and participants, or in litigation. Key business issues discussed in this chapter include:

Managing Plan Costs and Company Expense

- *Hard-dollar costs*—Depending upon the situation, hard-dollar plan costs may change. One example is for the employer's contribution expense to go up or down depending on changes in the workforce population, demographics, or plan design. Other considerations may include changes in internal benefits staff expense, or out-of-pocket fees for recordkeeping service providers, other plan vendors or professional advisors.

- *Soft-Dollar Issues*—Opportunity costs can change for diverted (or additional) internal staff or leaders required to handle internal and external activity, including communications with employees and plan participants. Changes in indirect costs can also result from a change of service providers. Another soft-dollar implication involves the plan's investments. Changes in the plan's total asset value or average participant account balance can impact which investments the plan will have access to after the restructure. This may result in higher or lower investment related expenses depending on how the plan changes.

Managing Risk

Every 401(k) plan must comply with the requirements of the IRS and the DOL. Understanding what obligations and technical deadlines apply can greatly reduce your liability for errors and penalties. The following obligations are typically complicated by changes in your organization or plan, and are exacerbated by additional entities on your corporate ownership map:

- The determination of highly compensated employees
- Nondiscrimination testing
- Required contribution funding, and deferral deposit timing
- ERISA's fiduciary requirements
- Government reporting
- Participant notices

Mergers and acquisitions, divestitures, and even downsizing can give rise to changes in control. Change may be immediate, or shift over time. Examples of impact areas may include communications and decision making, plan operations and workflow, access to data, and ease of reporting. If you are not in a position of centralized control, you may be able to coordinate effectively across the other groups to:

- Provide that legal counsel and professional advisors are aware of all facts regarding the entities, existing retirement plans, and organizational objectives
- Request that a contact list and timeline be developed to ensure that all key players are aware of milestones and deadlines for plan changes and

communications, as well as technical due dates for existing plans' reporting and filing requirements

- Ensure consistent, complete employee data tracking for census dates, hours worked, union status, leaves of absence reasons, and military service

Maximizing Opportunity.   As your professional advisors and leadership are likely involved in the change process anyway, it is a wise move to ensure that the emerging retirement plan makes solid business sense for the new organization, while concurrently managing change in the current environment. The following questions may be useful for you to consider when designing your new plan.

- How will the company's financial changes affect our retirement budget? Do we need to realign along a total compensation budget?
- Does our plan reward the behaviors we value, for example, employee savings, or tenure?
- How does our business change affect our demographics, and how does that affect overall benefit adequacy? What might a workforce ill-prepared for retirement mean to our organization?
- What recruitment or retention issues can we anticipate related to our plan design or formulas? How does our plan benchmark against our hiring competitors?

Timing—Considerations in Prioritizing.   How to set priorities depends on your situation and is addressed in the sections that follow. Establishing goal dates early in the process can be critical because of:

- *Contribution Accruals*—Once a benefit has been earned for a given plan year, it cannot be taken away. For example, an organization intending to eliminate its nondiscretionary profit sharing contribution in a given year must amend its plan before that contribution is earned by any participant, such as by meeting a 1,000-hour requirement.
- *Vendor Capabilities*—The incumbent service provider(s) may or may not be willing or able to support the emerging retirement plan. It is very important to gauge as early as possible if the existing service platform is a good fit from a fiduciary perspective. If not, you may consider searching for a new recordkeeping service provider.
- *Contract Provisions*—It is critical that any contract language around service provider termination, notice requirements, or fees is known and incorporated into the timeline.
- *Complexities or Differing Plan Provisions*—If certain grandfathered or protected benefits must be maintained in the emerging plan, direct conversations with the service provider must occur to ensure that there are no concerns with accurate administration. Even benign issues such

as transitioning different vesting schedules require information gathering, decision making and coordination across several parties.

- *Considerations for Special Groups*—If your organization includes collectively bargained union groups, you will need to manage carefully any plan changes in light of the collectively bargained agreement requirements for the plan.
- *Technical Deadlines*—Every 401(k) plan, even in times of transition, must meet compliance deadlines for required plan amendments, government filings, and participant notices.

BUSINESS MERGERS AND ACQUISITIONS

Merger and acquisition (M&A) activity tends to be cyclical. M&A activity peaked during the 2000–2001 technology bubble. The economic and market conditions of 2008–2009 created unprecedented implications for most organizations' access to cash—with significant winners and losers at both ends of the spectrum. Regardless of the impetus, business transactions require careful attention to the parameters governing the future of any retirement plan.

Potential land mines lie in the regulations and the application of the rules. However, issues can be mitigated ahead of a business transaction. Key concepts follow.

- The term "controlled group" refers to a grouping of entities (corporations, partnerships, or sole proprietorships) in which certain common ownership thresholds are met (that is, parent-subsidiary groups, brother-sister organizations, and so forth). From the perspective of Code Section 414, a controlled group is treated for employee benefit purposes as a single employer.[1] For merging organizations, this will affect Code Section 410(b) testing for coverage. This test ensures that an appropriate ratio of non–highly compensated employees (NHCES) to highly compensated employees (HCES) benefit in each of the controlled group's qualified plans.
- The "qualified separate lines of business" (QSLOB) designation is governed by Code Section 414(r), which in certain circumstances, permits controlled group members that are separate and distinct businesses to be tested as separate employers.
- Regardless of QSLOB status, or of which controlled group members sponsor which plan covering which employees, the HCE determination is made across all controlled group members' employees.[2]

Asset versus Stock Sale

Typically, there are two important questions to answer initially. First, what are the specifics of the buy-sell agreement? And second, is the transaction an asset or a stock sale?

To answer the first, ensure that the buy-sell agreement specifically addresses intentions regarding sponsorship and the future of the target's 401(k) plan. If, after reading this outline, you have any concerns about whether the intentions or language in the buy-sell agreement are appropriate, seek professional advice.

Determining whether the transaction is an asset or a stock sale is critical because the asset sale is, in its essence, a pick-and-choose transaction: The retirement plan is technically a liability that does not automatically accompany the purchased assets. Stock sales usually result in the buyer assuming all assets and liabilities of the target, and accordingly, the retirement plan. In an asset sale, if nothing is done with a target's retirement plan, the plan normally remains with the seller. In a stock sale, the minute the transaction closes, both the target's employees and retirement plan become the employees and retirement plan of the buyer. This can cause immediate problems for the buyer's existing retirement plans. At a minimum, determinations must be made early as to who will be covered, and how compensation and prior service credit will be handled.[3]

For an asset sale, the key question is, will the buyer assume sponsorship of the target's plan? If the answer is yes, no distributable event has occurred for target plan participants; distributions and rollovers are not permitted. The plan continues uninterrupted, with the same service credit accruing for current participants. Contributions to the target plan could be frozen, however, and target participants could enter the buyer plan. This option can be attractive when a plan merger is an unappealing choice.

Alternatively, the target and buyer plans could be consolidated or merged. This option requires that the target plan get a clean bill of health from a due diligence standpoint. This topic is discussed in detail later in this chapter.

If the buyer does not assume sponsorship of the target plan, the target plan could be terminated. Plan termination provides a distributable event and allows participants to cash out, or roll over their plan accounts. This includes the option of rolling their accounts into the buyer's plan. Termination may be a viable option when target plans have problematic grandfathered provisions or compliance issues.[4]

Under a stock sale, the buyer assumes all liabilities of the target (which includes the plan), so there is no distributable event. If the plan is terminated by the target before the closing date of the sale, the buyer has no responsibility for the 401(k) plan.[5] In addition, the plan termination will constitute a distributable event which allows target plan participants to roll their accounts into the buyer's plan.

The decision to maintain separate plans must take into account the potential land mines outlined at the beginning of this section. Timely discussions regarding intentions, thorough data gathering, and involving professional advisors to forecast likely outcomes can provide solid support for decision making.

Cost is clearly a consideration, as separate plans mean additional expense, that is, additional plan documents to maintain, 5500s to prepare and audit, and so on. However, many decisions regarding benefits are often the result of a cost-benefit analysis. Maintaining separate plans for some controlled group members may be attractive in situations in which:

- Plan benefits provided under a collectively bargained agreement are best administered as a stand-alone plan
- Plan termination is not appealing, yet neither is a plan merger because of compliance concerns with the target's plan
- Protected benefits or plan provisions (for example, a more generous vesting schedule) create difficulty in administration or expense[6]

Implications of a merger or acquisition on the company's 401(k) plan are usually not primary considerations when these transactions are being considered. However, the outcomes that result from mismanaging plan transitions related to these business transactions can be costly and distracting to the organization at a time when neither is welcome. We look next at plan mergers.

Plan Mergers

Merging plans involves the consolidation of one plan into another. The discussion here is aimed at the type of transaction in which a company acquires another entity. Plans typically merge as result of an acquisition. A plan merger is one of the most cost-effective options that a buyer has in relation to the treatment of the seller's 401(k) plan. Most employers decide to merge plans rather than the alternative of terminating or freezing plans. They understand that sponsoring more than one 401(k) plan is costly and administratively onerous. Other alternatives include freezing or terminating the seller's plans and are discussed further on.

Thorough knowledge of the involved plans and an understanding of the buyer's and seller's intentions are helpful in making a merger successful. It is also important for the success of the plan merger to properly plan ahead by taking the time and effort to diligently review all aspects of the merger. There are several areas of consideration, including plan design, cost and expense, administration, compliance, legal, investments, and communications.

Considerations   One area of consideration is the timing of the merger relative to coverage requirements. When one company is acquired by another, the companies become part of the same controlled group and over the long run must satisfy coverage testing. These minimum coverage rules must be satisfied by all 401(k) plans as if there were only one employer. Code Section 410(b)(6)(C) provides a special rule for applying the minimum coverage requirements in situations involving certain acquisitions or dispositions. This special rule creates a transition period during which time a plan may be treated as satisfying Code Section 410(b) following an acquisition or disposition if the plan satisfies 410(b) immediately before the transaction and there is no significant change in the plan other than the acquisition or disposition. The transition period begins on the date of the change and ends on the last day of the first plan year beginning after the date of such change. For example, if the acquisition occurred in April 5, 2009, the transition period for a plan with a calendar plan year would end December 31, 2010. The transition period can be as short as a year or as long as up to almost two years depending on when the transaction takes place. It can give the buyer sufficient time to plan a successful merger. Although the Code provides for this relief from coverage testing, a buyer may still want to merge the plans as soon as possible so as to begin integrating benefits. The buyer may be required by the sale agreement to provide for similar benefits immediately following the acquisition. This might be the case so as to avoid an interruption of employee deferrals.

Advantages   Corporate transactions represent change and change generates opportunities and risks. There are many advantages of a plan merger. Merging can mitigate employer risk, reduce administrative cost, ease administration, create efficiencies, simplify legal compliance requirements, and simplify communications efforts. A plan merger is an opportunity for enhancing employee morale.[7] It contributes to harmonizing benefits and assimilation of cultures of the merging organizations. Most likely the buyer will be merging other benefits at the same time as well, such as health and welfare benefits, fringe benefits, compensation programs, and employee policy issues. Merging the 401(k) plans will most likely fall in line with the overall corporate strategy of uniformity, consistency, and the assimilation of cultures.

One area of risk that can be reduced by merging is fiduciary risk. Merging reduces your fiduciary risk because your fiduciary responsibility and oversight is limited to one plan and one service provider. This reduces the chance of error. There is also only one set of investment funds under a single plan to monitor. Oversight and control of information such as the payroll and census data are easier under one merged plan and reduce operational risk. There is less exposure to risk when you are responsible for maintaining a single set of documents for the plan, trust, required amendments, and services agreements. Your regulatory risk is also reduced because you will have annual reporting and disclosure requirements for only one plan and one plan audit requirement if your plan covers more than 100 participants. If benefits are different, there will be additional testing requirements, which introduces additional regulatory risk.

Cost can be minimized by merging the administration of the plans. There are economies of scale in a merger. If the assets are large enough, the plan becomes more attractive to the service provider and fee concessions can often be achieved. This reduction in fees can potentially trickle down into a participant's pockets, especially if the costs of the plan are paid from plan assets or if the investment expenses can be reduced. If you, as the plan sponsor, are paying the administrative fees, the reduction in fees will help you manage company expenses. Lower fees also help reduce your fiduciary liability exposure.

Not only can financial economies of scale be achieved but there may likely be administrative benefits to a merger. A larger plan may qualify for additional administrative services, a higher level of customer focus from the service provider, or more customization. There is no need to maintain separate benefit departments to administer separate plans. Employees can transfer between departments without the need to be concerned about different benefit structures. Lastly, uniform benefits eliminate potential employee relations issues, especially if the benefits are considerably unequal.

Potential Risks   One of the more significant areas and paramount to avoidance of potential risk is the timing of the merger. Timely and careful attention to the many financial, legal, administrative, plan design, and communications issues is critical to a successful transaction. A successful merger usually takes three months to plan. Clearly written advance notification to all providers of the intent of the transaction is important. Proper planning allows time for certain administrative considerations, including plan design changes and transitioning to one service provider. Time is also essential for the analyzing plan investments, blackout notice periods, completion of required legal documentation, projection compliance testing, and potentially additional due diligence on the seller's plan to avoid last minute operational compliance issues. If a compliance issue is uncovered during the due diligence process, a delay in the merger of the plans may occur until the seller's plan has been self-corrected or an IRS letter of plan compliance has been received. There may be termination fees, investment liquidation fees, or market value adjustments related to plan investments that may affect the timing of the plan merger.

A strategic or legal decision may be made to retain or grandfather some of the provisions of the seller's plan. This may result in separate benefit structures within the same plan. The risks associated here are numerous and they involve several interested parties. The recordkeeper is one such party who will be required to extensively program the system for different provisions for different groups of participants. Some legally protected provisions such as in-service withdrawals may be difficult for the recordkeeper to program or may not be profitable enough for them and thus they may decide to monitor the protected or grandfathered provisions manually. Your human resources department may also be asked to assist in monitoring the affected participants. Manual intervention leads to potential errors and compliance issues. If the benefits are not uniform, whether they are protected or not, additional testing is required to ensure that you are not providing more favorable benefits to the highly compensated employees. Legal assistance will be required to amend the plan for different provisions. This may take a prototype plan out of prototype status, converting the plan to an individually designed custom plan and document.

There is a potential cost, including the cost involved with a custom plan document, for different provisions. A custom plan document should be submitted for an IRS qualification letter. Amendments must be drafted individually as opposed to prototype document amendments that the service provider handles for all of the plans on its prototype. There is also the cost that the service provider and your payroll vendor may charge for additional programming. If there is a market value adjustment or other liquidation penalty on the seller's investments, the buyer may decide to transfer the assets anyway and make the participants whole by contributing the shortfall. Some providers may be willing to pick up the cost of the shortfall.

It is important to help mitigate costs to participants in a merger. Grandfathering loans is an important strategy in carrying this out. The ability to roll over loans along with account balances avoids loan defaults and resulting taxation to the participants. Continuation of the loan program mitigates risk to participants.

You will need the support of several professionals in order to manage the risks in a merger. The support of legal counsel will be required to guide you through the legal requirements and potential plan defect issues, a benefits consultant with experience with vendor and legal requirements to guide you through best practices and assist in compliance testing and benefit calculations, a communications consultant to assist in communicating important messages to your employees during this unsettled time, and an investment consultant to advise on appropriate investments for the merged plan and to mitigate liability. You will also need to involve your human resources staff and both the seller's and buyer's recordkeeping service providers.[8]

Some organizations may want to maintain separate plans. They may wish to provide different benefits to different groups to help in the recruitment and retention process of key executives. They may be required to honor executive employment contracts or collective bargaining requirements that dictate the level of benefits. Also, an organization may not want to amend its plan to incorporate protected benefits from the seller's plan such as a more generous vesting schedule or more generous benefits. Finally, and carrying the most serious potential risk, is if the seller's plan has any qualification defects, merging the plans would lead to potential tainting of the buyer's plan, too. This can lead to immediate taxability of participants' balances in both the buyer's and seller's plans, putting participants at jeopardy of unfortunate tax consequences. Furthermore, there may be excises taxes and penalties to the buyer and seller. Potential defects can be mitigated with proper and thorough due diligence before the merger transaction.

Ultimately, it is paramount to mitigate employee relations problems and to gain the trust of the employees at both organizations. To quote an Aon colleague in a recently published article, "Employees are the company's most valuable asset. Employee benefits and related matters are a critical element of and either an impediment to or a generator of employee goodwill and organizational success."[9] One of the most important issues to employees during this time of uncertainty and confusion is what happens to their benefit plans. Proper and ongoing proactive communications can help manage this risk and alleviate employee fears.

Requirements Since mergers involve several elements of risk, one of the initial steps to manage the process includes proper planning. Internal experts like the benefits and human resources professionals should be engaged initially and continuously through the transaction analysis. If possible, they should be engaged in the pre-deal discussions. Next is to identify a team of external experts to assist in the process, including benefits consultants, service providers, and legal counsel. These experts will be paramount in assisting you to successfully emerge as a combined entity.[10] Careful coordination between the experts of both the seller and buyer is critical for success. Once the appropriate team of resources is assembled, the next important activity in the merger planning is to map out the substantive steps and requirements. This can be done by creating a plan merger project timeline. Periodic meetings involving the team should be held to review each step and discuss issues and proposed resolutions. Every decision should be documented and continually updated. Identification of senior management and key decision makers is important to achieving timely resolution during the planning process. The process can be documented in a merger project timeline. A sample project timeline is shown in Table 10.1. The project plan

TABLE 10.1 Sample Project Steps

	Project Step	Resources	Category	Completion Date
1.	Assure plan merger is permissible according to the structure of the entities' merger.	Legal counsel or consultant	Legal	
2.	Obtain all required documentation, outlined later in this chapter, from the transferor plan.	Company	Legal	
3.	Review and confirm that the transferor plan is qualified under the IRS, meets all filing and disclosure requirements for the DOL, and is being administered according to plan provisions.	Consultant	Legal	
4.	Meet to decide a target date for the merger, discuss goals and issues, and identify necessary documents that need to be completed.	Company, in conjunction with service providers of both transferor and successor plans	Administrative	
5.	Sign corporate resolution documenting merger intention, before amending.	Board of directors, from preparation by service providers or counsel	Legal	
6.	Provide service agreement severance notices to current service provider and trustee of transferor plan.	Transferor company	Administrative	
7.	Review purchase and sales agreement to determine the level of benefits requirements, including contributions required before the merger.	Legal counsel	Legal/Administrative	

#	Task	Responsible	Category
8.	Determine date by which activity such as transfers and withdrawals must cease in transferor plan.	Company, in conjunction with service providers of both transferor and successor plans	Administrative
9.	Coordinate date and process for activity such as payroll contributions in successor plan for transferred employees.	Company, in conjunction with service providers of both transferor and successor plans	Administrative
10.	Develop process for handling new enrollees during the transition phase.	Company, in conjunction with service providers of both transferor and successor plans	Administrative
11.	Determine investment fund transfers by fund for mapping or reregistration.	Consultant and service provider	Administrative
12.	Restate or amend transferor plan document to memorialize legislation (if required), for termination (if desired) or for merger. *Merger amendment must be signed before merger date.*	Prototype sponsor (if applicable). If attorney drafted document, consultant of counsel.	Legal
13.	Restate or amend successor plan document to memorialize legislation (if required), and for merger provisions for assets and employees and participants. Service provider of the successor plan reviews and programs recordkeeping system to ensure administration of any new changes to plan provisions. *Merger amendment must be signed before merger date.*	Prototype sponsor (if applicable). If attorney drafted document, consultant of counsel.	Legal
14.	Ensure amendments address protected benefits and provisions improvements.	Prototype sponsor (if applicable). If attorney drafted document, consultant of counsel.	Legal

(Continued)

TABLE 10.1 *(Continued)*

	Project Step	Resources	Category	Completion Date
15.	Prepare ERISA 204(h) Notice (only for money purchase plans) to be provided *at least 15 days before* amendment effective date.	Prototype sponsor (if applicable). If attorney drafted document, consultant or counsel (electronic submission not allowed).	Legal	
16.	Review amendments and notice materials.	Counsel	Legal	
17.	Provide copies of resolution, adopted amendments to trustees and service providers of both plans.	Company	Legal	
18.	Communicate plan provisions, fund mapping, and timing to new plan participants—including Sarbanes-Oxley Notice.	Company, with consultant or service provider support	Communications	
19.	Review process for deferral elections, investment elections and new loans	Consultant or service provider	Administrative	
20.	Board of directors directs the trustee to merge and transfer 100% of transferor plan assets as of merger date.	Board of directors, in coordination with service providers of both plans	Administrative	
21.	Reconcile plan assets post-merger to assure a 100% transfer.	Successor service provider	Administrative	
22.	Distribute summary plan descriptions to new plan participants *within 90 days* of becoming participants.	Company or service provider (electronic rules apply)	Compliance	
23.	Complete nondiscrimination testing required for final year of transferor plan.	Consultant or service provider	Compliance	
24.	File Form 5500 marked "final" for transferor plan as of the year-end in which the merger occurred.	Consultant or service provider	Compliance	

will be divided into several categories: due diligence, legal, administrative, compliance, and communications. Each category should have its own time frame and all should be monitored simultaneously. Key will be to initially review the purchase agreement, which will dictate the seller's and buyer's benefits requirements after the sale.

Due Diligence   Preliminary assessment and due diligence of the seller's 401(k) plan is recommended. The objective of a benefits due diligence review is to identify any legal, administrative, or compliance defects, assess the risks, and assign responsibility for resolution through an action plan. Ultimately, a written agreement should be entered into between the seller and buyer that defines the agreed-upon commitments regarding the treatment of any plan noncompliance. Thorough due diligence should uncover the defects that would be uncovered if the plan were audited by the IRS.

Proper due diligence requires analysis of administrative and legal documents. A sample document request list is provided here. Many of these documents will be provided by the recordkeeping service providers. Review of these documents will confirm that the 401(k) plan in form and in operation is qualified under the Code and meets all filing and disclosure requirements of the DOL. A review should also confirm whether the plan is being administered in accordance with the plan's documented provisions.

Sample Document Request List for Due Diligence of Seller's 401(k) Plan
- List of all qualified plans sponsored by the company
- An overview of corporate ownership structure
- Plan documents and amendments to date include an adoption agreement, if applicable
- Trust agreements
- Summary plan descriptions
- Most recent IRS determination letter
- Copy of investment policy statement and any documentation with respect to ongoing monitoring of investment performance
- Any correspondence with the DOL or IRS regarding the plan
- Minutes of retirement plan committee meetings
- Copies of executed Form 5500 filing and accompanying audited financial statement of plan assets for the last two years
- Copies of investment fund/GIC contracts, if applicable
- Actual current year employer contributions and budgeted future year employer contributions
- Details on level of employer contribution for the current year and prior year (that is, matching or profit sharing formula)
- Details on timing of employer contributions (that is, payroll basis, monthly, annually)
- Details on financial statement presentation of employer contributions

- Records of average deferral percentage and average contribution percentage tests for the last two years
- Records of other required testing, including controlled group coverage testing and Code Section 415 testing
- Documentation that any corrective actions (that is, refunds) required by test failures have been completed by the time frames prescribed by law
- Forfeiture amount
- Employee census
- Detail on administrative costs paid by the company and by the plan
- Service agreements with current providers, including current fee schedule and information on any liquidation or contingent deferred sales charges
- Collective bargaining agreements relating to plan participation

401(k) Plans and Additional Information Needed for Certain Business Transactions

- Details on administrative function provided by the parent company as it relates to the 401(k) plan, including details on human resources, treasury, and payroll processes
- Details on how these processes will be replicated
- How are these administrative functions currently being billed to the Seller? Are actual costs used, or is an allocation method used?
- Provide total asset balances attributable to affected participants and the breakout of total assets by asset category (that is, company stock, GICs, mutual funds)
- Details on plan information for each affected participant, including all demographic information, current contribution percent, and investment election selection
- Detail on which locations will need enrollment or education meetings for the new plan

Items for Review

- Has the plan been updated for GUST, EGTRRA, PPA, and any other required regulations legislative and regulatory changes?
- Timing of employer contributions?
- Are tests passing?
- Did a significant percentage of employees leave the company or the plan (possibly triggering a partial plan termination)?
- Review fees and expenses on Form 5500.
- Has the final employer contribution been made?
- Is the profit sharing formula a safe harbor or does it need to be tested?
- Are any Puerto Rican employees covered?
- Does the plan contain company stock?
- Does the plan cover collective bargaining employees?

The ease or difficulty in obtaining the required documents from the seller or the service providers can be an indication of a potential problem. If the plan is found to have a disqualifying defect, action may be taken to reduce or eliminate the liability associated with the errors, including the IRS self-correction program or the DOL delinquent filer voluntary compliance program. If an issue has been uncovered during the due diligence process, it is prudent for the buyer to wait to merge the plan until the seller's plan is corrected.

Listed here are some potential failures and how to uncover them.

Potential Plan Document Failures

- *Missing a Recent IRS Qualification letter or Required Plan Amendments*—The date on the IRS letter will help determine if it has been submitted within the correct time frame. The plan should also have made any required plan amendments. Even if the plan has a current IRS determination letter and has been timely amended, qualification will also depend upon the plan being administered in accordance with the terms of the plan.
- *Coverage and Eligibility Determination Failures*—It must be determined that the proper groups of employees were included in the plan and whether eligibility and entry dates for the plan were correctly determined. A review of the plan eligibility provisions and a sample administrative audit of dates of hire can help to determine failures.
- *Failure to Use the Correct Definition of Compensation for All Plan Provisions*—Compensation may be defined differently for the determination of highly compensated, determination of benefits, and testing. Some common mistakes include not determining compensation for the correct period of time. Eligible compensation, for example, may be determined for only the part of the year the employee was eligible, although the plan provides that such compensation is to be determined for the entire plan year. Some plans exclude certain items from the definition of plan compensation such as bonuses or commissions. The plan may not actually be administered that way, however. In addition, compensation, such as severance pay or nonqualified deferred compensation pay may be included for all purposes when these items should be excluded in certain cases. A review of participant contribution calculations and review of the testing can help determine failures.
- *Failure to Apply the Code Limits*—There are also limits (such as dollar and discrimination limits) on the amount of contributions that can be made under the plan. A review of participant contribution calculations and review of the testing can help determine failures.
- *Failure to Perform Required Testing or Failure to Properly or Timely Correct if Tests Fail*—This includes ADP testing of employee before-tax

deferrals, ACP testing of employer match and after-tax deferrals, and nondiscrimination testing on nonelective contributions that are not based on a uniform allocation such as age or service basis. Compensation testing must be performed if the definition of compensation is not a safe-harbor definition. For example, if the plan excludes certain types of pay that only non-highly compensated employees typically receive. Coverage testing to determine a sufficient percentage of non-highly compensated employees are covered under the plan. This would be done typically in a controlled group situation. Another test that may be required is a benefits rights features test if eligibility for certain benefits is not uniform.

- *Failure to Correctly Determine Vesting*—A review of a sample of distribution calculations can help determine if the vesting, which is based on years of service, is done properly.
- *Failure to Timely Submit the Annual Form 5500 Filing and Accountant's Report*—Proof of timely filing should be obtained; for example, a copy of the signed and dated filing.

Protected Benefits   Before a merger, you will need to perform a thorough review of the plan provisions of each of the 401(k) plans to ensure that certain protected benefits are not cut back. The following provisions are the benefits that must be reviewed.

- *Vesting of Employer Contributions*—The vesting provisions may be more generous in one plan. For administrative ease, the more generous vesting should be adopted. This can be costly, however. Alternatively, maintaining two vesting schedules can add recordkeeping cost.
- *In-Service Withdrawals*—In-service withdrawals at age 59½ are a protected benefit. For administrative ease, it is better to add this provision rather than monitoring two groups of participants.
- *Normal Retirement Age (NRA)*—At NRA, a participant becomes fully vested in employer contributions. The NRA is typically 65, but if a plan has a younger NRA, the younger age should be adopted, otherwise the recordkeeper may be required to track both features.
- *Vesting and Eligibility Computation Periods*—Plans can track service by counting hours or use an elapsed time basis. Elapsed time is when completed years are counted. Careful review must be done to determine which is more favorable and to ensure that no participant's service will be cut back when merging plans.
- *Distribution Options*—Many 401(k) plans have lump sum only as the form of distribution. Some plans offer installments or annuities. Since many plans differ in the way distribution options are set up, protecting this benefit in a merger may be the most difficult administratively of

the protected benefits to maintain. Optional forms of benefits may be taken away for benefits that accrue after the merger. The following are exceptions:

- Elimination of redundant options
- Elimination of noncore options in which core options remain
- Elimination of all non-lump sum options in a profit sharing plan (joint and survivor options may not be eliminated from money purchase plans)
- *Contribution Accruals through the Merger Date*—This issue arises with employer contributions that have accrued during the plan year of the merger, but have not yet been funded or allocated.
- *Definition of What Constitutes a Disability under the Plan*

Plan Design   A merger is an opportunity for redesigning the plan to align it better with corporate objectives as well as the demands of the marketplace, competition, and recruitment. It is also an opportunity to simplify provisions such as elimination of certain distribution requirements or implement new services that the provider may be offering. Establishing clear plan objectives when reviewing the plan design ensures that the plan matches your desired level of benefit adequacy for participants. It is a good time to benchmark the plan design to reduce the risk of turnover due to uncompetitive benefits. A review of collectively bargained agreements and other obligations are necessary in order to ascertain obligations to honor existing contracts still in force as well as legal obligations to bargain with union groups over changes related to or necessitated by the merger.

The plan design can have an effect on the type of plan document that will be required. This can affect the cost as well. If the buyer has a custom plan document in force already, then there is less plan design constraint and more flexibility with plan design. It is more costly, however, to have a custom plan document prepared and maintained as well as additional cost to have it reviewed by the IRS. If the buyer has a prototype plan document, then a simpler plan design may be desired. A review of the adoption agreement will be required to ensure that the prototype can support the new design.

Merger Amendments   The merger of a plan and associated assets cannot take effect until a corporate resolution is adopted to merge the plans. The resolution will outline how the transaction will occur and will describe the timing of the merger and other details such as the agreement to transfer loans from one plan to another or to transfer investment and deferral elections. It will also need to document any plan design changes such as incorporating required protected benefits as well as to name the new recordkeeper and trustee. The seller's trustee will need a notification of acceptance as trustee from the buyer's trustee. A review of the plans should be made to better determine any amendments that may be needed before the merger. A final Form 5500 will be needed for the seller's plan after the assets are transferred.

Operational Considerations   Coordination and accuracy of data between internal and external parties is critical to a smooth and accurate transition. External parties involved are the prior and new recordkeepers and payroll providers. Internally, the administrative staffs of both the buyer and seller need to have accurate data. The buyer's recordkeeper will require indicative data such as name, Social Security number, dates of birth and hire, hours worked each year, and rehire dates. These data can be obtained by either the prior recordkeeper or human resources group, depending upon which system is more current and accurate. Other data needs are compensation, loan data, hardship withdrawal available dollars, employee and employer contributions (if merging plans midyear), and deferral and investment elections (assuming employees of the seller will not be reenrolling under the buyer's plan. The transfer of assets and recordkeeping accounts by participant will be coordinated by the recordkeepers and trustees. Since employee deferrals are limited by plan year and not by plan, monitoring that no one exceeds the 402(g) limit (for example, $16,500 for 2009 and 2010) will be something that may need to be coordinated by the payroll vendors. Plan forfeitures are required to be used (either allocated to participants or to pay plan expenses) before the transfer of balances. So the seller needs to make sure the recordkeeper determines this. The elimination of unallocated accounts such as forfeitures may eliminate the requirement to file IRS Form 5310-A filing. (Notice of Plan Merger or Consolidation, Spinoff, or Transfer of Plan Assets or Liabilities; Notice of Qualified Separate Lines of Business.)

Investment Issues   An investment issue that arises is the treatment of the seller's participants' balances during a merger. One option is for the assets to become distributable. This means that participants have the option of taking a distribution, rolling over into an IRA, or rolling over into the buyer's plan. Buyers may choose this option to avoid the possibility of merging in tainted balances. Participants in this type of corporate transaction may not be able to leave their accounts under the seller's plan because it may not exist after the transaction.

A second option is that the assets and loan balances be transferred in a trust-to-trust transfer and participants are not permitted to elect a rollover or distribution.

There are two approaches to transferring assets in a trust-to-trust transfer. One approach is to map assets from the seller's plan into like investments in the buyer's plan. Alternatively, all assets would be liquidated in the seller's plan and participants reelect investment options under the buyer's plan. The assets for those employees who do not proactively make an investment election would be defaulted into the buyer's plan's qualified default investment alternative (QDIA). The buyer's QDIA may be different than the participant's asset allocation under the seller's plan. Fund mapping is beneficial because the assets remain invested in similar style funds. In a situation in which there are investments in the seller's plan that are unlike the investments in the buyer's plan, it may be prudent to have participants reelect their investment options. An outside investment consultant is recommended to advise as to which alternative best suits your situation and to select the appropriate like funds for mapping.

In addition to mapping existing balances into like funds, it is best practice to map investment elections for future contributions as well. It is more efficient administratively and a timelier approach when compared to soliciting new investment elections from all participants. In addition, it is best practice to map employee salary deferral elections as well. If each employee had to reenroll by completing all new elections, it could take several weeks, if not months, during which time there would be a cessation of deferrals. This is not in the best interest of participants.

Regardless of which alternative is used, there will be a period of time, a blackout period, during which certain participant transactions cannot be made. Most likely this blackout period will be minimal. See Chapter 8 for a more detailed discussion regarding blackout requirements.

An issue that should be researched at the time of investment review is to determine if there are any investments in the seller's plan that are illiquid or that cannot be mapped because there is a liquidation fee or market value adjustment. This is typical in certain stable value investment products. Also, a separate determination will be required if there is company stock involved. Frequently, the seller's stock is converted and held in the buyer's plan for a limited period of time also known as a sunset period so as not to force participants to liquidate at an inopportune time.

Service Provider Considerations   Once the recordkeeping service provider is notified of the merger, they typically want to promptly coordinate a face-to-face conversion meeting with human resources. It typically begins with a kickoff meeting during which time a draft merger conversion document that the service provider has prepared is reviewed. The merger document will contain details on the plan design and operation of the merged plan. The meeting will be followed up by regular conversion calls (often weekly) to review the timeline, outstanding issues, and plans for resolution.

Participant Communications and Notices   Merger transactions create a significant amount of uncertainty and potential confusion for employees. Corporate transactions are not typically disclosed to human resources until just before the transaction taking place. This means that human resources must act quickly following the announcement of the merger. Timely, thorough, and accurate disclosure of information is critical during this time of uncertainty. Thoughtful and reassuring responses to questions will translate into employee trust of the employer. A communications timeline is an important tool to use to help organize the rollout of an effective communications campaign. Communications pieces can take the form of a letter from the company's leadership, followed by a letter from human resources, and a follow-up with frequently asked questions memos. Communications of the 401(k) plan changes will most likely be coordinated with other benefits changes taking place. Buyers and sellers need to coordinate the timing and details of the communications. Input from the service providers will be essential. Call centers at both the buyer's and seller's recordkeeper will need to be involved as well as participants who will most likely call them with questions.

After the merger, a revised summary plan description or summary of material modification should be distributed that will reflect plan design changes. Participants will want to make sure that their final balances under the seller's plan per their last participant statement reconciles to the opening balances in their new plan's participant statements.

As mentioned earlier, there may be a time when participants will not have access to making transactions to their accounts. This period is frequently called the blackout period and a notification, in line with a Sarbanes-Oxley Act requirement, is required to be sent out at least 30 days before the blackout period.

Another required notification not just unique to a merger is the qualified default investment alternative (QDIA) notice. This notice communicates the plan's default investment option. Automatic enrollment and safe-harbor notices may also be required.

Conclusion   Merging plans is a complex procedure that affects companies in many ways and carries tremendous fiduciary risk. A successful merger can be accomplished by proper planning and due diligence, timely management and coordination, comprehensive and timely employee communications, and consultation and involvement with experts.

PLAN TERMINATIONS

Companies that find themselves in serious business distress may decide that they must terminate their 401(k) plan. Some companies involved in a business transaction or restructuring may deem it necessary to terminate the 401(k) plan. In a sale, the purchaser may not want to continue operation or merger of the seller's plan so as to not adversely affect the plan qualification of the buyer's plan. There are many complex considerations related to terminating a 401(k) plan, including legal, employee, and administrative considerations. There are also consequences that affect employees and the employer.

What Constitutes a Plan Termination?

Termination of the plan requires both the formal action to terminate the plan (for example, adoption of a corporate resolution), and the distribution of all of the plan assets as soon as administratively feasible after the formal decision to terminate. The IRS generally treats one year from the termination date as a reasonable period to distribute all of the plan assets.[11] If the employer applies for a determination letter soon after the decision to terminate the plan, however, the employer need not complete the final distribution assets until it receives a favorable determination letter from the IRS (even if the determination letter process takes more than one year). The requirement to terminate a plan by formal termination action followed by timely distribution of all plan assets has two effects:

- *Importance of Termination Date*—First, the employer's stated termination date will determine what amendments the employer must make to the plan. A terminating plan will need to be amended to include any required plan provision that is effective on or before the termination date even though in normal circumstances it would be appropriate to adopt the amendment at a later time. An IRS determination letter on plan termination assures the plan includes all necessary provisions.
- *Importance of Timely Distribution of All Assets*—The second effect of the timely distribution rule is that if the plan does not distribute the assets as soon as administratively feasible after the formal decision to terminate, the plan is not terminated as of the original stated termination date. In such a case, the employer may be required to establish a new termination date and additional amendments may be necessary to address any intervening legislative or regulatory changes. The general rule is that a qualified plan must be qualified both in form and in operation.

Consequences

Termination has serious consequences. Two of the most important are immediate vesting and taxation. A partial termination, complete plan termination, or complete discontinuance of employer contributions, will result in full and immediate vesting of benefits for affected participants. Consequently, potential forfeitures may become vested benefits.

During the operation of an active qualified plan, benefits grow on a tax-deferred basis. Upon plan termination, benefits generally become distributable. Unless rolled over to another qualified vehicle (plan or IRA), a distribution from the plan will be subject to income taxes, and if applicable, an early distribution penalty. Any loans outstanding become due or taxable because loans are seldom permitted to be rolled over. If a plan is retroactively disqualified, both employer and employees are negatively affected. The employer's deductions for contributions during the past years will be disallowed by the IRS and participants' benefits become retroactively taxable even if rolled over. Thus, the determination letter process, while not a legal requirement, is an important and permanent assurance as to the plan's qualified status on termination.

Allocating Unallocated Funds

When a plan terminates, the plan must provide a method for allocating any unallocated funds. Many plans use forfeitures to reduce or offset future employer contributions. If employer contributions cease, these forfeitures can be used, if the plan allows, to pay remaining allowable plan expenses. If forfeitures still remain after payment of allowable plan expenses, then the forfeitures must be allocated to participants.

Distributing Plan Assets

A plan sponsor may generally terminate a qualified plan at any time. Distributing all of the plan's assets, however, can be tricky. Code Section 411(a)(11) prohibits the distribution of a plan participant's account balance without his consent if the account balance exceeds $5,000 and the participant has not attained the later of age 62 or the plan's normal retirement age. If a plan participant does not consent to a distribution following termination of the plan, then the plan sponsor has several options available for shutting down the plan, as described next.

If the 401(k) plan has an annuity option, then the plan may purchase an annuity contract to provide for the participant's benefit and distribute the contract to the participant. If the 401(k) plan does not have an annuity option, then Treasury Regulation Section 1.411(d)-4, Q&A-2(b)(2)(vi) permits the plan sponsor to distribute the participant's account balance in a single lump sum without the participant's consent, provided that the plan sponsor does not maintain any other defined contribution plan. Alternatively, if the plan sponsor also maintains another defined contribution plan, the terminating plan may transfer the participant's account balance to the other plan. Of course, all of the Code Section 411(d)(6) protected benefits must be preserved under the transferee plan.

Missing Participants

When plan administrators need to distribute information or assets to missing participants, it can be an administrative headache. This is especially true when a plan is terminated and there is a benefit to be distributed to the missing participant. The plan administrator has a fiduciary duty to protect the benefits for the participant. How the administrator carries out that duty with respect to lost employees or employees who cannot be located is not directly addressed by ERISA. The DOL has stated that the steps a fiduciary must take to locate missing participants are inherently facts-and-circumstances determinations. The DOL reasons that each fiduciary must determine whether the steps it takes to locate missing participants satisfy the fiduciary's obligations under ERISA. Some common techniques administrators can use to locate missing participants include mailing a notice to the last known address, searching internal records, and using locator services, including the services of the Social Security Administration and the IRS. A private locator service will, for a fee, attempt to locate a person using information that the plan administrator provides.

Termination and Winding-Up Process

The DOL's Employee Benefits Security Administration (EBSA) regulations establish specific procedures that administrators must follow. The regulations establish a fiduciary safe harbor for distributions from terminating individual account plans (whether or not abandoned) on behalf of missing participants. In most cases, the account of a missing participant will be transferred directly to an individual retirement plan. In some cases, accounts of $1,000 or less may be distributed to a bank account or a state's unclaimed property fund on behalf of the missing participant.[12]

Employee Communications

As part of the determination letter process and in accordance with IRS procedures, notice that an application for a determination letter is to be made must be given to all interested parties. The notice must be given not less than 10 days or more than 24 days before the day the application for a determination is made. Interested parties in a plan termination generally include:

- All present employees of the employer with accrued benefits under the plan
- All former employees with vested benefits under the plan
- All beneficiaries of deceased former employees currently receiving benefits under the plan

This required notice identifies whom to contact for additional information. A more user-friendly communications method may be considered that would mitigate employee concerns and relieve employee anxiety.

Ongoing Administration

The plan sponsor should coordinate with service providers to ensure that the plan is properly administered from the time termination resolutions are adopted until the assets of the plan are finally distributed. This includes the filing of a final Form 5500 within 210 days after such final distribution.

Conclusion

Terminating a 401(k) plan is an involved procedure. Effective planning and coordination during the plan termination process is important for the success of the plan termination and mitigates risk. Professional advisors and legal experts experienced in plan terminations can help ensure a smooth and successful plan termination. We provide a checklist here for you to use when terminating a 401(k) plan.

401(k) Plan Termination Checklist
Initial Decisions
☐ Determine the official date of plan termination.
☐ If a method for distribution can be an annuity, determine as early as possible which insurance company will provide the annuity contracts.

Actions Necessary to Terminate the Plan
☐ Prepare an agreement or declaration amending and terminating the plan to set forth precisely what steps will be taken and how distributions will be made.
☐ Obtain action authorizing the termination by the board of directors or executive committee of the board of directors of the company (or other body with authority to terminate the plan).
☐ Notify the plan trustee of the anticipated plan termination.
☐ Determine if the plan will be filed for an IRS determination letter upon termination.
☐ Prepare and post a notice to interested parties before submitting a request for a determination letter to the IRS informing participants of the plan termination.

☐ Notify the IRS and the DOL of the plan termination. This is done by reporting the termination on the appropriate line item of Form 5500 for the plan year in which the termination occurred.

☐ Submit Form 5310 to the Internal Revenue Service requesting a determination letter with respect to the plan termination.

Documents to be Submitted to the IRS with Request for Determination Letter

☐ Form 5310

☐ Form 6088 (Required only for underfunded money purchase plans; information for the prior two years is reflected on this form.)

☐ Agreement amending and terminating the plan.

☐ Resolution of the board of directors or executive committee approving the termination.

☐ Power of attorney, if required.

Prepare to Distribute Assets to Participants

☐ Work with the plan recordkeeper and with the plan trustee to determine a reasonable date for making distributions to the plan participants.

☐ When the distribution date is determined, the trustee should prepare to place the plan assets in a guaranteed interest-bearing account so that the final trust asset amount can be known in advance for allocation purposes.

☐ Prepare distribution election forms to give participants, including all spousal consent forms needed for the joint and survivor annuity options, if applicable.

☐ Mail distribution election forms to plan participants. (Give participants two to three weeks to complete these forms.)

Distribute Assets

☐ Transmit employee distribution request forms to the recordkeeper at least one month before the date distributions are to be made.

☐ Obtain a final accounting from the plan trustee at least one month before the date distributions will be made.

☐ Determine which employees want to receive annuities and arrange for their purchase.

☐ Coordinate with the trustee and the recordkeeper for the final checks.

Reporting and Disclosure

☐ Ensure that all information returns are prepared for distributions as usual. Form 1099-R, and the appropriate transmittal forms, will be required as for any distribution from an ongoing plan.

☐ File annual report with the DOL. The Form 5500 would be filed for each plan year until assets are distributed. A final Form 5500 would be filed for the plan year or portion of the plan year in which the assets are distributed.

DIVESTITURES AND DOWNSIZING

Not all situations result in plans being combined into larger plans or being terminated altogether. In some cases, the result is a plan that is a fraction of what it used to be. This can result from organizations spinning off divisions or parts of their firm into separate entities. It can also be the result of a company downsizing significantly after which the resulting organization is much smaller than it was before the event. Both of these types of events will have an impact on the organization's 401(k) plan. This section discusses the effect divestitures and downsizing events have on 401(k) plans.

Divestitures and Plan Spinoffs

In the event an organization sells a division, it typically spins off that portion of the retirement plan as well. For purposes of this discussion, we are addressing situations in which a new entity is created, not where a buyer assumed a spun-off target company. Assume for our discussion that a large organization completely divests itself of a smaller part, so that there is no common ownership or controlled group to consider.

The Code rules governing plan spin-offs are in Code Section 414(l). To be considered a spin-off, it must be demonstrated that:

- Participant account balances *before* the spin-off were equal to participant balances *immediately after* the spin-off.
- Participant account balances *after* the spin-off were equal to the total plan assets *immediately after* the spin-off; for example, there was no unallocated suspense account.

If it can also be demonstrated that the participant account balances *before* the spin-off were equal to total plan assets at the same time, Form 5310-A is not required to be filed. Otherwise, the original plan from before the spin-off must file Form 5310-A.[13] Multiple filings for multiple plans may be required.

The biggest challenge for the spun-off plan is in establishing ongoing plan operations with minimal disruption, and with, ideally, an insignificant change in the service provider's platform and investment architecture requirements.

How might plan operations be affected? If the spun-off plan is smaller than the service provider is willing to administer, it may be impossible, or unreasonably costly, to maintain the spun-off plan with them. If the spun-off group used its larger organization's centralized resources for human resources systems and payroll processing, it will be necessary to meet new requirements in data sharing and workflow with the service provider.

As with any significant business change, getting outside help to execute the change is a good idea. Steps to minimizing risk in a plan spin-off include:

- Effective project management with agreement on timelines and milestone goals
- Explicit understanding of the service model, investment menu restrictions or requirements, and fees with the larger plan's provider
- Solutions for any illiquid or semi-illiquid assets; for example, stable value or guaranteed investment contracts
- A vendor search, if necessary, ideally beginning six months ahead of the go-live date for the spun off plan
- Implementation of the new plan, including an investment menu recommended by an independent third party advisor
- Coordination between HR and payroll (including programmers) and the service provider early in the process
- A well-crafted communication plan led by the service provider, including timelines for certain notices such as Sarbanes-Oxley, if applicable
- Fiduciary governance structure and training for the new fiduciary committee members

Downsizing and Partial Plan Terminations

A partial plan termination can be the result of a plan sponsor decision or the result of facts and circumstances. Absent a decision by the plan sponsor to partially terminate the plan, businesses facing reductions in force (RIFs) need to be keenly aware of what percentage of their workforce is potentially affected by a planned RIF, as well as how their benefit programs are affected.

The general rule, according to IRS Revenue Ruling 2007–43 is that a "partial plan termination" occurs if the employer initiates separations from service of at least 20 percent of plan participants during the applicable period. The "applicable period" is not specifically defined, but refers to the impetus underlying the RIFs. Conceivably, the applicable period could cover a one-time event, or span more than one plan year.[14]

Plan sponsors anticipating RIFs need to be aware of two implications for qualified plans:

1. Partial plan terminations require full vesting of the RIFed participants.
2. Collectively bargained agreements covering plan participants may call for special benefits, such as service enhancements.

This section covered issues related to organizations that become smaller because of a divestiture or downsizing event. We explore in the next section options employers have regarding their plan when they are facing difficult business conditions.

OPTIONS FOR DISTRESSED ORGANIZATIONS

Employers in financial distress often reassess, even if temporarily, their level of plan contribution and other expenses. Reducing a discretionary match or other employer contribution may require a plan amendment and summary of material modifications (if the formula is discussed explicitly in the plan's document).

Be aware that contributions, once earned, cannot be taken back. Assume an example in which a plan sponsor provides a required contribution on December 31 for all participants who earned a year of service (1,000 hours) in the plan year. Eliminating or reducing that provision cannot likely occur in August (as most participants earned the benefit sometime in late June); however, it could have been eliminated in March for most, if not all, participants. A last-day of the plan year requirement avoids much of this.

Less commonly explored is the idea of changing the allocation conditions for sharing in the employer contribution. If, for example, the profit sharing contribution was made per payroll or quarterly, it might prospectively be modified to apply only to those earning a year of service, or meeting a "last day of the plan year" service requirement.

Regardless of the specific decisions made, plan design changes require coordination with payroll teams and the plan's service provider. Participant communication materials addressing this and any other changes can help reduce participant concerns.

A plan sponsor of a retirement program that has undergone a partial plan termination, or has otherwise significantly reduced its asset base may be faced with new challenges, including:

- A different service platform, and less leverage with the service provider
- Less effective pricing; fixed expenses remain for compliance testing and Form 5500, but less revenue generated by plan assets to offset the service provider's fees
- Potential for negative cash flow due to increased loan activity and hardship distributions and reduced contribution levels

At some point, the employer may decide that a 401(k) plan is no longer the best form of retirement plan for their organization. Many recordkeeping service providers specialize in certain sizes and types of retirement plans. Initiating a search within the segment of service providers best suited for the new plan's size and type is recommended.

If the employer decides on exploring an alternative plan structure, two options and their high-level requirements are listed here.[15]

Savings Incentive Match Plan for Employees (SIMPLE) 401(k):
- Requires a plan amendment
- Is only permitted to cover the calendar year, that is, a plan with a December 31 plan year-end
- Permitted for employers with 100 or fewer employees in the controlled group who earned over $5,000 in the preceding year
- Requires a lower annual deferral limit than a traditional 401(k)
- Mandates employer contributions of 2 percent of eligible employee compensation, or a 3 percent match
- Eliminates ADP/ACP testing and is not subject to top-heavy testing

SIMPLE IRA
- Requires a SIMPLE IRA document; IRS provides a model document
- Uses the same rules as a SIMPLE 401(k) plan, but all contributions are deposited into SIMPLE IRAs
- Permits the sponsor to require that a certain IRA institution will be used, provided participants are given written instructions on how to transfer their balance to an institution they choose, and that transfers are permitted at no cost to the participant
- Allows the participant to take distributions at any time
- Eliminates the need for filing Form 5500

Adopting an alternative retirement plan model can simplify administration and recordkeeping. However, such a change requires very careful planning to ensure that the existing retirement plan is appropriately handled through the transition, as well as to ensure that timelines and due dates are well-managed. Professional support can be key to an effective result.

CONCLUSION

This chapter focuses on major structural changes to a sponsoring organization such as a merger and acquisition and the impact these changes have on the organization's 401(k) plans. While not always at the top of a manager's mind when contemplating a structural change, business transactions can trigger a tremendous amount of work related to the sponsor's 401(k) plan. This chapter covers the plan issues related to mergers and acquisitions, plan terminations, divestitures and downsizing, and companies experiencing business distress. The information provided here should give you a solid understanding of the necessary tasks related to any of these business transactions.

CHAPTER 11

Financial Communication and Education for Participants

The past few years have not been kind to the 401(k). WorldCom. DotCom. Lehman Brothers. Bailouts. Real estate busts; not to mention AIG. We've all heard the joke about the 401(k) becoming a 201(k). But it hasn't been all bad. A recent survey found the economic crisis has served as a wake-up call for many employees, with almost half (46 percent) reporting that recent economic events made them realize they need to take more control of their retirement savings.[1]

As companies increasingly move away from the provision of DB pension offerings, the burden is now more than ever on the individual to manage his retirement. As a result, financial communication and education has never been more important.

A survey of corporate executives found 66 percent believe that providing broader financial education in the workplace is more important to employees now than it was a year ago. The survey showed 63 percent of the executives say employee concerns over personal finances are creating a more difficult work environment. It also shows that companies are more committed to playing a lead role in providing people access to financial education.[2] Another survey identified a similar trend—increasing demand from employees for help with managing their finances. Fifty-one percent of all workers—and 55 percent of older boomers—indicate an interest in access to financial planners for retirement through their employers—up from 44 percent in 2007 and 29 percent in 2006.[3]

As we saw in Chapter 3, only about 60 percent of employees participate in plans where no automatic enrollment is used. For plans using automatic enrollment, 84 percent of employees on average participate. In addition, 22 percent of participants do not contribute enough to maximize their employer matching contribution, and only 35 percent of employees were definitely aware that their employer even offered matching contributions.[4] Furthermore, only 2 percent of workers say they are very knowledgeable about investing.[5]

The reality is that millions of workers don't contribute to a retirement plan even though one is offered at work, and studies have shown that large numbers of those who participate don't contribute enough to take advantage of the employer match. Without a successful plan design, financial education will not be effective, and even a well-structured plan can fail to achieve retirement savings goals without financial education and communication.

For some companies, the primary goal is to push employees to save enough so they have financial security as they head toward retirement. The idea is to get your employees more engaged in planning for retirement. PPA broadened your ability, as a retirement plan provider, to offer advice to help your employees evaluate their retirement plan investment options. Now it's time to take action.

This chapter offers ideas for taking an active role in educating employees on the value of your 401(k) plan as part of your total rewards strategy and employment deal. You'll see how a minimal increase in your level of outreach to employees can increase the perception of value, impact retention, and provide an even stronger return on investment (ROI) on your 401(k) plan. But first, take a look at your company's reasons for offering a 401(k) plan to your workforce.

WHY DO YOU OFFER A 401(k) PLAN?

Ask a CEO why his company offers a retirement plan and you'll hear answers ranging from the altruistic (help them prepare for the future) to the fierce (must offer an employment deal better than the competition). Why do you offer a 401(k)? Clearly, any effective communication strategy and implementation plan must begin with the answer to that question.

Consider the company's investment in the 401(k) plan—the administrative fees your company pays for and your company match. Now think about how much you invest in communicating the value of this benefit to your employees or educating them about the importance of saving for retirement. It's probably not much.

While the burden for preparing for retirement rests heavily on each employee's shoulders, there are a few reasons employers should care about ensuring their employees are fully engaged in preparing for retirement and actively participating in the 401(k) plan:

- Productivity: the link between financial stress and absenteeism or presenteeism

- Employee morale and retention: your retirement offering is an important part of your employment deal
- Competitive value

Financial education is necessary for employees to understand how retirement savings programs work and how they can use them to achieve adequate retirement savings. For example, many workers do not correctly use target date funds; rather than being the only fund held in a portfolio, they are often combined with separate stock and bond funds. This reflects a lack of financial education even where an effective plan design exists.

Also, even if a plan design does not produce high participation or contribution rates, research indicates that education provided to employees can help increase those rates. Numerous surveys have found that frequent educational events, particularly seminars, with consistent messages produce the largest effects on retirement savings. Where employee groups are known to have lower levels of financial knowledge, efforts to focus financial education on those groups may be an efficient use of company or plan resources. Finally, financial education can provide beneficial effects even after an employee separates from a firm. In particular, discussions of adequate retirement income are important in preventing individuals from consuming their retirement savings (that is, spending lump-sum distributions) before they reach retirement age.

Research has found improvements in employees' motivation, loyalty, and morale by demonstrating concern for their welfare; communicating the substantial value of retirement benefits; or responding to employees' request for assistance with financial planning.[6]

The challenge of rebuilding retirement security may seem very complex, but there are practical steps you can take as a plan sponsor to begin addressing this critical employee need. So, what can you do? It starts with an effective communication strategy and implementation plan.

COMMUNICATION STRATEGY

Success begins with a communication strategy. Building a proactive communication strategy can help you maximize your return on investment. In fact, employee communications can cost less than increasing company contributions to the plan.[7]

The most effective financial communication and education initiatives are ones with the following characteristics:

- Personalized: focused on the individual's situation
- Ongoing: more than a single point in time, the most effective campaigns are ongoing
- Targeted: identifies what to communicate to different types of groups within your audience based on their unique, diverse needs

So what are the elements of the communication strategy? There are seven simple steps:

1. Defining goals
2. Articulating key messages
3. Identifying audiences
4. Reaching your audiences
5. Mitigating challenges
6. Defining success and dependencies
7. Monitoring performance

Defining Goals

Ask yourself what you hope to accomplish. How can communication help to drive or reinforce the desired change or outcome? What actions are required of your employees? How can you make your communication more effective? What do current statistics tell you (diversification, rates of participation, level of deferrals)? Where do you need to improve? What do employees tell you (focus groups, surveys, employee meetings)?

The Great Places to Work Institute has developed a model for what makes a great place to work. Their model has three dimension: Trust, Pride and Camaraderie. Within the first dimension of trust they've identified the elements of credibility, respect, and fairness as essential to developing trust between employers and employees. Further, they have found that open and accessible communications is an effective way of establishing credibility.[8]

How you communicate with your employees may change depending on where they are in their career. Table 11.1 shows how the key topics you communicate may vary according to the audience's stage of career.

Articulating Key Messages

What do you want employees to know? What do they need to know? Why should employees care? Why is this program an important part of the employment deal? What do you want to reinforce about your employment experience? Where have you seen low levels of awareness, appreciation, or understanding?

TABLE 11.1 Communication Topics by Career Stage

Early Career	Mid Career	Late Career
– Participating in the plan – Increasing contribution rates with career progression – Focusing on long-term investment objectives	– Adjusting retirement savings based on other savings needs such as college education	– Managing how money should be distributed when leaving employment – Changing investment allocations to avoid potential large losses close to retirement

Employees need to understand what their retirement income will consist of (Social Security, pensions, personal savings, and so on) and set goals for how much they need to put in their 401(k) plan to ensure that all retirement income combined will result in an adequate replacement ratio.

Overall key messages should include:

- Importance of plan participation
- Contribution levels
- Asset allocation and diversification
- Time horizon for retirement savings

Other relevant topics can include basic investment terminology, a general explanation of your retirement program (pension and defined contribution, if offered), understanding of risk and risk tolerance, and the impact of pre-retirement withdrawals on retirement income (see the previous section on distributions).

Areas you may want to focus on when developing your communication and education include:

- Providing education to help employees realize and prepare for the costs associated with retirement, as well as how to create guaranteed income for life
- Recognizing that there may be an interest in this type of information earlier than traditional pre-retiree ages
- Communicating the benefits that are important to encourage participation such as employer match, advantages of dollar cost averaging, and tax advantages
- Offering retirement education programs that help employees realize and prepare for the costs associated with retirement such as health care, prescription drug costs, and long-term care

Identifying Audiences

Who are your key audiences? What are their needs? What messages does each audience need to hear? What are the concerns, risks, and fears of each group? What questions need to be answered? What is the value proposition for each group? What channels should be used? Should we be targeting our communication based on each audience groups level of financial acumen, education, age, or proximity to retirement?

Research has shown vast differences in the way individual employees manage their 401(k) plans. A recent study by the Ariel Education Initiative and consulting firm Hewitt Associates found significant differences in the savings behavior of different racial and ethnic groups even when comparing groups in similar age and income brackets.[9] Research commissioned by the FDIC found individuals with less financial knowledge tend to be minority, single, younger or older than average, low earners, and less educated. Those who need comprehensive financial education covering *all* basic topics (that is, cash flow, savings, and investments) were more likely to be single females, black or Hispanic, live in larger households, have less formal education, and have lower household income.[10]

It is also important to recognize that the needs of your audiences may change over time. For example, employees' perception of their proximity to retirement may change over time. A MetLife survey found that while more than half of workers 21 to 30 years old say they plan to retire by age 61, that figure drops to only 15 percent among those who are now ages 51 to 60.[11] That's why it's important to review and modify your communication plan on an ongoing basis.

Reaching Your Audiences

How will you reach your intended audience? Which channels are working best? Which are not? How could the communication channels be improved? What feedback do you have from employees?

Employee financial communication and education can include everything from classroom or one-on-one sessions to web-based calculators, podcasts, and savings blogs to boost employee's financial acumen. It's up to you to decide what will work best for your audience. It is also important to recognize that the best communication strategy and implementation plans are highly targeted to the needs of your audience. In building your communication strategy, you should determine the level of personalization and customization you can provide. Can you offer different educational sessions based on the specific needs of your audience? Does your vendor partner offer customized tools for retirement planning or one-on-one counseling sessions for your employees? Have you taken advantage of all that's available through the agreement with your vendor partner?

According to the 2002 Retirement Confidence Survey conducted by the Employee Benefit Research Institute (EBRI), 82 percent of workers receive benefit statements, 82 percent receive brochures, and 68 percent receive either newsletters or magazines.[12] The same study finds that 61 percent of employees have access to a financial planner and 66 percent are eligible to attend seminars. Online materials are available to 47 percent of employees at firms with educational offerings, 14 percent have access to computer software, and 14 percent have access to informational videos. A more recent Retirement Confidence Survey found that 61 percent of workers have referenced plan benefit statements, 52 percent have used information found over the Internet, 28 percent have used computer software, and 21 percent have used information obtained from seminars when making retirement savings and investment decisions.[13]

HR consultancy Watson Wyatt Worldwide found that both generic newsletters and material specific to the employer's retirement savings plan can raise participation rates. If used together, they can increase participation rates 36 percentage points. The survey also found that generic newsletters have no effect on contribution rates and that financial information specifically tailored to the employer's plan raises contribution rates approximately 2 points.[14]

The frequency with which employee communication is delivered can affect whether employees are using their retirement savings plan in the most beneficial way. Researchers have found that frequent seminars have a consistent and positive effect on participation in self-directed plans. They find that among lower-paid workers, frequent seminars are associated with participation rates that are 11.5 percentage points higher than the rates for plans with no seminars. For higher-paid workers, frequent seminars are associated with participation rates that are 6.4 percentage points higher than the rates for plans with no seminars.[15]

Mitigating Challenges

What do you see as the biggest communication challenges? Are there possible solutions? Will certain audiences be harder to communicate to than others? Why?

Companies that provide financial education in the workplace are not necessarily reaping the rewards for doing so. More employers report offering programs than employees report such awareness. Mid- and large-size companies have the biggest gap between retirement seminar offerings and awareness, with 55 percent of companies with 5,000 to 9,999 employees reporting offering seminars, while only 40 percent of their employees are aware of them. For companies with more than 10,000 employees, the chasm is even wider, with 63 percent of employers offering seminars while only 45 percent of their workers are aware of them.[16] These statistics highlight the importance of effectively promoting your program on an ongoing basis to ensure it gets noticed and has the desired results.

Defining Success and Dependencies

What needs to be established or put into place to ensure the goals are met? How can your vendor partners support your efforts?

The first measurement many of us consider in thinking about the success of a 401(k) is the level of employee participation. After all, the initial hurdle is getting people into the plan; only then can you encourage them to save at greater levels and teach them to invest wisely. The growing prevalence of automatic enrollment allows employers to take advantage of the power of inertia. The Deloitte 2009 401(k) Benchmarking Survey indicates that 52 percent of employers have an auto-enrollment feature (up from 42 percent the year before), and 14 percent are considering adding an auto-enrollment feature.[17]

Of course, employees must be permitted to opt out of plan participation, and you will want to track how many are electing to do so. In the Deloitte survey, 12 percent of employers saw an increase in opt-outs from auto enrollment programs.

Why is it so important to engage your workforce in planning and saving for retirement? Many studies have shown a connection between financial education and productivity. It's no surprise that money woes are a significant distraction, but does a healthy financial situation lead to a more focused employee? A study conducted by Jinhee Kim and E. Thomas Garman found statistically significant evidence that employees in a "high financial stress" group used more work time handling financial matters and were more frequently absent from work than those in moderate or low financial stress groups.[18]

How difficult is it to entice your employees to save now for the future? Research conducted by David Laibson explored the tension between "seizing available rewards in the present, and being patient for rewards in the future." Mr. Laibson has run educational sessions with employees, walking them through calculations, showing them what they are doing wrong. "Almost all of them *still* don't invest," Mr. Laibson says. "People find these kinds of financial transactions unpleasant and confusing, and they are happier with the idea of doing it tomorrow."[19]

How then can you motivate your employees to take advantage of your generous offer of matching contributions, free investment education, and the opportunity to be financially independent in retirement? Consider the following:

- Build workforce readiness for change.
- Gain leadership support and ownership.
- Define the risks and opportunities to focus on the strategy.
- Gather insights on employees' understanding, capabilities, and feelings.
- Identify key stakeholders and shape tactics around them.
- Develop clear positioning and consistent messages.
- Involve employees in the process to build credibility and acceptance.
- Implement through multiple change drivers, including communication and measurement.

Monitoring Performance

Success requires continuous measurement and fine-tuning. How will you define success? What metrics can you use? How have you measured success in the past? Without a starting point and a means of measurement, you will be unable to claim success. This is true of any venture, including your 401(k) plan.

Here a few simple metrics to consider:

- Are employees joining the plan immediately upon becoming eligible? Getting an early start gives an employee a huge boost in potential wealth accumulation.
- How much are employees contributing? Encourage employees to save as much as they can, at least up to the point required to receive the maximum employer match.
- Are employees making sound investment decisions? Employees should have a basic knowledge of risk and reward and how it applies to their personal situation, as well as an understanding of how basic financial principles such as dollar cost averaging and rebalancing can affect their savings.
- Are employees leaving their money in the plan? How much ground is being lost to loans and hardship withdrawals? Employees should understand how these actions hinder account growth over the long term.

Although knowing the numbers is crucial, they give you only half the story. Conduct stakeholder research. Ask leadership if the 401(k) plan helps them recruit qualified candidates. Is the plan doing its job as a retention tool? Do you see a pattern of coincident vesting dates and terminations? Direct your HR staff to ask questions about the 401(k) during exit interviews and compare responses with what they hear at new hire orientations. Is the 401(k) instrumental in employees' decision to join your company?

Do employees see the match as part of indirect pay or total rewards? Conduct quick pulse surveys and polls. Ask employees how they like to receive information, and whether they learned anything from a recent seminar. Then share your findings, take action to improve, and be sure to take credit when there's a success story.

Does your 401(k) vendor have a call center? What type of reporting is provided regarding the types of questions they are being asked? The same goes for the web site—statistics should be available on what employees are doing. If you note a trend, address those issues. Measure again, and see if you've gained any improvement.

THE IMPLEMENTATION PLAN

Now it's time to turn your overall strategy into a tactical plan for implementation. You can tackle this by quarter, by year, or in a multi-year approach. The key will be deciding how and when you will launch communication based on what you are trying to accomplish.

The steps are organized in the following four categories:
1. Channel: Determine your media mix. How you will use print, electronic and face-to-face media to reach your audience. What do you currently have in place? What does your vendor partner offer? (Examples of media: e-mail, frequently asked questions, web site, blog, manager talking points, all hands meetings, educational seminars)
2. Objective: What do you hope to accomplish? What is the desired action or outcomes?
3. Targeted message: What message needs to be communicated? What information do employees need to have? What happens if no action is taken?
4. Timing: Detailed timing with start and finish dates for the communication tactics.

As you implement your plan, you will be presented with opportunities to improve the branding of your program, vendor communications, and methods of communication.

BRANDING YOUR PROGRAM

Do your employees associate your retirement plan with the vendor who administers the plan instead of your company? If so, you may be in trouble when performance issues or cost constraints drive you to make a change in who administers the plan. If your employees are more likely to talk about the Fidelity, Vanguard, or State Street plan than the name of your company, you may want to consider branding your plan to align it more closely with your overall total rewards offering and employment deal.

If you are depending on your plan administrator to provide effective communication for your employees, a study from AARP Financial suggests you may want to reevaluate that approach. The survey found:

- 41 percent say information from financial services companies is not helpful.
- 67 percent give the industry below-average marks for explaining saving and investing concepts.
- The vast majority, 73 percent, said financial services professionals use more jargon than car mechanics.

Vendors can work with you to customize a communication plan that will meet the needs of your employee audiences. Depending on the vendor, content can range from highly effective, award-winning materials to a confusing, overwhelming barrage of promotional materials. As the plan sponsor, your job is to simplify the communication your employees receive from plan providers and to ensure it is meeting the goals and objectives of your plan. You should be an active participant in communication planning with your vendors—determining how to leverage their content, resources, and expertise in a way that maximizes your employees' understanding, appreciation, engagement, and participation in the program.

MANAGING VENDOR COMMUNICATIONS

Let's face it. The 401(k) industry is very sophisticated—plan vendors know the more contributions (employees and companies) make, the more money they have to manage and the more revenue they can generate in fees and commissions. They have a lot to offer in the way of communication (think: postcards, webcasts, articles, and so on), but as the plan administrator, it is up to you to manage that content in a way that reinforces your communication strategy. The key is to leverage vendor communication and participant outreach and integrate it into your ongoing communication and education plan.

THREE TIMES...THREE WAYS

For your financial education and communication plan to work, it should be provided to employees regularly to reinforce the goals of the retirement savings plan. We use a simple mantra of *three times...three ways*. That means, communicate the information at least three times using three different channels (such as e-mail, web site, meetings, and mailings).

No one communication channel alone reaches all participants all of the time. Each channel has its own strengths. Fidelity Investments, in a 2009 research brief, outlines the following strengths of each channel:[20]

- Print: facilitates personalized and targeted messaging that improves response rates
- E-mail: builds on the advantages of print and facilitates immediate action and a high level of personalization
- Web site: enables access to in-depth information, answers to frequently asked questions and helpful planning tools
- Phone: blends voice-activated menus providing easy access to basic information and live help that connects employees with experienced communicators
- On-site: provides in-person interaction for those who wish to engage face to face

CONCLUSION

Effective communications requires a clear strategy and implementation plan. This chapter has hopefully provided you with the information to do both. Individuals today have many activities competing for their attention and dollars. Done well, communications can cut through the noise and cause more people to save for retirement, and for those who are saving, to save more.

CHAPTER 12

Helping Participants Manage Their Retirement Income

For decades, employers have been assisting their employees in accumulating wealth for retirement through sponsorship of 401(k) plans. As more individuals become aware that their personal savings and 401(k) accounts will play a meaningful role in their retirement security, thoughts turn to the next phase of retirement, the income phase. To be precise, the *income phase* of retirement is when the individual begins drawing down their savings to meet their financial needs once they are no longer earning a paycheck (or, when their paycheck no longer meets all of their current financial needs).

Employers who sponsor 401(k) plans are beginning to ask themselves, "What should (or could) we do to help our employees prepare for the income phase of their retirement?" There are many issues that need to be considered when addressing this question and the issues are complex. This chapter attempts to organize the issues in a logical format so as to provide the DC plan sponsor a structured guide to thinking through an answer.

IN PLAN OR OUT?

One fundamental consideration is whether to provide the solution within the 401(k) plan or separately outside the plan. Key to this decision is the level of fiduciary responsibility the plan sponsor wishes to take in connection with the solutions. Offering the solution within the plan heightens the fiduciary's responsibility regarding the selection and monitoring of the product. How integrated should the solution be with the accumulation phase of the plan (pre-retirement) will also influence the decision. Some products today have a portion of the participant's regular contributions invested in an annuity during the accumulation phase. In this example, the retirement income product is seamlessly integrated. Another consideration is how automated does the plan sponsor want the solution to be (compulsory, semi-compulsory, or discretionary). Should plan participants be defaulted into the product or should they be required to make an active decision to buy into the product? Finally, how individualized should the solution be? Should it be a one-size-fits-all solution or a suite of solutions that can be customized to each participant's exact needs?

RISKS OF MANAGING RETIREMENT INCOME

To put some organization around the evaluation of retirement income solutions we start with identifying the risks that are inherent in managing retirement income; there are nine that we have identified and described. We then look at eight product types and evaluate them for how they address each of these risks. At the end of the chapter there are additional product features to be considered. This will give plan sponsors both context and a framework for thinking through their decision about what type of retirement income solution to offer to plan participants.

1. *Investment Risk*—Experiencing lower or more volatile investment returns than expected. This can be due to the individual being invested in a portfolio that is inappropriate, considering their investment objectives and risk tolerances. It can also be due to poor quality investments relative to available alternatives.
2. *Longevity Risk*—Living longer than expected. Longevity risk can arise from the individual living longer than average or, if the individual lives a normal length of time, the individual being unaware of their normal longevity. A compounding issue with longevity risk is that most individuals reach retirement as a couple. So, they are not only subject to the risk that they will live longer than expected, there is an even higher chance that one of the two of the couple will live longer than average.
3. *Inflation Risk*—Losing purchasing power of your income because of inflation. As the cost of goods and services increase over time, retirees whose income is fixed will lose purchasing power. Health care costs in the past have experienced inflation rates far exceeding that of core inflation. Retirees who spend a meaningful portion of their income on health care are acutely exposed to this risk.
4. *Planning Risk*—The failure to plan or to plan accurately. An individual has a substantially better chance of meeting his financial needs in retirement if he has a plan. Products should be evaluated on the basis of the ability of the individual to use them in a sound planning process. Tenets of sound retirement planning include:
   The plan Itself—There should be a plan and it should be of sufficient detail to be meaningful.

Individualized—The plan should be individualized to the person or couple considering their unique level of wealth as well as their specific spending and bequest needs.

Risk Tolerances—The plan should consider the individual or couple's tolerance for the risks described in this chapter.

Frequency of Review—The plan should be reviewed and adjusted (if necessary) on a regular basis. In addition, if conditions or planning assumptions change significantly or rapidly, a review of the plan should take place regardless of the preplanned review frequency.

Flexibility—The plan should be designed and implemented with a sensible amount of flexibility allowing for plan changes without incurring unnecessary fees or penalties.

Age Appropriate—In general, younger retirees have more energy and mental acuity to manage their financial life than older retirees. A plan that is complex and requires frequent review and decision making may be fine for a 65-year-old who has the ability and interest to manage such a plan. That plan may not be appropriate for the very same retiree when she is 85. A sensible plan should anticipate and accommodate these realities.

5. *Spending Risk*—Spending at a rate too high to be sustainable. A sensible spending plan is one of the cornerstones of a solid retirement income foundation. There are at least three variations of spending risks that retirees need to protect against. First, the retiree could be spending at a rate he thinks is sustainable, yet due to ignorance or miscalculation, he is spending too quickly. Second, there is the risk that the retiree lacks the discipline to stay within the spending guidelines that are appropriate for his level of wealth and potential length of life. And finally, there is the risk of unexpected and uncontrollable expenses that are beyond the budgeted spending plan.

6. *Counter-Party Risk*—The risk the insurer is unable to pay benefits. With every insured or guaranteed product there is the risk that the entity underwriting the risk may not be able to make good on their promise. Counter-party risk is usually inversely relative to the strength of the underwriting entity. An insurance company with strong credit ratings and a history on never defaulting on a promise is generally less of a counter-party risk than an insurance company with poor credit ratings and a history of defaults. However, history and credit ratings are no guarantee. While all 50 states, the District of Columbia, and Puerto Rico have life and health guaranty associations that provide some protection against insurer insolvency, this risk should not be ignored when making product decisions.

7. *Provider Portability Risk*—The risk of not being able to change the underlying product provider. Portability between providers is almost

unheard-of with insured products. This is less of a risk with pure investment products. In most cases, the investment manager of an investment portfolio can be replaced. In some cases, there are timing restrictions or penalty clauses related to changing an investment manager, but rarely, if ever, is the investor stuck with an investment manager indefinitely.

8. *Complexity Risk*—The product being too complex to understand or manage. All of the design considerations discussed in this chapter need to be weighed against the need for simplicity. The solution must be simple to understand, simple to buy, simple to own, and simple to explain. If there is one thing we've learned through our decades of DC accumulation experience, it is that complexity creates anxiety and anxiety creates suboptimal behavior. This risk is of particular concern as retirees begin to lose mental acuity in their later years.

9. *Maverick Risk*—The risk of being the first (or one of the first) to try a product or service. Maverick risk is rarely discussed but it influences many important decisions. A client said to me once that no one wants "to be served the first pancake off the griddle." New and innovative products can deliver great benefits to those who adopt them early. They can also create anxiety and suffer from low take-up rates as people wait to see how the product will fare under real-life conditions and multiple market cycles. Plan sponsors may not want to risk second-guessing or criticism by participants if a new product or service does not work out as well as planned.

These nine risks make up what we believe to be the major risks involved in managing income in retirement and thus give us a sound framework for evaluating retirement income product types.

RETIREMENT INCOME PRODUCT TYPES

In the book *The Retirement Plan Solution*, the authors set out a matrix for categorizing asset types along two types of risk: longevity risk and investment risk, as shown here in Table 12.1.[1]

TABLE 12.1 Basic Asset Types to Consider (Examples Shown for Each Category)

		Investment Characteristics	
		Risk Free	Risky
Longevity Protection Characteristic	Risk-Free	Conventional lifetime annuity	Variable lifetime annuity
	Risky	Treasury bills	Equities

In this section we expand on this classification method by evaluating eight retirement income product types based on the nine risks we've just described.

Traditional Investment Portfolio

A traditional investment portfolio is not guaranteed, meaning the investor can lose some or all of their principal amount. By its nature though, there are no fees paid to an insurance company to provide a guarantee. Therefore, for those individuals who have enough wealth at retirement to self-insure their longevity risk, a nonguaranteed investment portfolio is typically the least expensive way to go.

A traditional investment portfolio may hold any type of investments and may range in risk profile from absolutely no risk (Treasury securities) to very aggressive (100 percent equities). The makeup of the underlying assets is determined by the investment objective and risk tolerance of the retiree (preferably with the help of a financial professional).

Traditional Investment Portfolio

Risk	
Investment	Risk is based on the underlying investments. A risk-free portfolio could be constructed by investing in Treasury securities.
Longevity	There is no longevity protection inherent in traditional investment portfolios. Longevity must be managed through spending rate.
Inflation	Level of inflation protection is determined by the correlation between inflation and the portfolio's asset allocation. Inflation protection can be accomplished by investing directly in Treasury Inflation-Protected Securities (TIPS).
Planning	Uncertainty of returns makes it necessary to review and revise the plan frequently in times of high volatility.
Spending	The product itself does not provide any explicit spending risk protection because the entire principal is readily available.
Counter-party	Little or no counter-party risk.
Provider portability	Provider can be easily replaced.

| Complexity | Level of complexity can range from very simple to very complex. |
| Maverick | No maverick risk. |

Fixed End Date Fund

This is the first of two types of investment portfolios we describe that have distribution oriented objectives. Rather than having an investment objective that is based on risk tolerance (conservative, moderate, aggressive, and so on), these portfolios have a distribution objective that guides their asset allocation. These funds are typically managed by a professional investment manager whose team has the level of expertise required to make adjustments to the portfolio to give the fund the best chance at meeting its objective.

A fixed end date fund has an objective to pay out substantially equal monthly payments to the shareholders until a predetermined end date at which time the fund intends to have no residual value left. Since this fund is not guaranteed, the monthly payments may fluctuate in line with the actual investment returns experienced by the fund. The primary use for a fund such as this is for a retiree to satisfy a specific amount of income for a specific time frame without having to buy an annuity and while retaining some potential investment upside. Of course, without a guarantee, the retiree is exposed to investment downside as well.

Fixed End Date Fund

Risk	
Investment	Moderate level of investment risk, as the underlying portfolio is being constantly monitored by a professional investment manager.
Longevity	This product type is designed to intentionally run out of money at a certain end date. Therefore, there is no longevity protection in the product. The retiree would likely combine this product with a product that has a pure longevity protection characteristic such as an advanced deferred life annuity (described later in this chapter).
Inflation	Inflation protection can be built into this product type by setting the distribution objective to deliver substantially equal payments to the investor in real

(Continued)

Fixed End Date Fund   *(Continued)*

Risk

	dollar terms. Although the portfolio may be managed to this objective, inflation risk is still present, as the actual returns may fall short of the expected returns.
Planning	Theoretically, there should be a greater level of certainty of income with this product type. Actual investment returns, however, may vary significantly, causing the need to review and revise the plan more frequently than expected.
Spending	The nature of the product encourages spending discipline. Given that the entire principal is liquid and available at all times, however, spending risk still exists.
Counter-party	Little or no counter-party risk.
Provider portability	Provider can be easily replaced.
Complexity	This product type is relatively easy to use, yet the underlying investment process may be complex. As the markets change, the portfolio manager will adjust the portfolio's asset allocation to best meet the objectives of the fund.
Maverick	Moderate to high maverick risk with this product type.

Fixed Distribution Rate Fund

A fixed distribution rate fund has a predetermined end date just like the fixed end date fund we just described. The fixed distribution rate fund, however, has an objective of distributing a fixed amount each month until the end of the predetermined period. The difference here is that the fixed distribution rate fund is likely to have a residual of principal that is distributed to the retiree at the end of the period. The residual principal can then be used for any purpose, such as buying a lifetime annuity.

The primary use for this type of fund is also for a retiree to satisfy a specific amount of income for a specific time frame without having to buy an annuity. In this case, the retiree has greater certainty of the monthly payment amount (as compared to the fixed end date fund), yet has less certainty around the residual capital amount.

Fixed Distribution Rate Fund

Risk

Investment	Moderate level of investment risk, as the underlying portfolio is being constantly monitored by a professional investment manager.
Longevity	This product type is typically designed to distribute a fixed amount of principal each month for a predetermined number of years at which time it returns any residual principal to the investor. Therefore, the longevity protection is relative to the size of the principal returned at the end of the period (which is affected by the actual investment returns experienced by the fund).
Inflation	Inflation protection can be built in to this product type by setting the distribution objective to deliver equal payments to the investor in real dollar terms. Although the portfolio may be managed to this objective, inflation risk is still present, as the actual returns may fall short of the expected returns.
Planning	Theoretically, there should be a greater level of certainty of distributions with this product type. Actual investment returns, however, may vary significantly the amount of residual capital that is left over at the end of the period, causing the need to review and revise the plan more frequently than expected.
Spending	The nature of the product encourages spending discipline. Given that the entire principal is liquid and available at all times, however, spending risk still exists.
Counter-party	Little or no counter-party risk.
Provider portability	Provider can be easily replaced.
Complexity	This product type is relatively easy to use, yet the underlying investment process may be complex. As the markets change, the portfolio manager will adjust the portfolio's asset allocation to best meet the objectives of the fund.
Maverick	Moderate to high maverick risk with this product type.

Conventional Lifetime Annuity

In its purest form, a conventional lifetime annuity involves a single amount paid to an insurance company, which in turn pays the annuitant a fixed amount each month for as long as the annuitant lives.

Conventional Lifetime Annuity

Risk	
Investment	Conventional lifetime annuities are not exposed to investment risk yet the buyers of these annuities are exposed to interest rate risk at the time of purchase. To manage this risk a retiree may consider buying annuities in smaller amounts over a period of years rather than buying the entire amount needed in a single purchase at a single point-in-time.
Longevity	Maximum longevity protection.
Inflation	No inflation protection, therefore high inflation risk.
Planning	Low planning risk because future payments are predetermined.
Spending	Low spending risk because the principal cannot be accessed.
Counter-party	Counter-party risk is determined by the financial strength of the insurance carrier.
Provider portability	Provider cannot be changed.
Complexity	Very simple.
Maverick	Very little maverick risk.

Indexed Lifetime Annuity

An indexed lifetime annuity is the same as a conventional lifetime annuity with the exception that the monthly payment increases with the rate of inflation. The initial monthly payment from an indexed lifetime annuity is lower than with a conventional annuity.

Indexed Lifetime Annuity

Risk	
Investment	Indexed lifetime annuities are not exposed to investment risk yet the buyers of these annuities are exposed to interest rate risk at the time of purchase. To manage this risk a retiree may consider buying annuities in smaller amounts over a period of years rather than buying the entire amount needed in a single purchase at a single point-in-time.
Longevity	Maximum longevity protection.
Inflation	High level of inflation protection.
Planning	Low planning risk because future payments are predetermined.
Spending	Low spending risk because the principal cannot be accessed.
Counter-party	Counter-party risk is determined by the financial strength of the insurance carrier.
Provider portability	Provider cannot be changed.
Complexity	Very simple.
Maverick	Very little maverick risk.

Variable Annuity

Variable annuities allow the annuitant to direct the investment of the annuity's underlying value. This exposes the annuity value to investment risk and can result in the annuity value (and thus the benefit payments) to fluctuate.

Variable Annuity

Risk	
Investment	Investment risk varies depending on the underlying investments.
Longevity	High level of longevity protection.
Inflation	The makeup of the underlying investment portfolio will determine how much inflation protection is provided.

(Continued)

Variable Annuity   *(Continued)*

Risk	
Planning	Moderate level of income certainty.
Spending	Depends on the product specifications. Generally, there are high penalties to access the principal above a certain level, so there is some spending risk protection built in.
Counter-party	Counter-party risk is determined by the financial strength of the insurance carrier.
Provider portability	Provider cannot be changed.
Complexity	Products can range in complexity.
Maverick	Depends on the combination of product features.

Guaranteed Minimum Withdrawal Benefit (GMWB)

GMWBs are a variety of variable annuity. You pay a lump sum or a series of payments to an insurance company. The insurance company gives you a range of options for how your account is invested. You choose the funds from an available lineup. The investment portion of this product type is not purely a fixed income vehicle, but it lets you choose an investment approach that reflects your desired level of investment risk.

Periodically (monthly, quarterly, annually—as agreed in advance) you receive a distribution from the annuity. The distribution may be constant or vary with the return on the fund. If you want to, you can withdraw more than this minimum amount provided you do not withdraw more than a specified maximum amount every year. If you stay under this predetermined maximum, the insurer guarantees that that amount will continue for the rest of your life. This is true even if the remaining value of the investment declines to zero. In effect, there is a lifetime cash flow guarantee. If you withdraw more than the maximum, the longevity protection is not lost, but the guaranteed cash flow is reduced.

In some GMWB contracts, investment experience is reviewed periodically and, if the experience has been favorable, the guaranteed level of lifetime income is reset upward (and so cannot be reduced subsequently if future investment experience is poor).

In addition to getting the guaranteed lifetime cash flow, you remain the owner of the remaining investment in the fund. This means that the balance of the account is available to your heirs. It also means that you have not been forced to annuitize the investment irrevocably, and retain the ability at any time to terminate the investment.[2]

Guaranteed Minimum Withdrawal Benefit (GMWB)

Risk	
Investment	The policyholder is typically protected on the downside, yet gives up some of the upside market potential.
Longevity	High level of longevity protection.
Inflation	Unless the prearranged minimum withdrawal benefit is indexed to inflation, this type of product carries a moderate level of inflation risk.
Planning	Low planning risk because minimum benefit levels are predetermined.
Spending	Moderate spending risk because the principal can be accessed above the minimum withdrawal benefit.
Counter-party	Counter-party risk is determined by the financial strength of the insurance carrier.
Provider portability	Provider cannot be changed.
Complexity	This is a relatively simple product concept.
Maverick	Low-to-moderate maverick risk.

Advanced Life Deferred Annuity (ALDA)

Advanced life deferred annuities (ALDAs) are designed for retirees who have enough money to support their standard of living for some time (10 to 20 years, let's say), and don't want to pay for longevity protection in those first years, nor do they want to risk losing life and capital at the same time during these early years. In exchange for a lump sum amount paid today, the insurance company agrees to make monthly payments beginning at a predetermined future date (perhaps 10 or 20 years from now). At that future date, if the retiree is still alive, the prearranged payments begin, and are guaranteed to continue until the annuitant dies.

Because no payouts are made until the advanced age is reached, the cost of this annuity is dramatically lower than that of a conventional lifetime annuity. If the buyer dies during the deferral period, the ALDA can accommodate either no payment at all or some specified payment (for example, a return of the initial lump sum). The smaller the death benefit in the deferral period, the lower the cost of a given amount of cash flow from the advanced age.

This type of product is aimed at reducing the objection that a conventional lifetime annuity is unnecessarily capital intensive, because the unwanted protection in the early years is not a part of the payout stream. For this reason, an ALDA is sometimes called pure longevity insurance because it offers that protection in a pure form, paying out only if longevity is really long.

Advanced Life Deferred Annuity

Risk	
Investment	No investment risk.
Longevity	Maximum longevity protection, therefore no longevity risk.
Inflation	Unless the prearranged payment is indexed to inflation, this type of product carries some inflation risk.
Planning	Low planning risk because future payments are predetermined.
Spending	Low spending risk because the principal cannot be accessed.
Counter-party	Same counter-party risk as any insured product with the additional risk of having to stay in contact with the provider during the deferral period.
Provider portability	Provider cannot be changed.
Complexity	This is a relatively simple product concept.
Maverick	Academic literature has extolled the virtues of this product concept, yet few of these products exist today.[3]

ADDITIONAL PRODUCT FEATURES

We have just reviewed each product type based on how they address each of the risks involved in managing retirement income. There are other product characteristics that should be considered as well.

Optional—Many retirement income solutions require a long-term commitment on the part of the participant for the participant to experience the benefits of the solution. In some cases, early withdrawal or cancellation can be excessively wasteful for the participant. This is why, unlike an accumulation investment decision, the decision to participate in a retirement income solution should be an active decision on the part of the participant rather than a passive decision (such as defaulting).

Account Portability—Different from provider portability discussed earlier in this chapter, account portability refers to the ability of the individual to move his account with him if he leaves his employer. As an example, if a product can be held only in an account that is record kept by the employer's plan administrator, the participant would not be able to roll over this portion of his account into an IRA when he leaves the employer. Lack of account portability would likely be a deterrent to adoption by plan participants.

Fees—Where solutions are offered to a group (as opposed to individuals), the group should benefit through lower fees. Employers should use their buying power to ensure group or institutional rates for products they make available to their employees, whether inside or outside the plan. There should be clear transparency of all fees related to the product, and fee transparency should extend to the discrete features of the solution. For example, in a product with both investment management and longevity protection packaged together, it should be clear how much of the total fee is going toward providing each of these product features. It should be clear who is receiving the fees and what value each party is delivering for the fees they are receiving. Also, where multiple parties are involved in the manufacturing or distribution of the product, cross-subsidies (if any) should be transparent.

Survivor Options—Knowing that many people reach retirement as a couple rather than as individuals, consideration should be given for options that allow income to continue (in whole or in part) beyond the life of the first-to-die of the couple. An annuity that has joint-and-survivor benefit (meaning the surviving spouse continues to receive an annuity payment when one of the couple dies) is an example of a product with a survivor option.

Period Certain Payments—One of the biggest concerns people have about buying an annuity is the risk of losing both life and capital at the same time. The nightmare scenario is buying a lifetime annuity and then dying the next day. In this situation, there is no capital preserved for the individual's heirs. A way around this problem is to build *period certain* payments into the annuity. For example, an annuity with a 10-year period certain payment will pay the annuitant or her heirs for at least 10 years even if the annuitant dies within the first 10 years of owning the annuity. A variation on this feature is a return-of-purchase-price clause. This feature would guarantee that the sum of all payments to the annuitant or her heirs would equal at least the value of the original purchase price of the annuity. With these product variations, the monthly annuity payments will be lower than if the features were not part of the product to help fund the cost of the feature.

Riders—Other benefit add-ons may be considered as part of the solution design. One example is a long-term care (LTC) rider. The idea behind this feature is that the cost of long-term care can greatly exceed the normal living cost of a retiree. Therefore, if the retiree comes to need long-term care, their normal annuity income will not be enough. An annuity with a long-term care rider pays a smaller monthly income amount and uses the difference to insure against the need for long-term care. The retiree could buy these two types of coverage separately but purchasing the two in one policy might result in better pricing.

This list of additional product features contains items to consider when evaluating retirement income products in addition to how each product manages the nine risks we described in detail at the beginning of this chapter. As financial institutions create new products, there will inevitably be other product features to add to this list.

CONCLUSION

401(k) plans have for decades been designed and managed for the accumulation of wealth for retirement. Now, as a wave of retirees begin to draw on their 401(k) accounts for income, attention needs to be given to how we can help them do this in an effective and efficient manner. In many cases, the decision to invest in a retirement income product is an irreversible decision. Or, if the decision is reversible, it comes with a very high cost. This is why the evaluation and selection of retirement income products requires a high level of up-front due diligence and scrutiny.

Notes

CHAPTER 1   The Importance of the 401(k) Plan

1. U.S. Census Bureau, "Current Population Survey, Annual Social and Economic Supplement," 2008.
2. Elizabeth Arias, "United States Life Tables," Centers for Disease Control and Prevention, *National Vital Statistics Report* 51(3) (2000): 29.
3. Cerulli Associates Quantitative Update, "Retirement Markets 2006."
4. James Poterba, Steven Venti, and David Wise, "New Estimates of the Future Path of 401(k) Assets," National Bureau of Economic Research Working Paper 13083, May 2007.
5. Elizabeth Arias, "United States Life Tables," Centers for Disease Control and Prevention, *National Vital Statistics Report* 51(3) (2000): 29.
6. Congressional Research Service, "Age Dependency Ratios and Social Security Solvency," October 27, 2006.
7. www.socialsecurity.gov/OACT/ProgData/nra.html.
8. The Social Security Old-Age, Survivors, and Disability Insurance (OASDI) tax rate is only applied to income up to a certain percent. In 2010, the maximum income subject to the OASDI tax rate was $106,800.
9. Social Security web site: www.ssa.gov/OACT/ProgData/taxRates.html.
10. Traditional defined contribution accounts are subject to minimum required distributions starting at age 70½. This only requires the participant to take a distribution from the account and pay taxes on the distribution. It does not require the money to be spent.
11. Bureau of Economic Analysis web site: www.bea.gov/national/NIPAweb/Nipa-FRB.asp.
12. www.nobelprize.org.

CHAPTER 2   The Role of the Employer

1. Deloitte Consulting LLP, International Foundation of Employee Benefit Plans, and International Society of Certified Employee Benefit Specialists, "401(k) Benchmarking Survey," 2009 edition.
2. E. Thomas Garman, "The Business Case for Financial Education" *Personal Finance and Worker Productivity*, vol. 2, No. 1, (1998): 81–93.
3. Richard H. Thaler and Cass R. Sunstein, *Nudge: Improving Decisions about Health, Wealth, and Happiness* (New York: Penguin Books, 2009).
4. The Vanguard Group, Inc., "How America Saves," 2009.

CHAPTER 3   Measuring Retirement Readiness

1. The Vanguard Group, Inc., "How America Saves," 2009.
2. McDonald's Corporation implemented automatic enrollment in 1984, according to John Beshears, James Choi, David Laibson, Brigitte Madrian, and Brian Weller, "Public Policy and Saving for Retirement: The 'Autosave' Features of the Pension Protection Act of 2006," in *Better Living through Economics*, 2007, 8.
3. The Vanguard Group, Inc., "How America Saves," 2009.
4. Don Ezra, Bob Collie, and Matthew X. Smith, *The Retirement Plan Solution: The Reinvention of Defined Contribution* (Hoboken, NJ: John Wiley & Sons, 2009).
5. Burgess and Associates, study performed for John Hancock, covering 2001–2005. News release, Boston, August 14, 2006.

CHAPTER 4   Establishing a 401(k) Plan

1. ERISA §403.

CHAPTER 5   Plan Governance and Fiduciary Issues

1. A pension plan includes any plan, fund, or program that provides retirement income to employees or results in the deferral of income by employees for periods extending to or beyond the termination of employment (ERISA §3(2)(A)). The rules do not apply, however, to unfunded plans maintained primarily to provide deferred compensation for a select group of management or highly compensated employees and partnership agreements that provide payments to retired or deceased partners or deceased partners' successors (ERISA §401(a)).
2. H.R. 3763; P.L. 107–204 (July 30, 2002).
3. Bankruptcy Code §523(a)(4).
4. ERISA §3(21)(A).
5. ERISA §403(a).
6. 29 CFR §2509.75–8, D-3.
7. ERISA §404(c).
8. ERISA §405(b)(1)(B).
9. ERISA §405(b)(3)(A).
10. ERISA §402(a)(2).
11. ERISA §3(16).
12. 29 CFR §2509.75–8, D-3.
13. *Donovan v. Mercer*, 747 F.2d 304 (5th Cir. 1984).
14. *Parker v. Bain*, 68 F.3d 1131 (9th Cir. 1995).
15. ERISA §404(a)(1).
16. ERISA §404(a)(1)(A).
17. DOL opinion letter to Kirk F. Maldonado, March 2, 1987.

18. *Donovan v. Bierwirth*, 680 F.2d 263 (2nd Cir.), cert. denied, 459 U.S. 1069 (1982).
19. ERISA §404(a)(1)(B).
20. Remarks prepared for delivery by U.S. Secretary of Labor Elaine L. Chao, "Get it Right: Responsibilities of an ERISA Fiduciary," May 28, 2004.
21. ERISA §404(a)(1)(C).
22. ERISA §404(a)(1)(D).
23. See, for example, *Heady v. Dawn Food Products, Inc.*, 2003 WL 22859994 (W.D. Ky. 2003) (the terms of a plan's summary plan description (SPD) govern when it conflicts with the plan document even if there is a disclaimer in the SPD to the contrary); *Burstein v. Retirement Account Plan for Employees of Allegheny Health Education and Research Foundation*, 334 F.3d 365 (3rd Cir. 2003) (an SPD will control when it conflicts with the ERISA plan document); *Charter Canyon Treatment Center v. Pool Co.* 153 F.3d 1132 (10th Cir. 1998) (although an SPD trumps conflicting language found in a plan document, an SPD that is silent on a specific term will not prevail over a plan document that addresses it).
24. ERISA §404(a)(1)(D).
25. *Burke v. Latrobe Steel Co.*, 775 F.2d 88 (3rd Cir. 1985); *Morgan v. Independent Drivers Association Pension Plan*, 975 F.2d 1467 (10th Cir. 1992).
26. ERISA §405(c)(1)(B).
27. ERISA §§402(c)(2) and (3).
28. ERISA §405(c)(2).
29. Outside fiduciaries will have liability under ERISA. Shifting responsibility back to the fiduciary committee and its members may frustrate the purpose of retaining the outside fiduciary.
30. The authors found the description of ERISA section 3(38) and 3(21) fiduciaries by W. Scott Simon useful in developing this content. W. Scott Simon, "The Different Flavors of ERISA Fiduciaries," *MornigstarAdvisor*, December 3, 2009.
31. ERISA §405(a).
32. ERISA §406, ERISA §3(14), IRC §4975(e)(2), and IRC §4975(c)(l).
33. ERISA §§406(a) and (b).
34. IRC §4975(c)(1).
35. ERISA §3(14) and IRC §4975(e)(2).
36. ERISA §407.
37. ERISA §408(b).
38. Under ERISA §408, the DOL is authorized to exempt classes of transactions and individual transactions under the Code and ERISA if it is administratively feasible, is in the interest of the plan and the participants and beneficiaries, and protects the rights of the plan's participants and beneficiaries.
39. ERISA §408(b)(2).
40. As defined under IRC §414(q).
41. ERISA §408(b)(1).
42. ERISA §408(b)(3); 29 CFR §2550.408b-3.
43. Ibid.

44. ERISA §§408(b)(4), (6), and (8).
45. 29 CFR §2570.31(b).
46. Prohibited Transaction Exemption 77–3.
47. 29 CFR §§2570.30–2570.52.
48. IRC §§4975(a) and (f)(2).
49. ERISA §502(l)(1).
50. ERISA §502(l)(3).
51. ERISA §405(c)(1)(B).
52. ERISA §404(a)(1)(A)(ii).
53. Chapter 5 is intended to be a general guide in determining which expenses can be paid from plan assets, however fiduciaries should seek further counsel in making final determinations.
54. DOL, "Guidance on Settler v. Plan Expenses," www.dol.gov/ebsa/regs/AOs/settler.guidance.html.
55. Ibid.
56. Ibid.
57. Ibid.
58. ERISA §404(a)(1)(D).
59. DOL, "Guidance on Settler v. Plan Expenses," www.dol.gov/ebsa/regs/AOs/settler.guidance.html.
60. ERISA §408(b)(2).
61. 29 CFR §2550.408c-2(b)(3).
62. DOL Opinion 89–09A; DOL Opinion 86–01A; DOL Opinion 93–06A.
63. DOL Opinion 92–32A.
64. Field Assistance Bulletin 2003–3.
65. *Tittle v. Enron Corp.*, 284 F. Supp. 2d 511, 555 (D. Texas 2003).
66. *Watson v. Deaconess Waltham Hosp.*, 298 F.3d., 102, 115 (1st Cir. 2002); *Harte v. Bethlehem Steel Corp.*, 213 F.3d 446 (3d. Cir. 2000); *McDonald v. Provident Indemnity Life Insurance Co.*, 60 F.3d 234, 237 (5th Cir. 1995); *Bixler v. Central Pennsylvania Teamsters Health and Welfare Fund*, 12 F.3d. 1292, 1300 (3d. Cir. 1993).

CHAPTER 6   Protecting Plan Fiduciaries

1. *Tittle v. Enron Corp.*, 284 F. Supp. 2d 511 (D. Texas 2003). This opinion was delivered in a ruling on more than 20 motions to dismiss. In a motion to dismiss, the defendant in a litigation requests that the case be ended without further consideration because under all circumstances, the defendant will prevail, making all further evaluation of the matter unnecessary. While routinely filed, motions to dismiss are infrequently granted.
2. DOL's amicus brief in *Tittle v. Enron Corp.*, filed on August 30, 2002, in Civil Action No. H-01–3913, U.S. District Court for the Southern District of Texas, Houston Division.
3. Remarks prepared for delivery by U.S. Secretary of Labor Elaine L. Chao, "Get it Right: Responsibilities of an ERISA Fiduciary," May 28, 2004.

4. In her May 28, 2004, speech, DOL's Secretary of Labor, Elaine Chao, stated, "Fiduciaries who do not live up to their responsibilities may be personally liable to restore the plan's losses."
5. Bankruptcy Code §523(a)(4).
6. DOL's amicus brief in *Tittle v. Enron Corp.*, filed on August 30, 2002, in Civil Action No. H-01–3913, U.S. District Court for the Southern District of Texas, Houston Division, 31.
7. *Tittle v. Enron Corp.*, 284 F. Supp. 2d 511, 566.
8. Ibid. at 601.
9. WorldCom, Inc. ERISA Litigation, 354 F. Supp. 2d 423 (S.D.N.Y. 2005).
10. For more specific detail on the consequences of a breach of fiduciary duty, see ERISA Sections 409, 501, and 502.
11. www.dol.gov/ebsa/newsroom/fs2006vfcp.html.
12. It is important to note that many fiduciary breaches will also trigger violations under the IRS rules and regulations, which may lead to significant penalties and the risk of plan disqualification and loss of tax deductions. It is strongly recommended that any such breaches and operational plan defects be corrected as soon as the violation is detected.
13. ERISA §502(l).
14. Federal Register, "*Adoption of Voluntary Fiduciary Correction Program*," 67 (60), March 28, 2002.
15. PTE 2002–51.
16. Amendment to PTE 2002–51, 71 Fed. Reg. 20135 (April 19, 2006).
17. IRS Announcement 2002–31.
18. ERISA §412(a).
19. The term "funds or other property" of a plan is intended to encompass all property which is used or may be used as a source for the payment of benefits to plan participants. 29 CFR §2580.412–4. This definition covers all assets of a plan, including cash, real property, mortgages, and all securities, including employer securities. It does not include permanent assets used in the operation of the plan, such as land and buildings and furniture and fixtures.
20. ERISA §412(a); 29 CFR §§2580.412–1.
21. Ibid.
22. 29 CFR 2580. 75–5, Question FR-8.
23. ERISA §410.2(a).
24. Ibid.
25. DOL Opinion No. 2001–01A.
26. 29 CFR §2580.412–19(a).
27. 29 CFR §2580.412–19(b).
28. ERISA §412(a)(1).
29. 29 CFR §2580.412–6(b)(7)
30. Under ERISA §412(a)(2) and 29 CFR §§2580.412–23 through 32, no bond is required of any fiduciary that is a corporation organized and doing business under the laws of the United States or any state; is authorized to exercise trust powers or to conduct insurance business; is subject to federal and state supervision; and has at all times a combined capital and surplus in excess of such a

minimum amount as may be established by regulations issued by the Secretary, which amount shall be at least $1,000,000.

31. ERISA §409.
32. ERISA §410.
33. ERISA §410(b).

CHAPTER 7　Establishing and Managing Plan Investments

1. 29 CFR §2509.94–2, the DOL's Interpretive Bulletin relating to written statements of investment policies, including proxy voting policies or guidelines. At least one federal court has concluded that the failure of a plan to have an IPS was a breach of its fiduciary duties. *Liss v. Smith*, 991 F.Supp. 278 (S.D.N.Y. 1998).

2. For a more detailed discussion on this topic, please see Chapter 10 of Don Ezra, Bob Collie, and Matthew X. Smith, *The Retirement Plan Solution: The Reinvention of Defined Contribution* (John Wiley & Sons, Hoboken, NJ: 2009).

3. 29 CFR §2550.404a-1(b).

4. The term *investment manager* means any fiduciary, other than a trustee or named fiduciary, who:

- Has the power to manage, acquire, or dispose of any asset of a plan
  - Is registered as an investment advisor under the Investment Advisers Act of 1940 (Act)
  - Is registered as an investment advisor under the laws of the state in which it maintains its principal office and place of business because it cannot register under the Act, and, at the time the fiduciary last filed its most recent registration form, also filed a copy of such form with the Secretary of Labor
  - Is a bank, as defined in the Act or is a qualified insurance company
- Has acknowledged in writing that he is a fiduciary with respect to the plan (ERISA §3(38)).

5. ERISA §405(d)(1).
6. DOL Technical Release 86–1.
7. Other asset-based fees include shareholder servicing fees and sub-transfer agency fees.
8. DOL Advisory Opinion 97–15A.
9. DOL Advisory Opinion 97–16A.
10. The DOL later issued a similar ruling: DOL Advisory Opinion 2003–09A.
11. 29 CFR §2550.404c-1(b)(2)(i)(A).
12. 29 CFR §2550.404c-1(b)(2)(i)(B).
13. 29 CFR §2550.404c-1(b)(3)(i)(B).
14. Ibid.
15. 29 CFR §2550.404c-1(b)(2)(ii)(C)(1).
16. 29 CFR §2550.404c-1(d)(2)(ii)(E)(4)(iii).
17. 29 CFR §2550.404c-1(b)(2)(i)(B)(1).
18. 29 CFR §2550.404c-1(b)(2)(i)(B)(2).

19. Bankruptcy Code §523(a)(4).
20. ERISA §407.
21. Ibid.
22. 29 CFR §2550. 404c-1(d)(2)(ii)(E)(4).
23. According to Vanguard's 2009 report "How America Saves," (page 19), 87 percent of employers who automatically enroll their employees into a 401(k) plan use a target date fund as their default. Another 11 percent use some other balanced fund as their default with the remaining 2 percent using a stable value or money market fund as their default.
24. Revenue Ruling 2000–8 (specifies the criteria to be met in order to automatically reduce an employee's compensation by a certain amount and have that amount contributed as an elective deferral to an employer's 401(k) plan).
25. Preamble to the DOL Reg. §2550.404c-1 at 57 Fed. Reg. 46906 (October 13, 1992); IRS Rev. Rul. 2000–8, footnote 1.
26. Federal Register, Final Rule, "Default Alternatives Under Participant Directed Individual Account Plans," October 24, 2007.
27. Stephanie Bennett and Fred Reish, "DOL Issues the Final QDIA Regulation," November 8, 2007.
28. 29 CFR 2550.404(a)-1(b).
29. Preamble to the DOL Reg. §2550.404c-1 at 57 Fed. Reg. 46906 (October 13, 1992); IRS Rev. Rul. 2000–8, footnote 1.
30. Pension Protection Act of 2006.
31. ERISA §3(21)(A)(ii).
32. 29 CFR 2509.96–1; 61 Fed. Reg. 29585 (June 11, 1996).
33. Investment Advisers Act Release No. 1406 (March 16, 1994).
34. DOL Advisory Opinion 2001–09A. The investment manager was SunAmerica.
35. Essentially, the program had three parts. First, at a conceptual level, the financial expert would develop asset allocation models with different risk-and-return characteristics using the expert's methodology based on generally accepted principles of modern portfolio theory. Second, the financial expert would apply the asset allocation models to the investments available to plan participants under a particular 401(k) plan and develop computer programs to facilitate providing advice to plan participants. The financial expert would determine whether a particular plan has enough different asset classes to implement the asset allocation models. The investment manager would merely inform the plan sponsor whether this requirement has been satisfied. The financial expert would also design a worksheet to collect participant data on their retirement needs. Third, data would be collected and fed into computer programs that generate asset allocation advice that meet the participant's retirement needs.
36. The arrangements included the fees paid to the financial expert by the investment manager would not exceed 5 percent of the financial expert's gross income on an annual basis; the financial expert's fees would not depend upon how the participants allocate their investments; neither the investment manager's choice of the financial expert nor its decision to continue or terminate the relationship with the financial expert will depend upon its investment management fees generated by 401(k) plans that used its asset allocation advice program; the

financial expert retains sole control over the asset allocation models and computer programs, including the staff programming the computers; and other than the asset allocation advice program, there are no other relationships between the investment manager and financial expert that would allow the investment manager to influence the financial expert or affect the financial expert's ability to act independently of the investment manager.

37. DOL Advisory Opinion 2001–09A.
38. The description of the proposed investment advice regulation was derived from the DOL's fact sheet which can be found at www.dol.gov/ebsa/newsroom/fsinvestmentadvice.html.
39. FINRA stands for the Financial Industry Regulatory Authority. FINRA is a private corporation acting as a self-regulatory organization for brokerage firms and trading markets. The excerpt of the managed account description can be found at www.apps.finra.org/investor_Information/smart/401k/3011082.asp.
40. The Vanguard Group, Inc., "How America Saves," (page 51), 2009.
41. A fiduciary should be aware of potential nondiscrimination issues against favoring highly compensated employees for qualified plans under the Internal Revenue Code and ERISA in setting a minimum balance requirement.
42. DOL Opinion 98–04A; 124 DOL Interpretive Bulletin 94–1.
43. DOL Interpretive Bulletin 08–1, known as the "ETI Bulletin," CFR 2509.08–1.

CHAPTER 8   Managing Your Plan's Operations

1. The final rule was published by the DOL in the Federal Register, Vol. 75, No. 9, January 14, 2010.
2. 402(g) is the Internal Revenue Code Section that defines the maximum elective deferral dollar amount an individual can contribute to a 401(k) plan. In 2010, the 402(g) limit was $16,500.
3. www.dol.gov/ebsa/newsroom/fs2006vfcp.html.
4. IRS Publication 4531.
5. www.irs.gov/retirement/article/0,,id=96907,00.html.
6. ERISA §402(a)(1).
7. ERISA §104(b)(1).
8. DOL Reg. §2520.104b–2(b)(2).
9. ERISA §502(c)(1).

CHAPTER 9   Design and Management of Distribution Options

1. Judith A. Sankey, ed., *Employee Benefit Plans: A Glossary of Terms* (Brookfield, WI: International Foundation of Employee Benefit Plans, 2000).
2. IRC §411(a)(2)(B)(ii).
3. IRC §411(a)(2)(B)(iii).
4. Deloitte Consulting LLP, International Foundation of Employee Benefit Plans, and International Society of Certified Employee Benefit Specialists, "Annual 401(k) Benchmarking Survey," 2008 edition.

5. Hewitt Associates, "Research Highlights: Trends and Experience in 401(k) Plans," 2007.
6. Profit Sharing/401(k) Council of America, "401(k) and Profit Sharing Plan Eligibility Survey," 2008.
7. Judith A. Sankey, ed., *Employee Benefit Plans: A Glossary of Terms* (Brookfield, WI: International Foundation of Employee Benefit Plans, 2000).
8. Treas. Reg. §1.401(a)-14(a).
9. IRC §401(a)(9)(A).
10. IRC §401(a)(9)(B)(ii).
11. Treas. Reg. §1.401(a)(9)-3.
12. Ibid.
13. Ibid.
14. Treas. Reg. §1.401(a)(9)-5, Q&A-5 2(c).
15. IRC §401(a)(9)(B)(ii).
16. Treas. Reg. §1.411(d)-4, Q&A-4.
17. IRC §401(a)(11)(B)(iii).
18. Craig Copeland, "More Detail on Lump-Sum Distributions of Workers Who Have Left a Job, 2006," *ebri.org Notes* 30(7) (2009): 2–5.
19. Ibid.
20. DOL Reg. §2550.408b-1.
21. Treas. Reg. §1.401(a)(4)-4(b)(2)(ii)(E).
22. IRC §72(p)(2).
23. Treas. Reg. §1.401(k)-1(d)(3)(iii)(B).
24. Treas. Reg. §1.402(c)-2.

CHAPTER 10　How Business Transactions Affect 401(k) Plans

1. Temp. Treas. Reg. §1.414(q)-1T, Q&A-6(a).
2. Temp. Treas. Reg. §1.414(q)-1T, Q&A-6(c).
3. Kevin G. Long, *Employee Benefit Plans in Mergers and Acquisitions—Should I Stay or Should I Go?* (Folsom, CA: Chang, Ruthenberg, and Long, PC, 2008).
4. David P. Boucher, "How a 401(k) Plan Can Affect a Merger or Acquisition," *Employee Benefit Plan Review* 63(8) (2009): 12–13.
5. Ibid.
6. Ibid.
7. Scott J. Macey and Thomas W. Meagher, "Strategies and Risks in Business Transactions—All's Well That Ends Well," *N.Y.U. Review of Employee Benefits*, Chapter 13 (October 2008): ¶13.01 p.6.
8. Ibid. ¶13.02 p.8.
9. Ibid. ¶13.01 p.6.
10. Ibid. ¶13.02[1] p.9.
11. IRS, "401(k) Resource Guide—Plan Participants—Plan Termination." http://www.irs.gov/retirement/participant/article/0,,id=151798,00.html.
12. DOL, "Fact Sheet: Abandoned Individual Account Plan Final Regulations and Class Exemption," www.dol.gov/ebsa/newsroom/fsabandonedplan.html.

13. Joan Gucciardi and Ilene Fereczy, *Plan Termination Answer Book* (New York: Aspen Publishers, 2009), 14.3–14.9.
14. Morgan Lewis, "Workforce Reduction Planning," April 2009, www.morganlewis.com/pubs/ML_WorkforceChangeInsight_April2009.pdf.
15. Stephan J. Krass, *The 2008 Pension Answer Book* (New York: Aspen Publishers, 2008), 33.1–33.22.

CHAPTER 11 Financial Communication and Education for Participants

1. MetLife—2009 Press Release; Many Employees and Employers Out of Synch On Range of Retirement Issues, April 7, 2009.
2. Charles Schwab/CFO Research Services Report—June 2009, Getting Retirement Savings Back on Track.
3. MetLife—2009 Press Release; Many Employees and Employers Out of Synch On Range of Retirement Issues, April 7, 2009.
4. Anya Olsen and Kevin Whitman, *Social Security Bulletin*, Vol. 67, No 3, 2007; Effective Retirement Savings Programs: Design Features and Financial Education.
5. Daniel Gross, "911 for 401(k)s: Why We're So Stupid About Retirement Investing." *Slate*, March 1, 2005.
6. Patrick J. Bayer, B. Douglas Bernheim, and Daniel M. Garrett, "The Effects of Financial Education in the Workplace: Evidence from a Survey of Employers," 2008.
7. Watson Wyatt Worldwide Insider Newsletter 2009. Increasing Employees' 2008. Appreciation of Their Retirement Programs, page 3.
8. Great Place To Work Institute; www.greatplacetowork.com.
9. Ariel Education Initiative and Hewitt Associates, 401(k) Plans in Living Color: A Study of 401(k) Savings Disparities Across Racial and Ethnic Groups.
10. Susan Burhouse, Donna Grambrell, and Angelisa Harris (2004). Delivery Systems for Financial Education in Theory and Practice.
11. MetLife, Study of Employee Benefits Trends Survey—Seventh Annual, page 51.
12. Employee Benefit Research Institute, 2002 Retirement Confidence Survey.
13. Employee Benefit Research Institute, 2007 Retirement Confidence Survey.
14. Anya Olsen and Kevin Whitman, *Social Security Bulletin*, Vol. 67, No 3, 2007; Effective Retirement Savings Programs: Design Features and Financial Education.
15. Patrick Bayer, Douglas Bernheim, and J. Karl Scholz (1996)—Chapter 4 of *Private Pensions and Public Policies*.
16. MetLife, Study of Employee Benefits Trends Survey—Seventh Annual, page 47.
17. Deloitte Consulting LLP, International Foundation of Employee Benefit Plans, and International Society of Certified Employee Benefit Specialists, "401(k) Benchmarking Survey," 2009 edition.
18. Jinhee Kim and E. Thomas Garman, "Financial Stress, Pay Satisfaction and Workplace Performance," *Compensation and Benefits Review* 36(1) (2004): 69–76.

19. Craig Lambert, "The Marketplace of Perceptions," *Harvard* magazine March–April 2006.
20. Fidelity Investments, "Helping All Employees Achieve Retirement Readiness" (Boston: Fidelity Perspectives: Employee Engagement, Spring 2009).

CHAPTER 12   Helping Participants Manage Their Retirement Income

1. Don Ezra, Bob Collie, and Matthew X. Smith, *The Retirement Plan Solution: The Reinvention of Defined Contribution* (John Wiley & Sons, Hoboken, NJ: 2009).
2. Ibid.
3. Guan Gong, Anthony Webb, and Wei Sun, "An Annuity People Might Actually Buy," (Chestnut Hill, MA: Boston College Center for Retirement Research, 2007).

Index